Ingmar Bergman at the Crossroads

Ingmar Bergman at the Crossroads

Between Theory and Practice

Edited by
Maaret Koskinen and Louise Wallenberg

BLOOMSBURY ACADEMIC
NEW YORK · LONDON · OXFORD · NEW DELHI · SYDNEY

BLOOMSBURY ACADEMIC
Bloomsbury Publishing Inc
1385 Broadway, New York, NY 10018, USA
50 Bedford Square, London, WC1B 3DP, UK
29 Earlsfort Terrace, Dublin 2, Ireland

BLOOMSBURY, BLOOMSBURY ACADEMIC and the Diana logo are trademarks of
Bloomsbury Publishing Plc

First published in the United States of America 2023
Paperback edition published 2024

Volume Editor's Part of the Work © Maaret Koskinen and Louise Wallenberg

Each chapter © of Contributors

For legal purposes the Acknowledgments on p. xi constitute an extension
of this copyright page.

Cover design: Eleanor Rose
Cover image © AB Svensk Filmindustri (1963) Photograph: Rolf Holmqvist

All rights reserved. No part of this publication may be reproduced or transmitted
in any form or by any means, electronic or mechanical, including photocopying,
recording, or any information storage or retrieval system, without prior
permission in writing from the publishers.

Bloomsbury Publishing Inc does not have any control over, or responsibility for, any
third-party websites referred to or in this book. All internet addresses given in this
book were correct at the time of going to press. The author and publisher regret any
inconvenience caused if addresses have changed or sites have ceased to exist,
but can accept no responsibility for any such changes.

Library of Congress Cataloging-in-Publication Data

Names: Koskinen, Maaret, editor. | Wallenberg, Louise, editor.
Title: Ingmar Bergman at the crossroads: between theory and practice / edited by Maaret
Koskinen and Louise Wallenberg.
Description: New York: Bloomsbury Academic, 2022. | Includes bibliographical references
and index. | Summary: "Offers new and insightful perspectives on Ingmar Bergman's work
as a film and theatre director as well as writer of fiction, through the coming together of an
internationally prominent group of academic scholars and artistic practitioners who have
worked on and/or with Bergman"– Provided by publisher.
Identifiers: LCCN 2022019225 (print) | LCCN 2022019226 (ebook) | ISBN 9781501389641
(hardback) | ISBN 9781501389610 (paperback) | ISBN 9781501389627 (epub) |
ISBN 9781501389634 (pdf) | ISBN 9781501389603
Subjects: LCSH: Bergman, Ingmar, 1918-2007–Criticism and interpretation. |
Motion picture producers and directors–Sweden–Biography. | Screenwriters–Sweden–
Biography. | Motion pictures–Sweden–History.
Classification: LCC PN1998.3.B47 I543 2022 (print) | LCC PN1998.3.B47 (ebook) |
DDC 791.4302/33092 [B]–dc23/eng/20220815
LC record available at https://lccn.loc.gov/2022019225
LC ebook record available at https://lccn.loc.gov/2022019226

ISBN: HB: 978-1-5013-8964-1
PB: 978-1-5013-8961-0
ePDF: 978-1-5013-8963-4
eBook: 978-1-5013-8962-7

Typeset by Deanta Global Publishing Services, Chennai, India

To find out more about our authors and books visit www.bloomsbury.com and
sign up for our newsletters.

Contents

List of Figures	vii
Foreword	ix
Acknowledgments	xi

Introduction: Why Bergman, Why Now? *Maaret Koskinen and Louise Wallenberg* — 1

1. *Hour of the Wolf*: Nightmares and Creativity *Margarethe von Trotta* — 15
2. Working with Bergman: Interview with Film and Television Producers Katinka Faragó and Måns Reuterswärd *Maaret Koskinen and Louise Wallenberg* — 19
3. Ambiguity and the Making of *Nattvardsgästerna/Winter Light* *Paisley Livingston* — 37
4. *The Passion of Anna*: The Wondrous Alchemy between Actors and Landscape, Interview with Atom Egoyan *Maaret Koskinen and Louise Wallenberg* — 53
5. Scenes from on and off the Set: Ingmar Bergman, Power, and MeToo *Maaret Koskinen* — 69
6. For Good or for Bad?: Bergman's Ambivalent Influence—Some Observations *Linus Tunström* — 91
7. Jacobi's Burden: "Jewish" Figurations in *Fanny och Alexander* *Jonathan Rozenkrantz* — 103
8. Producing *The Magic Flute* (1975): Conversation with Måns Reuterswärd and Katinka Faragó *Maaret Koskinen and Louise Wallenberg* — 121
9. Metareference, Metalepsis, and Music in Liv Ullmann's and Ingmar Bergman's *Faithless* *Alexis Luko* — 137
10. Bergman's *The Magician*: The Art of Creating Illusions *Allan Havis* — 169
11. Author, Auteur, Actor: Twenty-one Fragments on Bergman, Ullmann, and *Persona* *James Schamus* — 183
12. *Dear Director*: Adapting Bergman's Failures and Leftovers into a Play, and a Fan-letter into a Film *Marcus Lindeen* — 205
13. Making (the) Silence Speak: Remake, Retake, Rectify *Louise Wallenberg* — 215

Conclusion *Maaret Koskinen and Louise Wallenberg* — 229

Bibliography — 233
Filmography — 243
List of Editors and Contributors — 245
Index — 249

Figures

1.1	The director as demon on the film set of *Vargtimmen/Hour of the Wolf* (1968)	17
2.1	Faragó, Lindholm, Bergman, and unknown on the film set of *Smultronstället/Wild Strawberries* (1957)	23
2.2	Director, actors, and film crew laughing and joking in between anxiety-ridden takes on the film set of *Tystnaden/The Silence* (1963)	27
2.3	Måns Reuterswärd and Katinka Faragó at their home in Stockholm during one of our interviews held in 2018–19	35
3.1	Ambiguity on many levels in *Nattvardsgästerna/Winter Light* (1968)	46
4.1	Bergman's quartet of actors in the film poster for *En Passion/The Passion of Anna* (1969)	55
4.2	On the film set of *En passion/The Passion of Anna* (1969) with Erland Josephson as the cynical Elis and Liv Ullmann as Anna	56
5.1	Bergman to Nykvist: "Don't you dare leave in the midst of the shoot!" Here in harmonious times, on the shoot of *From the Life of the Marionettes*	76
6.1	From Linus Tunström's theater production of *Fanny and Alexander* at Uppsala City Theater in 2012	92
7.1	Isak Jacobi enacting a stereotypical "Jewish usurer" in his encounter with Bishop Vergérus	105
7.2	Isak Jacobi and Helena Ekdahl as two old lovers sharing memories during Christmas night	111
8.1	Ingmar Bergman and conductor and musical director Eric Ericson instructing the orchestra during the film set of *The Magic Flute* (1975)	122
9.1	Marianne (Lena Endre) and "Bergman" Erland Josephson in *Trolösa/Faithless* (2000)	138
9.2	Diegetic and extradiegetic narrative circles of *Faithless*	147
9.3	Love pairs in *Faithless*	149
9.4	Meta-moment where "Bergman" (Erland Josephson) touches "David" (Krister Henriksson), a younger version of himself	150

10.1	Perpetual performance by the charming cinematic creatures in *The Magician* (1958)	171
11.1	Still from the opening credits of *Persona* (1966)	193
12.1	Marcus Lindeen and Kazzrie Jaxen	213
13.1	Lindblom refusing nudity in the bathroom scene in *The Silence* to Bergman's dismay (1963)	221
13.2	Anna (Nina Gunke) and Ester (Anki Lidén) about to kiss in a take evoking the iconic shot in *Persona*	225

Foreword

Ang Lee

I was eighteen years old, a student at the Academy of Arts in Taipei, when, one winter evening, I had my first experience of cinema as an art form—back then, I watched movies like everyone else, more for entertainment than for enlightenment. That night, almost fifty years ago, I sat in the screening room and watched Ingmar Bergman's *The Virgin Spring*, and my life changed forever. I was electrified and dumbfounded. When the lights came up after the film ended, I sat, immobile and awestruck. I had no idea what had hit me, but I did know I was not going anywhere. I stayed in my seat and watched the entire film again. Afterward, I wandered the streets of the city, alone, lost, but also touched, in connection with someone and something new, something that would stay with me for the rest of my life. I was not a religious person but had been raised in such a way that God's existence was never questioned. But that night, I had experienced something I recognized as true art and beauty, but also something that dared raise the question: Where is God? I had a sense that those two things—absolute beauty on the one hand, and terrifying doubt on the other—were somehow related, maybe even the same thing. But I could not have said how. Decades later, I still can't say. But I know that Ingmar Bergman showed this to me, and still shows me, and I am indebted to his example.

In a sense, Bergman's work is relatable to me as a Chinese artist who works in relation to the traditional and still widely held understanding in Chinese culture of art's threefold purpose:

真: truth
善: virtue
美: beauty

On the surface these just seem like clichés. But to me their relationship is subtle and difficult. Beauty is not simply prettiness. Virtue or goodness is not simply being nice. The artist achieves beauty only by first testing themselves against, and facing, the truth (even if the truth is unknowable), no matter how painful or difficult, and thus achieving the virtue that makes them capable of producing real art. This process can lead to beauty that is not necessarily pretty (according to your aesthetic sense, for example, is Picasso's *Weeping Woman* beautiful or ugly?). So, 真善美 is always a struggle, a journey. But it seems like Bergman just basks in all three of them all at once and all the time, serenely, like breathing.

I remember in particular two moments in *The Virgin Spring* that show this. The first is when the character played by Max von Sydow is about to go through the ritual as he prepares to kill his child's murderer. He walks up a hill and begins to push against a single small tree. It is a very simple elongated shot. That was an epiphany to me—why did Bergman do that shot, and make it so simple and functional? One man and a tree—like in De Sica's *Bicycle Thieves* when, in a high contrast shot, the father stands, pausing, before the bicycle, thinking about whether to steal it. It's one man and one object, one man making a decision. In *The Virgin Spring*, the shot is very gloomy, overcast, Scandinavian—again, very simple. Anybody today can do prettier shots. But that is not Bergman's intention with this lengthy shot—his intention is for you to feel the possible presence of God, even if his characters can't.

The other scene is near the end of the film, before the miracle of the spring, when von Sydow's character explicitly questions God's existence. It was a high-angle shot of the actor's head in one-quarter profile (and even though I was not sophisticated with film lange I notced it). Years later, when I started making movies, and I wanted to shoot someone thinking, contemplating, asking an existential question, my camera angle would always be high, and I often shoot the actor from behind.

When I was in the midst of preparing a very difficult film, *Lust, Caution*, I jumped at the invitation to travel to the island of Fårö to meet Ingmar Bergman. It was summer, and the light was tranquil, but I was not. I arrived to meet Bergman after years of work and study, always thinking of him as a kind of artistic father figure, but also associating him with the wrath of the father. But when we finally met and embraced, he was soft—he was like a mother. All of a sudden all the questions I had, all the struggles in art, they all kind of melted in the mother's arms. The ultimate father figure to me held also within himself the mother—and told me I was going to be ok. Perhaps he was right. Perhaps he was wrong. I don't know. But I do know that every day I work as a filmmaker is a day that continues the journey I began when I left that theater in Taipei half a century ago.

Acknowledgments

First, we wish to express our gratitude to the contributors of this collection, all of whom have shared both their experiences, their memories and/or their creative and analytical skills and without whom this collection would never have been compiled. We wish also to thank Krister Collin at the Swedish Film Institute, who kindly has helped us access the many beautiful images that accompany most of the chapters. The Department of Media Studies at Stockholm University has generously financed the cost for the images, and we are grateful for this. A sincere thank you also goes to Riksbankens Jubileumsfond, who generously helped finance our writing retreat held at the Bergman estate on Fårö in October 2019. A warm thank you also to the Bergman Estate and to Kerstin Kalström, who generously housed us for an entire month. Finally, we wish to thank our editors at Bloomsbury, Katie Gallof and Stephanie Grace-Petinos, for their untiring support throughout the publishing process.

Introduction

Why Bergman, Why Now?

Maaret Koskinen and Louise Wallenberg

Much has been published on Ingmar Bergman since he became an international name in the 1950s with films like *Sommaren med Monika/Summer with Monika* (1953), *Det sjunde inseglet/The Seventh Seal* (1957), and *Fanny och Alexander/Fanny and Alexander* (1982–3). His rich legacy as director/writer of about 50 features, and well over 150 plays, as well as author of short stories, novels, and plays, has attracted scholars from a multitude of academic and interdisciplinary approaches (for instance theater and performance studies, literature studies, gender studies, philosophy, religion, and musicology), while also having been the object of serious film critique.[1]

Yet the scholarly or, for that matter, public interest for his work is not in decline—rather the opposite.[2] A telling sign is that in 2018, the year of the Bergman Centennial, there were no less than 798 Bergman-related events (exhibitions, stage performances, retrospectives, seminars, etc.) in 84 countries worldwide. Furthermore, Bergman is not only (still) influential in the West, but outside of it as well: in 2018 retrospectives of Bergman's films were screened on five continents, for example in Kampala, Uganda; in Seoul, South Korea; and in Buenos Aires, Argentina.

Not least importantly, these festivities were undertaken not in adulation of a monument of a bygone era, but rather in celebration of a living artist. In fact, Bergman is at present the internationally most performed Scandinavian writer for the stage, as reported by the Bergman Foundation, while Norstedts, where Bergman published all his written work, has launched several volumes of his previous as well as hitherto unknown writings.[3] In short, Bergman still wields both a national and international impact: for example, in 2021 Hagai Levi's HBO-series *Scenes from a Marriage*, starring Jessica Chastain and Oscar Isaac, premiered, the same year that another relational drama, *Bergman Island*, by Mia

Hansen-Löve and starring Tim Roth and Vicky Krieps, was shot in and around Bergman's estate on the Baltic island of Fårö.[4]

* * *

But there still remains untold stories, and much to be said and explored. One decidedly under-researched area is Ingmar Bergman's work behind the scene. For one, the publications that do exist, tend to be quite old, for instance the interviews undertaken with Bergman's cinematographer Sven Nykvist, and the book-length interview with the director himself, in *Bergman on Bergman* from 1970 (which was also in part censored by Bergman).[5] In addition, the one truly in-depth behind-the-scene work, *L-136: dagbok med Ingmar Bergman* from 1963 by Swedish filmmaker Vilgot Sjöman, is limited to the shoot of one film, while the dominant part of empirical research in this area consists of innumerable interviews with actors, such as Bibi Andersson, Harriet Andersson, Max von Sydow, and Liv Ullmann.

In this book, there is certainly good reason to return to previous scholarship, but in that case through the lens not only of newly acquired empirical information, but through forays into theoretical frameworks. Hence, while parts of new research presented here may have been acquired in traditional ways, for instance in the Ingmar Bergman Foundation archive (located in Stockholm), these forays into Bergman's work behind the scenes are even further enhanced by being contextualized and put in new perspectives by the field of production studies.

As pointed out by film and media scholar Patrick Vonderau et al., over the past twenty years production studies has turned into a consistent field of research, with the aim of exploring media as production cultures.[6] Studying production specifically as a culture involves gathering empirical data about the lived realities of people involved in various kinds of media production, including working conditions, daily routines, and rituals, as well as relationships between and within different professions, and not least contracts. Methodologically speaking, then, the study of production as a culture is normally based on empirical evidence given by people who have been involved with or still are involved in various production areas (film, television, theater, etc.). Such evidence can range from large issues such as national production systems to the minutest observations regarding the practices and routines prevalent in those systems.

This is precisely what our book provides, not least through our in-depth interviews with Bergman's longtime collaborators Katinka Faragó (b. 1936) and Måns Reuterswärd (b. 1932). Both have firsthand, intimate experience of working with Bergman as producers, Faragó in film and Reuterswärd in television (which also included theater and opera works), which they did over no less than five decades. In fact, meeting these two formidable individuals, who also as married form a formidable power couple in the Swedish media at large, prompted us to launch a four-week study and writing retreat. To this retreat we decided to invite practitioners, such as Faragó and Reuterswärd, as well as academics, in order to think, talk, and write on Ingmar Bergman's work. The aim of the retreat, then, was to bring international scholars and practitioners together to discuss Bergman from different angles and experiences, and to openly exchange perspectives and competences, transgressing the often-rigid boundary between theorists and practitioners—in short, to explore what theory and practice can "do" for each other.

This retreat was held in October 2019 at the Bergman estate on Fårö in the Baltic Sea. Our invited co-authors consisted of both established and renowned Bergman scholars, coming from different areas and disciplines, and equally renowned practitioners in film, theater, and television production, who have one thing in common: they all have worked with Bergman and/or on Bergman's oeuvre. In bridging the abyss between practice and theory, and through this bridging, engaging, and expanding the theoretical issues concerning film and media production studies, our collection is both unique and novel in the way it involves filmmakers, theater directors, and/or producers with film scholars, and as such it takes the existent research on Ingmar Bergman in new directions.

Bergman through the Lens of Production Studies

The notion of production studies, then, forms an important framework for this book. In this context, let us cite Mette Hjort and Pietari Kääpä who in their editorial to the *Journal of Scandinavian Cinema* special issue on production studies note that "the scholarly study of media production has emerged as a vibrant field in contemporary media studies," and that production studies, "as envisaged in ground-breaking collections by authors such as Toby Miller (2001), John T. Caldwell (2008), Vicki Mayer et al. (2009), Vicki Mayer (2011) and Mark Deuze and Mirjan Prenger (2019), ask critical questions about the dynamics of power in the media industry."[7] While this, as intimated above, involves gathering empirical data about the lived realities of people in media production, it also means studying a very broad range of related issues—questions of national production systems, problems of work organization, studio histories, or the ever-changing transient borders between production and consumption. Production Studies thus involves the analytical work with texts and practices readily available: trade stories and interviews, screening "q & as," or even feature films disclosing the "behind the scenes."[8] Our book delves extensively into such areas as well, both interviews and behind-the-scenes films.[9] In this context it should also be noted that while Anglo-American scholarship has offered behind-the-scene studies in production cultures and production practices in various media, including film and television, what generally has been missing so far are studies dealing with historical and national aspects of production, especially regarding European contexts. In our book, such critical questions inform, either implicitly or explicitly, the experiences of the aforementioned Faragó and Reutersward.

However, the notion of production studies informs many other contributions in our book as well, for example Paisley Livingston's study into the filmmaker's attitudes and decisions during the shooting of *Nattvardsgästerna/Winter Light* (1962). Production studies also inform Jonathan Rozenkrantz's study on the representation of the "Jewishness" in *Fanny and Alexander* as he engages with Bergman's work books on the filming process. From a practitioner's perspective, Atom Egoyan offers an analysis of *En passion/The Passion of Anna* (1969), and he does so from the intimate knowledge and position as a director working with actors. In her short essay on *Vargtimmen/Hour of the Wolf* (1968), Margarethe von Trotta too regards the film from the director's point of view, as well as an understanding of the sources that inform Bergman's film, with a grounding in her own German culture. In this context it is particularly gratifying to have been able to include two members of the younger generation of Swedish directors, Linus Tunström and Markus Lindeen, who not only have worked with and for Bergman, but who both are theater and film directors as well.

Having mentioned the dual capacities of the last two contributors, it should be noted that the notion of intermediality as well is an important framework for this book.[10] This notion almost comes by default, as Bergman himself was a consummate practitioner in not only film (itself, arguably, defined as a *Gesamtkunstwerk*), but also in the theater (as mentioned, he was a prolific director for the stage, of both classics and his own plays from the early 1940s on), as well as in the opera, and in television—while also ending his career as a writer of novels as well as his highly literary autobiography. Not surprisingly, then, most of the texts by and interviews with our contributors in various ways delve into all of these artistic practices (film, opera, television, writing), and the relation between them. Thus examples of intermedial approaches can be found in for instance playwright and performance studies scholar Allan Havis's analysis of *Ansiktet/The Magician* (1958), and the film's intricate relations to the theater, including historical nineteenth-century acting troupes that traveled the roads. A similar intermedial approach is found in musicologist Alexis Luko's study of *Trolösa/Faithless* (2000), directed by Liv Ullmann but based on a manuscript by Bergman, in which Luko demonstrates how music is embedded in the cinematic story, bringing the intermedial relationship of the two media to the fore.

As for possible and desirable frameworks, one final caveat should be added. Inspired by the recent pioneering work of Daniel Humphrey and Hamish Ford, "Situating Ingmar Bergman and World Cinema," we realize that a reflection on the "none-issue" of race, that is, the very "whiteness" of our own collection, is necessary.[11] As for the existent Bergman scholarship, there are a few exceptions that take up race and/or ethnicity. For instance, in 1960, James Baldwin published an interview with Bergman, "The Northern Protestant," in *Esquire Magazine* (analyzed by Janet Staiger in Koskinen's collection *Ingmar Bergman Revisited* from 2008), and in 1998 Rochelle Wright published a monograph in which she analyzed images of Jews and other ethnicities in Bergman's film work.[12] Since then, however, very little has been written about race and ethnicity, whiteness included, in Bergman's films. In addition, there have been rather few major studies on the perception of Bergman's films and his role as director outside of the Western world, and those publications that do exist, have not been translated into English. Hence, the already mentioned special issue edited by Hamish Ford and Daniel Humphrey, which deals with global perspectives on Bergman's films, is indeed a groundbreaking publication.

While most of the contributors in our book do not engage with race, there are however, instances where issues of ethnicity (not least Bergman's contradictory attitudes toward Jewishness) are discussed in depth, as in Jonathan Rozenkrantz's contribution, or touched upon from personal experiences, as in our interview with Katinka Faragó. In addition, while we are well aware that the whiteness of this collection is embarrassingly discernible, it could be added that as we started to organize the writing retreat in early 2019, we did reach out to two influential and highly acclaimed non-white filmmakers, both of whom have expressed an affinity with and a fascination for Bergman's film work—but who unfortunately were not able to participate. All the better, then, that Rozenkrantz's analysis of *Fanny and Alexander* in such an evocative way mirrors the lived experience of Katinka Faragó—the very film about which Bergman announced that without her, it would never have been made.[13]

Outline of the Book

The collection is generally structured in an interweaving fashion, so that texts by practitioners are followed by those of academics, and in addition so that aspects of previous texts return in more depth in the following text.

An exception to this general rule is Margarethe von Trotta's evocative "*Hour of the Wolf*: Nightmares and Creativity," which serves well in setting the tone for what is to follow. Here she details the affinity between Bergman's film *Hour of the Wolf* (1968) and E. T. A. Hoffmann, the German Romantic writer of gothic stories. In particular she delves into mirrors, *Doppelgänger*, and inner demons such as jealousy (one favorite demon in Bergman)—but also the liberating and creative possibilities of insomnia and nightmares. In many ways, von Trotta's text is a letter from one film director to another.

In "Working with Bergman: Interview with Film and Television Producers Katinka Faragó and Måns Reuterswärd," further considerations from the practitioners' perspective are explored, in this case, as mentioned, by the two people who experienced working with Bergman on (and off) the film and television set for a longer time than anyone else. Faragó in particular is forever connected to Bergman, and vice versa, the two having worked together on no less than twenty-five pictures directed by Bergman, Faragó first in the positions of script girl, then production leader, and finally producer. At center here is her incredibly detailed first-person narrative, which reveals never-before published information on how it actually was to work with Bergman on and off the film set. As "his" script girl, she was both the center and the nexus on the set, and continued to be so as his production leader, and as producer. Just like his colleague and partner Faragó, Reuterswärd worked closely with Bergman over a long period of time, and he did so as his producer, particularly of Bergman's work for television toward the end of his career. Reuterswärd, who originally was trained as an artist, and who had started out as a technician in the infancy of national Swedish television (i.e., the early 1950s), came in the 1960s and early

1970s to produce a number of experimental and innovative shows on the arts, including dance and painting, using state of the art technology. This, it turned out, came into very good use when he produced *Trollflöjten/The Magic Flute* in 1975, as well as several of Bergman's plays written for the television.

In his contribution, "Ambiguity and the Making of *Nattvardsgästerna/Winter Light*," Paisley Livingston has honed in on a film in which Katinka Faragó was script girl. Here Livingston discusses how Vilgot Sjöman's book *L 136*, and behind-the-scenes film *Ingmar Bergman Makes a Film* on the making of Ingmar Bergman's feature (1961) can provide invaluable insight into the filmmakers' considerations during the shoot. In preparation for his book and film, Sjöman personally witnessed much of the making of *Winter Light*; he interviewed Bergman and many of his collaborators, reporting their responses to a variety of pertinent questions. In this chapter, Livingston brings some of this evidence to bear on interpretative and evaluative issues raised by this work, focusing in particular on significant, unresolved ambiguities pertaining to basic story facts, characterization, and religious themes.

If Paisley Livingston takes a close look at how one director (Sjöman) studies another director (not surprisingly, in 1962 Sjöman made his debut as feature film director), Atom Egoyan too was inspired by Bergman's films from the very beginning, when starting out as a young director. In our interview with him, he returns in particular to *En passion/The Passion of Anna* (1969) to discuss the "the Wondrous Alchemy Between Actors and Landscape." Here, Egoyan offers fascinating insights about how a film always reveals the very dynamics of the shoot, and describes how Bergman, in this specific film, played with this fact so as to make a meta-comment on the practice of filmmaking, not least on the complicated and volatile relations between real-life actors and the fictional characters in the script.

With her contribution, "Scenes from on and off the Set: Ingmar Bergman, Power, and MeToo," Maaret Koskinen enters yet another territory just as wrought with conflict, as well as violence, through the phenomenon of the MeToo-movement. While sexuality and violence, and sometimes the relations between the two, are not uncommon themes in Bergman's films, what is perhaps less known (at least internationally) is that in Sweden aspects of MeToo have been linked to Bergman as well. This has prompted Koskinen into an investigation of Bergman's undeniably domineering role in the Swedish film industry, and also in the theater, not least in wielding power over the access and careers of a whole generation of actors. In addition it could and should be asked whether this position of power involved gendered working conditions and asymmetrical power relations between actress and director.

In "For Good or For Bad? Bergman's Ambivalent Influence—Some Observations," theater and film director Linus Tunström enters, from the perspective of a younger generation, a similar volatile territory. He draws from his reactions from revisiting some of Ingmar Bergman's films, but also memories of meeting Bergman in person, as well as observations of the environments where he worked, in order to meditate upon Bergman's (undoubtedly strong, but also sometimes negative) influence on the Swedish theater and film scene. However, he also meditates on his own work as a director, and on the nature of creativity itself, detailing how the creative mind can work, looking for elements to feed the inner narrative, and how to make visible what is moving underneath, taking examples both from what he can deduct from relating to Bergman's work, and from his own artistic process.

Other potentially problematic areas in Bergman's oeuvre are class, whiteness, and ethnicity. In his chapter "Jacobi's Burden: 'Jewish' Figurations in *Fanny och Alexander*," Jonathan Rozenkrantz hones in on the representation of "Jewishness" in Bergman's last feature made for cinema theaters (1982) through the prism of Swedish anti-Semitism. His aim is to analyze the functions of its "Jewish" elements within a complex national, cultural, and historical context of a postwar Sweden where the presence of anti-Semitism was systematically denied while Jews on screen were virtually nonexistent. Engaging with Bergman's work books detailing the preproduction and the filming of *Fanny and Alexander*, Rozenkrantz offers a close reading of the film through key research on the expressions of Swedish anti-Semitism in film, visual culture, and media discourse and through studying the press coverage and reception of the film to find out whether—and how—said issues were addressed at the time of its making and release. Furthermore, the chapter investigates how the film engages with the two dichotomies on which Swedish anti-Semitism has been based, one religious (Christian/Jew) and the other racial (Swede/Jew).

If *Fanny and Alexander* made film history, both as what was (then) considered Ingmar Bergman's swan song, and as the winner of four Oscars, including best foreign film, the chapter "Producing *The Magic Flute* (1975): Conversation with Måns Reuterswärd and Katinka Faragó," enters Swedish television history. Reuterswärd is a crucial contributor to and part of Swedish television history, and in this interview he offers a detailed narrative of how Bergman worked and navigated in this still rather new medium, with its specific production demands.

Reuterswärd's detailed recollections and specific area of expertise form an important contribution to the existent research on Bergman.

With Alexis Luko's chapter "Metareference, Metalepsis, and Music in Liv Ullmann's and Ingmar Bergman's *Faithless*" we enter decidedly intermedial perspectives, as she approaches Bergman from a musicological perspective. Departing from the concept *narrative metalepsis*, that is, different narrative levels and stories embedded within stories, Luko investigates how music acts as a metaleptic agent in *Faithless*, transgressing boundaries between various narrative levels. Two high-level narrative levels investigated are Ullmann's and Bergman's personal stories, which infiltrate the diegesis, thus creating multiple layers of fact and fiction. Related to the topics of metareferences and metalepsis, she also focuses on how the film raises questions around auteurship through music and sound. If Luko in her previous work has argued that Bergman was a sonic auteur, a filmmaker who created distinct soundscapes, here her focus is locating Bergmanian sonic trademarks in moments where Liv Ullmann—whether purposefully or subconsciously—emulates, borrows, or pays homage to Bergman's sonic style.

Another facet in Bergman's films with strong intermedial implications is the theater. In his analysis of *The Magician*, Allan Havis explores the freedoms of rootless artists, and the powers of suggestion. Referring both to Bergman's residency as artistic director in the 1950s at the Malmö City Theatre, and the Gothenburg City Theater, where he staged G. K. Chesterton's play *Magic*, Havis places Bergman in a decidedly theatrical context. In line with this approach, he also compares Bergman's film to Buchner's play *Woyzeck* from 1833, as well as to Pirandello's stage characters, who like Bergman's screen characters in *The Magician* are enmeshed and assigned to a perpetual performance and on occasion are allowed to drop the masks of deceit and camouflage.

In "Author, Auteur, Actor: 21 Fragments on Bergman, Ullmann, and *Persona*," James Schamus elaborates on some of the most important *topoi* in recent Bergman criticism—the nature and conception of Bergman's often-contradictory notions of authorship, his indebtedness (and rivalry with) Strindberg, his distaste for "literary" films, and his aspirations toward literary writing—by focusing on Bergman's collaboration with Liv Ullmann in the making of *Persona* (1966). The actor's speaking—and silent—body is, in Bergman, the unavoidable site of the antinomy between text and image out of which cinematic authorship is forged. But actors, as Schamus puts it, say the darnest things, even when they are ostensibly written by the male auteur. Through a reading of Bergman and

Ullmann's many, various, and, over time, changing and contradictory accounts of their collaboration, Schamus aims to add further to the insights of critics such as Koskinen, Steene, Blackwell, and Rugg, while making the case for the specific contributions of Ullmann to Bergman's authorial persona, from *Persona* through to her perhaps less-than-faithful directorial adaptation of Bergman's screenplay, *Faithless*.

The remaining two chapters delineate in no uncertain terms the ongoing relevance of Bergman's work on a younger generation of directors, in both films and in the theater. The first one is film and theater director Marcus Lindeen's personal essay "*Dear Director*: Adapting Bergman's Failures and Leftovers into a Play, and a Fan-letter into a Film." It starts off with a description of his initial (and somewhat resistant) relation with Bergman's oeuvre as one marked by cultural saturation and an almost overwhelming respect. The essay then focuses on Lindeen's film *Dear Director* (2015), which besides being inspired by the unfinished script and the film that was made in connection to this script, also was inspired by a sixteen-pages-long letter found in the Bergman Foundation archive. This letter, written by American jazz pianist Kazzrie Jaxen, then Liz Gorill, also bears clear connections with *Life of the Marionettes* (1980): Jaxen wrote the letter after having watched the film in 1980, and it is a deeply personal letter in the form of a diary directed to the "director," describing how the film initiated a life crisis. In *Dear Director*, Jaxen appears as herself, thirty-five years later, letting the director (the author) into her life to discuss and explore life crises, unborn twins, and unfinished scripts.

In the final chapter of this collection, "Making (the) Silence Speak: Remake, Retake, Rectify," Louise Wallenberg follows a somewhat "accidental" trajectory of Bergman's control—but also influence and support—on contemporary younger women actors and filmmakers, from *Tystnaden/The Silence* (1963), via *Paradistorg/ Summer Paradise* (Gunnel Lindblom, 1977), to *Guds tystnad/God's Silence* (Lisa Aschan and Isabel Cruz Liljegren, 2018). The latter is the lesbian remake of *The Silence* that was produced as part of the "Bergman Revisited" series, a compilation of six short films produced by the Swedish Television and the Swedish Film Institute in conjunction with the Bergman Centennial in 2018. The unifying figure for this chapter is Lindblom, and via her, Wallenberg explores representation (and presence) as two folded: representation as in having agency and self-governance (on and off the film set), and as in how one is being represented on screen.

As editors of this collection, it is our hope that *Ingmar Bergman at the Crossroads* will not only offer novel insights into the multifaceted work and universe of Bergman, but also, that it will inspire scholars and practitioners to work together, be they film or theater directors, scriptwriters, playwrights, or television producers. The old divide between theory and practice, much enforced by the lingering, rather strict educational systems in both areas, has since long served to keep practitioners and scholars apart, despite the fact that we explore and study the very same art form. As the month-long writing retreat on Fårö, as well as the two-year-long work with finalizing our project in written form, have taught and shown us, we have lots to learn from one another.

Stockholm, March 10, 2022.
Maaret Koskinen and Louise Wallenberg

Notes

1 As for the many scholarly investigations into Bergman's film work, see for example Peter Cowie, *Ingmar Bergman* (Loughton, Essex: Motion, 1962); Cowie, *Swedish Cinema* (London: Barnes, 1966); Cowier, *Ingmar Bergman. A Critical Biography* (New York: Charles Scribner's Sons, 1982); Cowie, *Ingmar Bergman. A Critical Biography*, updated edition (London: Andre Deutsch, 1992); Jerry H. Gill, *Ingmar Bergman and the Search for Meaning*. Grand Rapids, MI: Eerdmans, 1969); Constance Penley, "*Cries and Whispers*" (orig. 1973), in *Movies and Methods*, ed. Bill Nichols (Berkley: University of California Press, 1976), 204–8; Bruce Kawin, *Mindscreen: Bergman, Godard and First-Person Film* (Princeton, NJ: Princeton University Press, 1981); Paisley Livingston, *Ingmar Bergman and the Rituals of Art* (Ithaca and London: Cornell University Press, 1982); Livingston, *Cinema, Philosophy, Bergman: On Film as Philosophy* (Oxford: Oxford University Press, 2009); Marilyn Johns Blackwell, *Persona: The Transcendent Image* (Chicago: University of Illinois Press, 1984), Johns Blackwell, *Gender and Representation in the Films of Ingmar Bergman* (Columbia, SC: Camden House, 1997); Frank Gado, *The Passion of Ingmar Bergman* (Durham, NC: Duke University Press, 1986); Charles. B. Ketcham, *The Influence of Existentialism on Ingmar Bergman: An Analysis of the Theological Ideas Shaping a Filmmaker's Art* (Lewiston/Oueenston and New York: Edwin Mellen Press, 1986); Egil Törnqvist, *Bergman's Muses: Aesthetic Versatility in Film, Theatre, Television and Radio* (Jefferson, NC and London: McFarland & Company, 2003); Törnqvist, *Between Stage and Screen: Ingmar Bergman Directs* (Amsterdam: Amsterdam University Press, 1995); Louise Vinge, "The Director as Writer. Some Observations on Ingmar Bergman's *Den goda viljan*," in *A Century of Swedish Narrative. Essays in Honour of Karin Petherick*, ed. Sarah Death and

Helena Forsås-Scot (Norwich: Norvik Press, 1994), 281–93; Rochelle Wright, *The Visible Wall: Jews and Other Ethnic Outsiders in Swedish Film* (Uppsala: Uppsala University, 1998), Wright, "The Imagined Past in Ingmar Bergman's *The Best Intentions*," in *Ingmar Bergman: An Artist's Journey: On Stage, On Screen, In Print*, ed. Roger W. Oliver (New York: Arcade Publishing, 1995), 116–25; Margareta Wirmark, ed., *Ingmar Bergman. Film och teater i växelverkan.* (Stockholm: Carlsson förlag, 1996); Marc Gervais, *Ingmar Bergman: Magician and Prophet* (Montreal and Kingston: McGill-Queen's University Press, 1999); Birgitta Steene, *Ingmar Bergman: A Reference Guide* (Amsterdam: Amsterdam University Press, 2005); Maaret Koskinen, ed., *Ingmar Bergman Revisited. Performance, Cinema and the Arts* (London and New York: Wallflower Press, 2008); Koskinen, *Ingmar Bergman's The Silence. Pictures in the Typewriter, Writings on the Screen* (Seattle: University of Washington Press and Copenhagen: Museum Tusculanum Press, 2010); Koskinen, "Multiple Adaptation Processes: The Case of Alexander Ahndoril's The Director and Its Predecessors in Feature Film, Television Documentary and Popular Print Media," *Journal of Scandinavian Cinema* 5, no. 1 (2015): 35–47; Thomas Elsaesser, "Ingmar Bergman in the Museum? Thresholds, Limits, Conditions of Possibility," *Journal of Aesthetics & Culture* 1, no. 1 (2009): doi:10.3402/jac.v1i0.2123.2009; and Peter Ohlin, *Wordless Secrets: Ingmar Bergman's Persona. Modernist Crisis & Canonical Status* (Cardiff: Wales Academic Press, 2011). And as for the more serious film critique that his oeuvre has attracted, see for example Georges Sadoul, "Ingmar Bergman et le cinéma suèdois," *Les lettres francaises*, no 626 (June 28, 1956): 6; Jacques Siclier, *Ingmar Bergman* (Brussels: Club du livre de cinema, 1958); Jean Béranger, *Ingmar Bergman et ses films* (Paris: Le terrain vague, 1959); Andrew Sarris, "Notes on the Auteur Theory in 1962," in *Film Theory and Criticism: Introductory Readings*, ed. Leo Braudy and Marshall Cohen (New York & London: Oxford University Press, 1999), 515–18; Susan Sontag, "Bergman's *Persona*," in *Styles of Radical Will* (New York: Farrar, Straus & Giroux, 1969), 123–45; Robin Wood, *Ingmar Bergman* (London: Studio Vista, 1969); Wood, *Ingmar Bergman*, 2nd edn. Rev. (Detroit: Wayne State University Press, 2013).

2 Daniel Humphrey, *Queer Bergman: Sexuality, Gender and the European Art Cinema* (Austin: University of Texas Press, 2013); John Orr, *The Demons of Modernity: Ingmar Bergman and European Art Cinema* (New York and Oxford: Berghahn Boos, 2014); Linda Haverty Rugg, *Self Projection: The Director's Image in Art Cinema*; Alexis Luko, *Sonatas, Screams, and Silence: Music and Sound in the Films of Ingmar Bergman* (New York and London: Routledge, 2015); Koskinen, *Ingmar Bergman's The Silence*; Koskinen, "Multiple Adaptation Processes"; Louise Wallenberg, "Magos's Magic," in *Fashion, Film, and the 1960s*, ed. Eugenia Paulicelli, Drake Stutesman, and Louise Wallenberg (Bloomington: Indiana University

Press, 2017); Erik Hedling, "Ingmar Bergman," in *Oxford Bibliographies*, ed. Karin Gabbard (Oxford: Oxford University Press, 2017), https://doi.org/10.1093/OBO /9780199791286-0222; and Hedling, ed., *Ingmar Bergman: An Enduring Legacy* (Lund and Manchester University Press, 2021). See also Humphrey and Ford, "Situating Ingmar Bergman and World Cinema," in a special issue titled Bergman World in *Popular Communication* 19, no. 2 (2021): 66–79.

3 So far in Swedish only—two volumes of Bergman's diaries, one volume of his essays and articles, and one of his unpublished and unfilmed manuscripts for films and plays. See: http://www.norstedts.se/nyheter/176284-norstedts-firar-bergmanaret -2018.

4 Remakes or interpretations of *Scenes from a Marriage* are common, both on screen and on stage: see for example *Marriage Story* by Noah Baumbach, starring Scarlett Johansen and Adam Driver from 2019, and Norma Aleandro's stage play *Escenas de la vida conyugal* with Ricardo Darín and Érica Rivas from 2015.

5 "A Passion for Light," *American Cinematographer* 53, no. 4 (1972). See also the following interviews with Nykvist: Andrew C. Bobrow, "Sven Nykvist Discusses Ingmar Bergman's 'Face to Face,'" *Filmmakers Newsletter* 9, no. 7 (1976) and "Dialogue on Film: Sven Nykvist," *American Film* 9, 9, no. 5 (1984).

6 See production Research. https://productionstudies.net.

7 See Pietari Kääpä and Mette Hjort, "Editorial," *Journal of Scandinavian Cinema* 10, no. 2 (2020): 89. https://doi.org/10.1386/jsca_00015_2.

8 See Patrick Vonderau et al. https://productionstudies.net. Accessed on September 7, 2021.

9 Ingmar Bergman made several behind-the-scenes films from his own shoots with the (then) state-of-the-art equipment, as early as the 1950, for example, from the shot of *The Seventh Seal* and *Wild Strawberries*.

10 See, for example, Lars Elleström, *Media Borders, Multimodality and Intermediality* (Houndmills: Palgrave Macmillan, 2010) and Elleström, *Transmedial Narration: Narratives and Stories in Different Media* (Cham: Palgrave Macmillan, 2019).

11 Humphrey and Ford, "Situating Ingmar Bergman and World Cinema."

12 James Baldwin, "The Northern Protestant," in *Ingmar Bergman Interviews*, ed. Raphael Shargel (Jackson: University Press of Mississippi, 2007), 10. Originally published in James Baldwin, "The Precarious Vogue of Ingmar Bergman." *Esquire* 53, no. 4 (1960): 128–32; Janet Staiger, "Analysing Self-Fashioning in Authoring and Reception," in Koskinen, *Ingmar Bergman Revisited*; and Wright, *The Visible Wall*.

13 Quotation IB Fårö Center.

1

Hour of the Wolf

Nightmares and Creativity

Margarethe von Trotta

As a young student, I was a big fan of E. T. A. Hoffmann, a very idiosyncratic German Romantic writer. Sometimes I even skipped my classes because I simply couldn't get myself to put down a book of his stories. Earlier, in Paris in the late 1950s, I had discovered the movie *Det sjunde inseglet/The Seventh Seal* (1957), which shook me to the core and turned me into a major admirer of Ingmar Bergman. It was only many years later that I saw *Vargtimmen/Hour of the Wolf* (1968) and sensed an affinity between it and the work of E. T. A. Hoffmann.

In the early 1960s, young directors in Germany had rebelled against the old guard of established filmmakers with the slogan: Grandpa's movies are dead. The so-called "Young German Film" was born, with Alexander Kluge, Volker Schlöndorff, and Edgar Reitz leading the way. It was a veritable revolution, just like the "Nouvelle Vague" in France had been before it. Since all eyes were now on the young rebels, Ingmar Bergman's films were somewhat sidelined. And then, in 1968, the movement became politicized: We wanted to change the world—Germany, that is—and, soon enough, some were even willing to use violent means to do so.

As far as I know, *Hour of the Wolf*, which was shot in 1967, wasn't an instant success in Sweden either—and maybe for the same reasons. At the time, everything was about political awareness, not self-reflection. Only *Persona* (1966) became and remains Bergman's recognized masterpiece, eclipsing the movies he made right afterward in many people's memories.

Since the Goteborg Film Festival asked me to present a movie for the 100th anniversary of the birth of Ingmar Bergman, I chose this one, because of the affinity between it and E. T. A. Hoffmann. I know that Bergman read Hoffmann's work—in German, even—and I think that in this movie he was trying to give shape to his nightmares. His choice of the title alone, "Vargtimmen"—the time between night and daybreak, which is rife with fear and obsessive thoughts for many people who suffer from insomnia—gives an idea of how he intended the movie to be read and understood. For years, I had trouble sleeping because my dead mother would appear in my dreams wanting to kill me, even though in life she had been an exceptionally loving mother. I would only manage to shake off my fears and finally fall asleep when the blackbirds' early song announced the break of dawn. In *Hour of the Wolf* this excruciating, uninvited wakefulness plagues Max von Sydow, alias Johan Borg, and his wife Alma (Liv Ullmann) keeps vigil with him, even though she can barely keep her eyes open from exhaustion. She wants to protect him from his demons.

Early on in the film, Max von Sydow shows Liv Ullmann how long a minute lasts on his watch. We see the time pass—or rather, stand still, it seems—on Liv's face, and this long lingering on her face already gives us an idea of what the story will demand of her and of us. In the story from his childhood, in which he, Johan Borg—Ingmar as a boy—was locked in a dark closet, scared half to death, he describes horrors experienced early on in life. E. T. A. Hoffman calls them "Nachtstücke."

Ingmar Bergman and Liv Ullmann were living together when the movie was shot. I suspect it was an important—and happy—time for them both. Even so, he suffered from insomnia. And jealousy. Jealousy also plays a role in the film, as does humiliation—a theme that recurs frequently in Bergman's cinematic oeuvre from the start. The climax comes when Borg meets his apparently dead former lover, who suddenly comes back to life, forcibly pulls him to her, and sinks her teeth into him. Passion and annihilation. The residents of the castle, the demons referred to as the cannibals, laugh derisively. Who isn't familiar with those nightmares in which you are laid bare and helplessly exposed to the ridicule of others? Undoubtedly this is something that affects artists in particular; it is material they can exploit in order to create. Exploit to the point of exhaustion. Can you drive away your fears by naming them? These are questions I asked myself while watching the movie. When, haunted by my dead mother's nightly persecutions, I finally went to see a psychoanalyst because I thought I was going crazy, after a few sessions she sent me home with the following advice: "Talk about everything you've told me here in your films. That will be your therapy." In "Torquato Tasso" Goethe wrote: "Where in their anguish other men fall silent, a god gave me the power to speak my pain." Bergman might well have said the same of himself.

Figure 1.1 The director as demon on the film set of *Vargtimmen/Hour of the Wolf* (1968).

One of E. T. A. Hoffmann's novellas is called "The Devil's Elixirs." In it, a monk encounters his doppelgänger, a paragon of depravity. The two men look at each other as though seeing themselves in a mirror and, soon, they no longer know which of them is the good one and which the bad. At one point in *Hour of the Wolf* Borg says: "The mirror is shattered, but what do the shards reflect?" Which of the two doppelgängers remains reflected in them? Johan Borg, the artist in the movie, loses touch with the real world. Bergman, on the other hand, was able to save himself by continuing to make movies (Figure 1.1).

2

Working with Bergman

Interview with Film and Television Producers Katinka Faragó and Måns Reuterswärd

Maaret Koskinen and Louise Wallenberg

In March 2018, the year of Ingmar Bergman's centennial, we were both invited to Moscow to speak at a Bergman symposium held at the Centre for Russian and Swedish Research at the Russian State University for the Humanities. One evening, the Swedish Embassy invited us out to dinner, and while the Ambassador, the Cultural Attaché, and their party were running late, we were on time. We were led to the tables where the Swedish party was supposed to dine, where we to our joy found Katinka Faragó (b. 1936)—who was in Moscow for another Bergman-related event. As one of Bergman's closest collaborators, Katinka had been invited to some thirty events and talks worldwide during the Bergman Centennial. We sat down with her, and the conversation and laughter started immediately: Maaret was overwhelmed, since Katinka is known for her integrity and larger-than-life personality, but so was Katinka, who told us that she had lived in fear of Maaret's sharp pen for years (while pursuing her academic career, Maaret was a film critic for the biggest Swedish daily newspaper from 1981 to 2011). After this unexpected meeting, we asked Katinka to talk to us about her career—and we also asked if we may interview her husband, the famous television producer Måns Reuterswärd (b. 1932). Måns, who first trained as a photographer, became involved in Swedish National Public Television (SVT) in the 1950s, first as a technician, learning the trade from scratch, and later as a producer. Between 1978 and 1980 he turned to producing feature films for the Swedish Film Institute (SFI), before returning to producing for SVT. Måns had been involved in a great number of music, ballet and opera productions, among them several dance programs for television with famous choreographer Birgit Cullberg. In 1971, their production *Rött vin i gröna glas/Red Wine in Green*

Glasses was awarded the Prix Italia. In 1993, he was nominated for an Emmy Award for his behind-the-scenes documentary on Bergman's operatic adaption of *The Bacchae* at the Royal Swedish Opera. In many ways, Katinka is Sweden's Ms. Film, just like Måns is Mr. Television—they definitively shaped the country's film and television. They also have exceptional experiences of working with Bergman over a period of no less than five decades. And so, a series of meetings and conversations started in the summer of 2018. During our retreat at Fårö in October 2019, we had another chance to interview them, this time specifically focusing on their joint collaboration on Bergman's *Trollflöjten/The Magic Flute* (1975). What follows are excerpts from our hour-long interviews, conducted at seven different occasions between June 2018 and August 2021.[1]

* * *

Katinka started working in the film industry as a script girl already at the age of 13 in 1950. She says that she started working in the industry through her father, scriptwriter Alexander Faragó, who for instance was involved in writing the script of Fred Astaire and Ginger Rogers's *Top Hat* (1935):

> **Katinka**: It was through my dad. We were Hungarian refugees, and he was a writer and managed to flog some screenplays although his Swedish wasn't great and he wrote some kind of German. Yet he managed to sell some screenplays and during the filming of *Loffe blir polis* [*Loffe Becomes a Cop*], with Elof Ahrle as director and in the title role, he once took me along to Nyköping. I was just about thirteen. The [movie] dog and I clicked. So, he went home and left me there, and I'm still there, in a way.
>
> **Louise**: But how did you come to Sweden?
>
> **Katinka**: We came to Sweden because of Hitler, or really because of Miklós Horthy, who was the fascist leader in Hungary then. Dad had written an article against Horthy in the main Budapest newspaper and was jailed, and at the time it was a question of a life sentence, or something worse.
>
> **Louise**: When was this?
>
> **Katinka**: This was in 1935 and they couldn't prove anything because editorials were anonymous, so they released him and then Mom and Dad immediately disappeared to Vienna. Then I was born in 1936 and he was doing well in Vienna; he wrote several plays that were staged for example at Burgtheater, a fine theater in Vienna. Yes, it was *the* theater in Vienna actually, at least at the time. We had a home in Vienna and everything went well, but then came the

Anschluss in 1938, and the next day we were already leaving, because someone had warned him. They sold 2,000 books and Persian rugs overnight and took the tram to Bratislava...

This is very vague; they never told me everything because this was a difficult time for my parents and we never spoke about it. Dad disappeared to Prague and Mom took me to a farm outside Bratislava. We could sleep there and in the morning she took me in a wheelbarrow toward the city and Dad came by car from Prague. Then we went to Warsaw by train. But that was also not a good place for us so eventually we came to Helsinki where we were during the Winter War. We stayed there for a year and Dad managed to sell some screenplays and he became good friends with Erik Blomberg, at the time a famous director in Finland. In 1940 we took a train that went around the entire Gulf of Bothnia. We first came to Haparanda, then to Eskilstuna, and finally to Stockholm. Dad said that we were Catholic so that we could enter Sweden: it wasn't popular to be Jewish. So, and I don't know how or why, we arrived in a camp in Eskilstuna. And eventually we ended up in Råsunda [just outside Stockholm], because you could get an apartment for free for three months. Then we lived for many years on 9 Östervägen in Råsunda.

Louise: Was this the case for all Jewish war refugees?

Katinka: Yes, I think so. And then Dad started selling screenplays for feature films and then the *Loffe* films came [made between 1948 and 1950]. There were three of them. And I was to go with him when I was around 12, 13, to one of these *Loffe* shoots. I'm very good with dogs so I fell in love with the dog in *Loffe blir polis* [Elof Ahrle, 1950]. Nothing is as boring as being at a shoot with nothing to do, so Dad left after a few days and left me there... Just over a year later they were going to do *Anderssonskans Kalle* [*Mrs. Anderson's Charlie*; Rolf Husberg, 1950], and then they called again and so I watched the dog again. There was a script boy there and he thought it was the most boring job he had ever had. He put the book in my lap and went out to smoke, so I learnt a bit of what it was about. And the people were very kind. The whole environment was warm and kind and there was no harassment. People were just so nice to me, and I got to know Harriet Andersson and we became friends. She was about four years older than me. But we played; we were shooting at a house out on Djursgården, so we went to Skansen during lunch, she and I, and we fed the monkeys and rode on the swings. It was fun with Harriet; we've had a long journey.

Louise: And in 1955, at the age of 17, you started working with Bergman. Didn't you feel chosen, and a bit special?

Katinka: No, I was scared to death! "Why should *I*?" I asked. "Nobody else wants to," they said. It was nice of them to say that to me.

Louise: You must've been really good at what you did?

Katinka: Nobody else wanted to.

Louise: Because being a script supervisor is not easy. You have to have total control, right? And that with Bergman?

Katinka: Ha, ha . . . Everyone at the studio just said "Ha! We'll see how that goes . . ."

Louise: On which film did you work together the first time?

Katinka: *Kvinnodröm* [*Dreams*; 1955]. And then I got to work with Harriet Andersson again. And they said: "If he spits on you, spit back. If he glares at you, glare back." Oh well. So I met him there at the studio in a narrow corridor outside the canteen, there at Gärdet [a green area in central Stockholm]. He stared and I stared. I thought it lasted an eternity, but it was probably just half a minute or so. "This will work out," he said and laughed. Then it worked out for thirty years. A very long time, but I did other things too and you went from film to film when you finally got there. He even took me to SF [Studios] for *Sommarnattens leende* [*Smiles of a Summer Night*, 1955]. Because I survived that, and it was hard . . . it was a large film and there were many people and scenes, and we did the film in ten days although it was planned to take three weeks.

Louise: You said that the atmosphere was so kind and agreeable at the shoots. Did you experience it that way at all these films?

Katinka: Yes, I actually think so. I've not had any great conflicts with people, you know. We had a fantastic camaraderie. You stuck together, worked, and didn't complain. It was a very nice work atmosphere, as I remember it. Others may think differently. But that's what I thought. And I was part of a community of wonderful actors. It was then that I learned to understand acting. For an actor, being in front of a camera is being naked. It means standing there naked. And there Bergman would sit listening, preferably under or beside the camera, and then they'd get some clothing on their bodies. He was a fantastic recipient, and they had never been as good as with Ingmar. And you wouldn't discuss lofty things; it was about *now*, the moment when you're standing there. And he was good at that. He once said: "You have to create the art at your desk, then you have to get things done in the studio." So there was no talk about art; there were no pretensions. He had a stomach ache, OK. And sometimes it became a bit violent. But now in these Me Too-times . . . I'd never seen him grope anyone. And if you'd sit there as a script supervisor, you're right in the thick of it and you'd know. If anything happens, you'd find out. You'd sit there eight hours a day. I'd never heard anything, and I've checked with Gunnel [Lindblom] and with Harriet [Andersson], and they agree and say that it wasn't like that. And they really want to say that he was gropey or slimy or I don't know what. I'll defend him to the death!

Louise: He loved women, but he didn't harass?

Katinka: Sitting with him alone when he was in a good mood . . . He later employed me for ten years. He was of course in Munich most of that time, but we spoke in Munich too; I was often in Munich. Suddenly he would do this with his hand [she shows], "Oh so beautiful, can't you do that one more time?" Do you see? And you'd feel, "Oh, me?" You'd say things to him that you wouldn't even say to your partner. You'd say things to him that you wouldn't even know you had thought. I don't know what he did.

Louise: He created trust?

Katinka: Trust, and love, without the body (Figure 2.1).

Louise: But I'm wondering if this camaraderie or that you stuck together and so on, do you think that it changed over time or when you made films later on, at the end of the eighties?

Katinka: Why should it have? With Ingmar we were often the same people as well. On the whole. Then I've worked with so many other directors. It also depends

Figure 2.1 Faragó, Lindholm, Bergman, and unknown on the film set of *Smultronstället/ Wild Strawberries* (1957).

on which tone the director sets. He is a very important person in this team. It also depends on how much trust he places in the people around him. There are also these dimwits who can do everything on their own. And then the team becomes, we'd get a bit tired, you could say . . . Erland Josephson who made two films with us, said during the first one: "I can't do this, can you help me?" and then we were all eager to give everything!

Louise: Katinka, you collaborated for thirty years, with you in different roles—first as a script supervisor, then as a production manager, and producer. Bergman must've depended a lot on you on set, but he must've also really needed you?

Katinka: It was so fantastic because when he died my one daughter called and said, "Mom," and she was of course grown up then, "Finally free."

Louise: What did she mean?

Katinka: When they were small, he would call on Sundays and then it had to be quiet, quiet, quiet . . . I was out working more or less the whole week and when you finally were home you had to keep your mouth shut too. So, he wasn't popular, let me tell you. Then when I stopped, Måns started working more intensely with him on TV and then he was here for dinner, I'll be damned! He was here quite often, so they were rather tired of Bergman.

Louise: So, he was always present, always demanded his place, and you had to make peace with that?

Katinka: Hmmm, but I remember that it wasn't the case when shooting *Fanny och Alexander* [*Fanny and Alexander*, 1982]. Then we were finally more compatible . . . we were friends during *Fanny och Alexander*, when we sat there on a couch on Fårö until 2 or 3 am and prepared the whole damn film. It was insane; it was the night of my life, you see. And yes, there's so much about him, there are so many other memories. And it was just then, *then* it passed, and of course I respected him. But I wasn't afraid of him anymore.

Louise: So you were afraid, Katinka?

Katinka: At the start I was afraid of him, of course I was.

Louise: For how long?

Katinka: For a few years, and it started with *Kvinnodröm*. You know, he had a method I first didn't get; I was actually very young. For example, when I'd sit on lower Götaplatsen [a public square in Gothenburg] and he'd be above talking to Eva Dahlbäck. Suddenly I'd be yelled at across the whole Götaplatsen. "Why the hell are you screaming? What have *I* done?" So I was sad, sad, sad and there were tears and all of that. . . . Then some years later we did *Smultronstället* [*Wild Strawberries*, 1957] and he'd get started; this happened many times, it did. And we were shooting at a gas station at Gränna and Max [von Sydow] was pumping gas and they're 50 meters away. And suddenly all hell broke loose. And I was being yelled at, and I thought "But what have *I* done, what is he fighting about?" I went completely cold. Then he called that evening. We weren't staying at the same place. So he called and said, "Come over for dinner." "No thanks, I'm not coming." "Come over!" "No, Ingmar, I don't want any dinner, I'm not coming." And then he maybe understood that I wasn't a complete ninny because if I had gone there, the same circus would've started up. I don't want to say that that was the end of that, but it became better. And I realized part of what it was. If he were to row with one of the actors, then she'd have had to get her makeup redone; crying and then getting new makeup takes an hour. So it's better to take it out on me; yes, that's my theory, and I'm convinced it was the case, because it had to get out! It had to get out; had he worked himself up he had to blow off steam. And I'm sure that it was like that; he was a very rational person. He thought that if he were to yell at the actor nothing will happen for an hour, and he couldn't afford that.

Louise: So, it was coldly deliberate?

Katinka: Yes.

Louise: He needed it?

Katinka: Yes.

Maaret: It must've helped you considerably that you spoke up so early: the king needs naysayers too to understand that not everyone is yes-men at whatever cost.

Katinka: Sometimes I actually dared, but it took time which we didn't always have. . . . When we did *Sommarnattens leende*, but that was before this. The last day we were having coffee outside the barn on the set. The barn was actually scenography and we had built something inside, and we were sitting on the grass. There weren't any wrap parties then. So it'd be coffee and thank you very much, "And we'll count all the mistakes Katinka made on this film." And then the sound guy said—yes, he [Bergman] was like that, he was mean, you know—so the sound guy, his name was P-O said, "Cue the taps," when I was supposed to start crying (laughs). But then he went round to the back of the house and apologized. He always apologized. But never in front of the team. So they thought I was an idiot. . . . Rather ". . . and you understand that I only want to teach you, I just want you to be able to do the job properly." His method was interesting, I have to say.

Maaret: Interesting, to say the least . . . So, it helped him to become kind of furious?

Katinka: Exactly, it helped in some situations. Talking straight . . . And I went back again the next morning, of course you did.

Louise: We're wondering about your transition from script supervisor to production manager. When and how did it happen?

Katinka: Ingmar called me in the morning, perhaps April 26, 1976, I think: "I'm leaving, and I want you to know before *Expressen* [a Swedish tabloid] comes out." That was when he was moving to Munich. And then Harry [Schein; CEO of SFI, 1963–1970 and 1972–1978] called me in the afternoon. We were about to do *Paradistorg* [*Summer Paradise*; Gunnel Lindblom, 1977] and Gunnel said, "I've been left behind alone." So, I asked her, "And me then, Gunnel?" with a debut director and quite a large film. "Oh, I didn't think about that." Exactly. But then Harry called and said, "Come up." We were in the basement of Filmhuset [the SFI building]. And then we shed a few tears about the situation!

Louise: The first film you made with Bergman was *Kvinnodröm*, and the last was *Fanny och Alexander* [and the 1984 TV play Bergman wrote, *Efter repetitionen* (*After the Rehearsal*)]. Between these you two made no less than nineteen films. At the same time, you also worked with many other directors, both in Sweden and internationally. One of the films you made with Bergman that gained international recognition was *Tystnaden* [*The Silence*, 1963]. What was it like to film such an anxiety-ridden story?

Katinka: During the breaks we told funny stories, roared with laughter and guffawed. And it worked. It was a method Ingmar used, and funny stories were often told, not just while filming *Tystnaden*, but in general. And then suddenly he'd stamp his foot: "OK, action, you guys!"

Måns: Yes, it was exactly like that! And then we'd watch TV every day for example, not just at teatime but during breaks too, while we were waiting on lighting and such. Then there'd be lots of chatting, a lot of gossip and many funny stories— and the actors leaving the studio was not appreciated, if they weren't in makeup or so. Once the lighting was done—"Action!" And then the atmosphere would just flip like this (gestures). He was good at that (Figure 2.2).

Katinka: I think he has even said somewhere that the more serious, the darker and harder the film, the more fun is being had between takes. An example is the behind-the-scenes documentary on *Viskningar och rop* [*Cries and Whispers*, 1973]. It's a horrid film in many ways, very dark—despite the color. And then you see the three actors [Liv Ullmann, Ingrid Thulin, and Harriet Andersson] sitting there and jumping on the bed and showing their breasts to each other.

Måns: Ingmar also had that, that curve I mean, and the effort starts right at the bottom: you almost break it down to the silliest little part, before you (claps his hands) take it to the max.

Maaret: Yes, that was a good way of putting it! But Måns, you have also worked in the film industry. Can you tell us a bit more?

Figure 2.2 Director, actors, and film crew laughing and joking in between anxiety-ridden takes on the film set of *Tystnaden/The Silence* (1963).

Måns: My stint in the film industry only lasted three years. That's where the so-called I Fund was, which was a fund we created to promote cooperation between SFI and SVT. There was no communication, and SVT sometimes invested in feature films, but sometimes not, and there was no real policy.
Katinka: Wasn't the film industry also involved in this?
Måns: Yes, it was a fund comprising money administrated by SFI, but we were also to practically handle the people who went to SVT and talk to them and suggest different topics and film projects. Ideas had to be approved by them and then by Harry [Schein]. The fund was started with Pelle Berglund [producer and director] and Jörn Donner [CEO of SFI, 1982–6], who each had their pool. So there were two people to use the money and they did that diligently enough, so after two or three years the funds started running out. Then Harry called me. "No," I said, "absolutely no way." Ingmar was plotting behind the scenes and thought I could do it. So he managed to convince me and I thought it was rather nice to get away [from the world of TV] and breathe some fresh air. So I took a leave of absence and started working there with Anna-Lena Wibom [SFI producer]. The funds have already run out by then, and Harry thought it was a bit embarrassing so he pulled some strings with the funds. I don't know how, but they had some G Funds and H Funds and you name it.

However, it happened, we all got some money to spend and then I would read [screenplays]. It was quite exciting.

But first I was forced to make a film I don't think was so successful. Sure, it was Kjell Grede, but the film, *Min älskade* [*My Beloved*, 1979] didn't turn out well. But it was a way for Ingmar to keep Cinematograph, his production house, going while he was in Munich. That meant that he had to ensure that it was produced and Katinka was also employed as a director of Cinematograph. So he had to get the screenplays funded by SFI. Then he sent me a screenplay: "It's a damn good screenplay, you see. This is much better than anything else you have read. . . ." I read it and thought yes, there are some good things and I was a great admirer . . . I wasn't a complete novice, so I thought it was fun. So, we had a go and we got started. And it wasn't hard to get through a screenplay that came via Bergman and Kjell Grede. But then some strange process started and I don't really know why. I've never understood it either. Then Kjell Grede and Ingmar sat in a hotel room in Oslo . . .

Katinka: We were making *Höstsonaten* [*Autumn Sonata*, 1978] at the time.

Måns: . . . and so he and Kjell sat and ripped the screenplay to shreds—and it was no good. Then Kjell would go to his room like a schoolboy and rewrite and come back and then [they] read. And in the end it disappeared. . .

Katinka: . . . yes, all that was characteristically Kjell, the small jokes and so on. Ingmar removed that.

Måns: But I had to give my blessing, and it premiered at Sture [a smaller movie theater in central Stockholm] and played for a week—and then it was over. You kind of got the feeling that you weren't tough enough for that industry . . . Yes, that was my stint at SFI. I thought it was fun and interesting, but unfortunately SVT turned down many good film projects. I had a finished screenplay based on Inger Alvfén's novel *S/Y Glädjen* [*S/Y Joy*, 1979], but they turned it down. I don't want to bad-mouth SVT, but it's easy to see that the difficulties weren't on the film side, but rather that civil servants, not from the industry, from two channels sat there refusing. I don't know what kind of films they had dreamt about, but nothing was up their alley. It was a bit sad at the same time, because I had to sit with my own old bosses and listen to their complaints . . . But it was a fun period, because I woke up to a world outside of TV and there were writers and directors in the film world and I actually felt more at home there. Then I had to go back to TV work, because I was employed there.

Maaret: Could it be that during this radically left-wing period at SVT, they simply resented authors and "the literary world"?

Måns: Exactly, I mean, they refused great authors. I thought: what could you do to produce new screenplays, and then you'd have to start with *the authors*. They're the ones writing, after all. Then they'll maybe invent something that a director could enjoy making a film of. So that was why I had many such feelers out and it takes time. I mean, you don't get a new screenplay in a week, but it must have time to germinate and maybe comes after a year or so. It's not done in a trice, so I didn't get to complete it. But it was sabotaged, I thought, when the idea was not even worth discussing. Sometimes SVT's way of communication could be so horribly negative—or *destructive*, more precisely. With general meetings and all that collective destructiveness. Everything was crap—*Trollflöjten* for example.

Maaret: In a way we are currently in a similar period, to simplify somewhat. You could actually draw some parallels: there are certain decrees, that films should have certain ideological content to interest producers. While the intentions may be good and you want new stories, fine—this is done through draconic measures. Much risks falling by the wayside as a result.

Måns: Yes, exactly.

* * *

Louise: And then came the 1990s and Bergman, once more.

Måns: Ingmar was done with film but clear on the fact that he wanted to do theater. And there was talk about freezing theater productions on TV but still trying to use transmissions, as they were called, from stage productions. And Ingmar thought that I should do it. I think it started with [Yukio] Mishima's *Madame de Sade* in 1992. I'd seen the play at the Royal Dramatic Theater as directed by Ingmar and thought, hell, such fine theater could become a very good TV production. Sometimes you kind of know what can be done, and this was so concentrated. It was so two-dimensional and so damn beautiful with the costumes. So I went to Ingrid Dahlberg who was the head of SVT Channel 1 Drama. I said, "You know Ingmar, you can speak to him because I think he should make TV from this play."

Louise: So it was on your initiative?

Måns: Yes. I planted the idea, in any case. Then I met Ingrid after a few days and she said Ingmar had refused: "This play is not for the inhabitants of small red cottages," as he put it. Some weeks passed, and then Ingrid called me to say that he had changed his mind, but "You should take the credit, so you are the one producing it." So we started. It was extremely enjoyable; we sat working—but then Ingmar Bergman suddenly got his famous 37.2 [°C; 98.96°F] fever. In other words, he was *extremely* ill. Awful. He lost consciousness and said, "Well, you see that I can't do it, you have to take over now." So we were working with his assistant as script supervisor when we had arrived at so-called camera solutions. You cluelessly tried to do the best possible. We thought it was very handsome and then Ingmar came snuffling, sat in a chair under a blanket and we went through a few minutes of scenes. Then I suddenly saw that the blanket was slipping down. "Listen, we'll do this instead, you see," and then he took over. There I had a lesson in film scenes and thought yes, damn, why didn't I know better . . . It was wonderful. He was so kind because he understood that I had some experience. When he lay down his scenes, he displayed the genius I see in all his films: using the simplest possible option. I call this economy footage or footage economy, in other words using one camera and one take for as long as possible. As long as you can create a scene or an expression using that camera. Then you can move around, zoom in, and zoom out. You can pan, you can move the actors—this was the art he displayed. Things would happen, but there are no unnecessary cuts. If it is a single cut, it has an important meaning. I think it is wonderful to see what I call a craft—*film craft*.

Maaret: So it took shape right there and then?

Måns: Yes, to me. I had a lesson. In any case, it became clear to me what he wanted. Then we continued working together on *The Bacchae* in 1993. It was an idea I threw out as soon as I heard rumors that he was doing another opera. I grabbed the telephone and said that we had to find some kind of TV partnership. The performance was a collaboration between the Royal Dramatic Theater and the Royal Swedish Opera, and then TV joined, so I could sit in on all the dress rehearsals at the Opera the entire fall. And then we did the behind-the-scenes documentary *Dokument Fanny och Alexander* [*Document Fanny and Alexander*, 1986], with Arne Carlsson filming. It was mostly material from the dress rehearsals and the actual opera performance, and after the opera premier we made a TV version.

Katinka: But you did discover Peter Mattei in some way?

Måns: It was modern music and not that easy to sing. But Mattei was just like the guy who played Tamino in *Trollflöjten*, he had recently finished school. So he was a rising star.

Maaret: Didn't he play the King of Thebes and Sylvia Lindenstrand was Dionysus?

Måns: Yes, and then those Dionysian Bacchae were to slaughter him. It was a horrendous story. Then Ingmar added new backstories or biographies for all twelve followers or Bacchae. That was a lot of fun, because those girls were so good and they made opera history. They had never had such fleshed-out roles—how they felt, what kind of persons they were. They were all different and had different stories. It was fantastic and it was only in the screenplay.

Maaret: What Bergman did in the TV version was so attractive, and can also be seen in your documentary on the shoot: first you see them rehearsing, but then you cut to sections of the complete TV production, when each one goes to the camera and presents themselves—"my name is," and so on—while at the same time appearing in medium shot.

Katinka: It's so funny in the film, when Peter Mattei admits to not understanding some words Ingmar had said. Do you remember that?

Måns: Yes, but he was such a natural talent, he had a great voice. But he was shocked by the directing, and Ingmar grabbed hold of him . . .

Katinka: . . . and pulled them both to the floor.

Måns: He got rolled around. He was such a fantastic person who could handle that really tricky role, he did it superbly. But the strange thing was that Bergman first had wanted to stage *The Bacchae* as a play at the Royal Dramatic Theater. But then he realized that no, I'm going to do an opera with Daniel Börtz as composer. He had long admired Daniel Börtz's music, and Ingmar was very curious about modern music. He would frequent the Berwald Hall [a concert hall in Stockholm] and they had liked each other too, so they had agreed. So they sat on the telephone between Fårö and somewhere in Närke where Daniel was in a cottage, and wrote the music—and then it was done! They'd never actually met in person before the rehearsals started. Then we recorded the music just for the heck of it at the Royal College of Music so that Ingmar had something to work with. We couldn't read music so he had to hear it with a small orchestra and some crooners, so it was just working material. Then we made the TV version and it was completely new; it was like starting all over again.

Then Ingmar was so delightfully curious about all new forms of expression and technical oddities and he really was like a child with a toy box—he was glad when I tweaked something. So I got the chance to show him different things he thought were interesting.

* * *

Louise: Then after *The Bacchae* came Bergman's own play, *Sista skriket* [*The Last Gasp*, 1995] which was shown at SFI, right?

Måns: Yes, that was the play about silent movie director Georg af Klercker. And then Ingmar and I talked about doing a TV version and we did that in a studio. But then he wanted me to do an introduction where we describe the history of SF [Swedish Film Industry, a production and distribution company] or Svenska Bio [Swedish Cinema] as they were called when they were located on Lidingö [an island in Stockholm]. I combed through all the images at SFI and did an introduction of about five minutes on the time when af Klercker was working and how it had been for Mauritz Stiller and those old geezers. In the play af Klercker is a director who approaches producer Charles Magnusson, who at the time was the director of Svenska Bio, with a screenplay that is refused. He was treated really badly, despite his talent. That was what Ingmar wanted to say, that af Klercker was a great talent who was never accepted. Anyway, that was what was so great about Ingmar, because as soon as he would do something he'd be so enthusiastic. And it may sound a bit cocky, but he kind of wanted me there specifically. He missed me when I wasn't there.

Katinka: I have to tell a story. A very short one. He always called on Sundays, as I said. And then one Sunday he called and asked: "Do you sometimes see your husband naked?" "Yes, it has happened," I answered. "But have you seen his angel's wings?" he asked. That was a sweet thing to say.

Måns: I don't know that I had any angel's wings, but that was exactly what was great, that you felt that he trusted you—that's perhaps the right word.

Katinka: Yes, Måns really helped him.

Måns: Arriving late to meet Ingmar was a mortal sin, as everyone knows. I knew that, but once I got stuck in a traffic jam. Usually if we were supposed to start at nine, everyone would sit outside the studio waiting for Ingmar to enter and then everyone would go in. And just when I came rushing in through the door at ten past nine, I heard someone asking, "What should we do, Måns isn't here yet?" and Ingmar answered: "No, but then we'll wait until he comes." And then he just looked up when I came and only said, "Well then, shall we get started?" There was a line: I thought that if you'd come so far that your being late is accepted, you're probably in the clear.

No, we never fell out. We had professional discussions, of course. We had many technical problems to solve, and *Trollflöjten* was a whole adventure as far as technology goes, with different types of film I wasn't so familiar with at first. But he was very loyal: as long as I could just explain why it was in a certain way, he'd say that he understood. But you couldn't concoct a story or lie, because he'd see through it immediately.

Maaret: There's a scene in Arne Carlsson's behind-the-scenes documentary on *Fanny och Alexander* where Sven Nykvist is struggling to formulate something. He first just mumbles something about it not working, and then he tries to explain. And then Bergman becomes impatient and clearly irritated—but then after a while Sven finds the words to describe the problem. "But why don't you speak up then?!"

Måns: Exactly, that's what it's about. Always presenting the truth. Or more correctly, never trying to explain away something but calling a spade a spade. I didn't think I'd survive the biggest setback I once had with him. That was when we were doing *The Bacchae* for TV and we had two studios. We had an earthquake scene. It was part of the theater production too, but when we were doing the TV show he had said: "Yes, it must shake you know. The whole damn place must shake." Our technical unit had built some kind of floating thing on wheels and boy, did it shake. We had four or five cameras each with its own recorder so that we could cut together everything afterwards. So it was pure action. Ingmar sat next to me in front of five monitors and directed all the cameras at the same time. All was well. Ingmar went home and the next day I went up to the cutting room to get all those video cassettes from all the cameras and the script supervisor was sitting there preparing. Ingmar was supposed to come at ten. Then I saw: it's all the same footage. . . . All the cameras, all five, only gave two different recordings! And I realized that three of the cameras' recordings were gone. Someone had wired it incorrectly in some check. We had technicians who were supposed to take care of it. And then . . .

Maaret: And then. Then you had to explain when he arrived. What happened?

Måns: Yes. So, I said "Here's the thing: I should've checked this yesterday." He just looked at me. "Oh well. Then we'll do this. I need three recordings, and we can do that." Silence. Not a peep about why the hell. No, he had solved it in his head, instead of just indulging in the disappointment of not getting all the great footage. But he could work out that he needed three angles, could you do that? So we called everyone in again, but it was easier because we could take one angle at a time. But I had a lump in my throat, I'll be damned. Because you felt like such a failure. He had trusted us to know what we do and it flopped. And I almost manically checked everything twice. I always had backups, there were spares in every nook and cranny. We knew that if something broke we could just take the next one, there were always backup solutions. But this, this was *too much*. But then I think he was extremely professional in the sense of not making the mess worse but solving it instead. So we solved it the next day, we called in people for an extra session and then we caught up and that was that.

* * *

Louise: And then finally it was Bergman's play *Larmar och gör sig till* [*In the Presence of a Clown*, 1997].

Måns: Yes, *Larmar* was actually supposed to be a theater production but at the last moment we decided to do TV instead. And it was great fun, but because Schubert was involved in the piece I felt damn, it's not fun seeing that Schubert was such a tragic figure, with his syphilis and illness and death agony. And then the clown who is Death. But he had that crazy figure Carl, actually based on Ingmar's uncle, who was a bit mad and some kind of technological inventor. So Ingmar wanted to do some type of travesty on *Singing in the Rain*, a story about a silent movie where you have to stand behind the scenes and speak out loud. We first filmed the silent movie inside the play where the actors stood off to the side and mimed to the footage. That was so much fun to do and we made sure to use a proper 35 mm film and special black-and-white film. And Ingmar was, let's say, in quite a good mood.

Maaret: Peter Stormare played the projectionist and it started burning and there the movie in the play had to stop.

Måns: Yes, Peter Stormare thought it was great: "here you can play and get paid for it too."

Katinka: He rapidly lost that attitude, let me tell you . . . sorry.

Maaret: But wait: you produced both the play itself and the behind-the-scenes documentary too?

Måns: Yes, we made the behind-the-scenes documentary, but it was Arne Carlsson. Then I sat on Fårö, I think, with Arne and cut and sorted material. Arne would film everything—because you never know, something may come of it. He said that it was like fishing, you sit with a rod and get a bite—and there you have your damn fish! Then you reel it in and suddenly you have a great bit, that connects to another part. But we had a mountain of material . . .

Maaret: I see. It's the fun part, but the hard part is also the editing and the material, but it means you have to have a photographer who knows what is important and what is good. . .

Måns: But it was a pity that Ingmar was so angry with him sometimes. I felt so bad for Arne, for example in *The Bacchae* when Arne was filming. He walked right across the stage with the camera: "What are you doing here? Leave!" Then later when I talked to Arne he just said, "No, I'm used to it." He was so quiet and unassuming in some way so he would always take it and swallow it, and I don't know how he's put together. But he could sneak around without being noticed, and it was because of that that he got to film. He had a way of becoming almost imperceptible, of being there without being seen and heard.

Katinka: You should actually interview him too sometime. He tells the story of how he and Sven Nykvist sat in a trailer somewhere waiting for the sheep to lamb and they sat there waiting night after night, while Sven told Arne the story of his life in that trailer—it's a wonderful anecdote. That's really nice. Sven taught him—not the worst of teachers!

Måns: Yes, Arne was kind of from the start one of the closest ones. It all started when he went pike fishing and then he went to Ingmar: "Do you want a pike?" Then Ingmar helped him financially and I think he is one of those inhabitants of Fårö that meant a lot to him.

Louise: And just think of the behind-the-scenes documentary on *Fanny och Alexander*, it's terrific.

Katinka: Just the fact that he never switched off the camera when Gunnar Björnstrand didn't know his lines, that's really fantastic.

Maaret: Yes, you sit there squirming for ten minutes. Arne just stands still and waits.

Måns: It's unbearable to watch. But holding the camera still, that's so nice. There's so much you'd like to say when they talk about film training and TV training. Today it doesn't matter how it looks or what you do. Now you film with cell phones and that's all and well, but there should be a reason, not just doing it because it's fun. And the imagery, everything that shows how a director thinks and visualizes. Take Ingmar's way of telling a story, that stability that makes the audience feel that I'm part of what I see. I don't have to hold on because things are all over the place; I'm like a fly on the ceiling looking down at someone who's standing and singing on a little patch. In this respect all visual storytelling has gone completely bananas. Especially on TV.

Maaret: Just think of when the drones came. Drones you use in war, and like so often technological developments unfortunately come from US warfare. Then we get loads of good stuff in peacetime. But when the drones came you suddenly had to take pictures from high above, in the weirdest of places.

Måns: Yes, but it's cool, and those cranes taking pictures from high above too. In my time we didn't have these. I remember the discussions when TV cameras were going to get zooms—imagine something so horrible! We were used to having five lenses that you cranked around. The visual storytelling was having lenses that could be combined in certain ways. I remember the arrival

Figure 2.3 Måns Reuterswärd and Katinka Faragó at their home in Stockholm during one of our interviews held in 2018–19.

of the zoom as a revolution—and we said no! Take it away, we don't want any damn zooms on the cameras. But then someone put zooms on every single camera.

Maaret: It changed the aesthetics and storytelling, it definitely did. But isn't it the case that when you have entered into the mayhem and tested everything, everything still settles in the end. People first thought 3D was so cool, but then you get tired of it.

Måns: That's why I think history is so important, because it's first then that you can go back and say "Now look at Bergman and how he made his films . . ." It's perhaps time to look at *how you do it*.

Katinka: At film school, for instance.

Måns: At film school. But there is such disdain for everything seen as old-fashioned: it's not possible today . . . Yet it's an artistic medium. I mean everyone still admires Rembrandt's painting technique. And painting portraits is still just as fantastic. Mozart's music is still being played, I'll be damned, and it works. You're throwing away all history just to run after the fad of the day . . .

Maaret: The baby with the bathwater.

Katinka: Listen here. I have to make dinner. (End.)

Note

1. We have chosen to include information gathered during an interview conducted by Louise and her colleague Maria Jansson for a project on women's experiences of working in the Swedish film industry. This interview took place in May 2018. The first interview conducted by Louise and Maaret took place in August 2018. It was followed by four more sessions in 2018 and 2019, with the last two conducted at Fårö during the retreat in October 2019.

3

Ambiguity and the Making of *Nattvardsgästerna/Winter Light*

Paisley Livingston

Knowledge of how and why a film has been made can make a huge difference to its understanding and appreciation. Unfortunately, in all too many cases, the available evidence only offers us glimpses of the long and complicated process through which a feature-length film has been created. It is often especially hard to learn much about the filmmakers' perspectives and intentions. One marvelous exception to that rule is Vilgot Sjöman's documentation of the making of Ingmar Bergman's *Nattvardsgästerna* [translated literally as *The Communicants*, but also distributed as *Winter Light*]. Sjöman personally witnessed much of the making of the film; he interviewed Bergman and many of his collaborators, reporting their responses to a variety of pertinent questions. The result was a book and documentary film that jointly give us invaluable insight into the filmmakers' attitudes and decisions. In what follows I bring some of this evidence to bear on some interpretative and evaluative issues raised by the film.

In the first part of his documentary, *Ingmar Bergman gör en film/Ingmar Bergman Makes a Film* (1963), Sjöman interviews Bergman on a sunny day on Fårö. He invites Bergman to talk about his writing of the script of *The Communicants*. Bergman begins by relating that his point of departure was something a rural pastor had told him. A member of the pastor's church had committed suicide, and the pastor had spoken to him just the day before this happened. The pastor related that he had been "impervious to the man's suffering," and "blamed himself mercilessly" for his death.

When he read the script, Sjöman noticed that Bergman had significantly revised this initial story idea. In the script, it seems that the pastor, Tomas Ericsson, may not actually have a private conversation with the depressed and suicidal fisherman, Jonas Persson. Instead, he appears to have only dreamt of having such a conversation. Here is how Sjöman reports his exchange with Bergman on this topic:

- "[I: Bergman] saw that I must get away from the church play. Out into reality instead. As realistic and true to life as possible."
- "In that case are you going to take out the oddities of the fisherman's second visit to Thomas? As you have written it now, we don't know whether Jonas is really there or not."
- "He is a vision. Has never been there."

I frown, not understanding.

- "But you've experienced that yourself, haven't you? One sits there and experiences something so intensely that it's just as if the person in question were there. Thomas sits there thinking so hard of what he is going to say to the fisherman that he imagines Jonas *is* there. He goes and asks Märta afterwards if she has seen Jonas."
- "That seems like a mystification to me. Especially if you're striving for everyday reality."[1]

Sjöman urges Bergman to eliminate what he called the "mystification." Bergman then comments that if he were to reframe the scene as representing an actual conversation, there would be temporal problems:

> If I make it so that it's not a dream talk, I'll be faced with a time problem of course: Jonas goes off; within two minutes he has shot himself. But good Lord! when have *I* ever bothered about realistic time. I can make a minute seem as long as an hour.[2]

It may be worth noting here that what Bergman initially described as a kind of extremely vivid thinking or imagining was then characterized by him as "a dream talk." Two months later, during the read through with the actors, the issue of the conversation's status in the story cropped up once more. Gunnar Björnstrand asks: "This is the dream sequence, isn't it?" At that point Bergman says: "When I wrote this I thought—only in a dream can one speak as openly as this"; he also says: "we are not to have the slightest suspicion of a dream mood. We must see it exactly as a reality."[3] Later in the conversation, Sjöman continued to advocate a realist alternative: "Couldn't the parson say all this just the same?" Bergman replies as follows:

> No, as I see it, he's a man with no contacts who can't speak so plainly. That's why this dream sequence comes in. *And I want to try out displacements in time, mazes*

among displacements in time. At any rate, it was an enormous help to me. The dream was an incubator. Now that I've lifted the baby out of the incubator, I can make it into a real episode, perhaps, and not a dream sequence.[4]

The "perhaps" in this last statement is quite significant. Bergman had been quite definite in reporting on his earlier intention to the effect that the conversation only took place in Tomas's mind. Yet it is also quite clear that Bergman reconsidered. He excised that part of the script that indicates that Tomas becomes convinced that Jonas never actually visited him. In the script, when Tomas goes out into the chancel and finds that Märta is there, waiting for him, he asks her whether she has seen Jonas. She shakes her head, to which he responds: "Then he won't be coming," the implication being that Tomas has decided that the conversation never really happened. In cutting this part of the script, Bergman opened up the possibility that Jonas had actually visited the sacristy. Yet it does not follow that Bergman had resolutely decided to shift entirely to a realistic understanding of the conversation. Whence the 'perhaps.'

If one closely scrutinizes the audiovisual sequence depicting the conversation between Tomas and Jonas in the sacristy, it would appear to be consistent with the two incompatible options. It could depict a conversation *dreamt* by Tomas, or it could depict a conversation that actually took place in the story. Arguably there is nothing in the audiovisual sequence alone that *requires* us to understand it in either one of these two ways. There is a close-up representing an exhausted Tomas at his desk, with his head down on his arms, as if he is about to fall asleep. After a moment he seems to awaken and looks up; then there is a cut to an image of Jonas standing before the pastor's desk. The scene in which the two men converse hardly looks to be a representation of someone's dream, especially in comparison with Bergman's representation of dreams in other works, such as *Smultronstället/ Wild Strawberries* (1957). This is unsurprising given Bergman's above-cited claim that there should be "not the slightest suspicion of a dream mood."

The conclusion that may be drawn at this point is that the scene in question is ambiguous. Its ambiguity is of a familiar kind. As is well known, an expression— be it verbal or visual—can be ambiguous in the sense that it can be used to express two or more incompatible things. For example, the noun, "bank," can refer standardly to the shore of a river, lake, or stream; but it can also refer to a long high mound, or to a financial institution. Longer linguistic and other expressions can also be ambiguous in the sense of serving divergent purposes equally well. This kind of ambiguity is a familiar feature of our means of expression. It is also well known that the ambiguity of an expression can be resolved in a particular context where it is put to use. For example, when stated with the right intention and in the right context, "Go to the bank!" can be used unambiguously to issue a command to visit a financial institution. The ambiguity of an audiovisual sequence can similarly be resolved within the context of the cinematic work of which it is a part. Many of the sequences that serve as "flashbacks" within a cinematic narrative are in themselves ambiguous between being depictions of what really happened at some earlier point in the story, and depictions of what some character wrongly recalls as having happened. In some cases spectators are given good reason to understand a particular flashback as belonging to only one of these two categories.

Returning now to the sequence in *The Communicants* depicting the conversation between Tomas and Jonas, we can observe that in the context of the film as a whole, there are only three salient options:

1. The ambiguity of the scene is resolved in favor of the conversation being dreamt;
2. The ambiguity of the scene is resolved in favor of the conversation's being real;
3. The ambiguity of the scene remains *unresolved* in the film as a whole.

Evidence pertaining to the film's critical reception can be taken as lending some support to the third option, since well-informed critics have been sharply divided with regard to the status of the scene. I hasten to add, however, that critics' entrenched disagreement is at best a symptom, but not proof, of an unresolved ambiguity.

Many interpreters write as though it were unproblematic to assume that the conversation really takes place. Their focus instead is on its consequences for the characterization of the pastor and for the overall story conveyed by the film.[5] For example, Bishop Lennart Koskinen remarked that in his conversation with the fisherman, Tomas makes every mistake a priest can possibly make.[6] Here is another rather strong statement made by a critic who believes that it is true in the fiction that the conversation took place:

> Bergman's depiction of the bad priest—the weakling shepherd—is thorough and pointed. Here the man who professes to serve as Christ served turns away the cripple (when the sexton first tries to speak to Tomas, the pastor cuts him off with a "Yes, yes") and cannot reach the fisherman Jonas (he tells the despairing man, "If God does not exist, what does it matter?"). After brutally sending the

fisherman to his death he repeats with horrible irony lines that Christ spoke as he gave himself sacrificially: "God, why has thou forsaken me?" Later he attends the fisherman's corpse with more diligence than he had his spirit.[7]

Other interpreters, however, appear to be quite certain that Tomas is innocent of any such wrongdoing, since they maintain that the conversation never actually takes place in the story. Frank Gado writes that it is "obvious" that Jonas does not really visit Tomas in the sacristy.[8] Egil Törnqvist agrees with the dream hypothesis, but does not think it obvious; instead, the spectator is meant to be initially taken in by the seeming realism of the sequence: "Characteristically, he [Bergman] avoids making it *clear when it occurs* that Jonas' second visit to Tomas is a visit only in Tomas' mind. By this procedure he is able to strengthen the spectator's identification with the protagonist, a goal that is constantly in his mind."[9]

Each of the two conflicting readings has many other advocates. Since it is possible that just one of these two conflicting readings squares best with the available evidence in the film as a whole, a brief survey of the evidence could be helpful.

The very best evidence in favor of the realist hypothesis is that the conversation is presented in the same style as the many ordinary realistic scenes that have preceded it. In such scenes, Bergman follows the standard cinematic convention whereby motion picture shots of an actor playing the part of some character are taken as depicting the actual actions of that character in the story. For example, when a shot depicts Ingrid Thulin, portraying Märta, as she blows her nose, it is "true in the fiction" that Märta blew her nose in the corresponding manner, unless, that is, some other sort of evidence indicates that this default convention has been be overturned. In the absence of such evidence, the spectator has every reason to assume that Jonas is really there, talking to Tomas.

In such a context, it is highly significant that Bergman cut elements from the script that were strongly incompatible with the default realist assumption. If he did not want the spectator to be able to entertain the possibility that the exchange actually took place, why would he cut out a seemingly crucial conversation in which Tomas discovers that he only dreamt or imagined that Jonas visited him? It may be worth pointing out that some of the advocates of the dream hypothesis cite the script without noting that Bergman made this key revision during the shooting of the film. It is fair to object against this procedure that what happens in the script does not always happen in the movie. Yet it should be noted as well that Bergman's wanting spectators to "entertain" the realist option is not the same thing as his expecting them to settle on it as the only plausible option.

The very best evidence in favor of the dream hypothesis is that it eliminates the temporal inconsistency mentioned above. If the conversation was only a dream, Jonas had plenty of time to fetch his shotgun, travel to the riverside, and kill himself. There was also time for Jonas's body to be discovered, and for the woman to walk to the church to inform the pastor. This is how Bergman reasoned about this aspect of the plot's structure, but he appears to have also thought this temporal problem was far from decisive.

Another sort of evidence that weighs somewhat in favor of the dream hypothesis is its inconsistency with the pastor's waking behavior. Tomas clearly has doubts about his religion and about his role in the church, but his failure to say anything remotely appropriate to the suicidal fisherman is extreme, and one might think, implausible. On this reading, his statements do not even indicate what he would have been likely to say, had Jonas kept his promise about coming to see him. At most it could be conjectured that the exchange was an involuntary expression of what Thomas might have wanted to say were he to take the liberty of speaking without reservation about his own doubts and anxieties. That Bergman thought along these lines was made clear in one of his above-cited remarks to Sjöman.

An advocate of the realist approach to the conversation might argue that the style of the film is consistently realistic, and that only the realist reading maintains this consistency. As was mentioned above, this was part of Sjöman's argument against what he called the "mystification." Bergman had opted for "everyday reality," and the pastor's having a vivid dream or imagination of a conversation could be deemed inconsistent with that choice.

It is certainly the case that the film has a realist quality, but not consistently so. A first exception is linguistic. Maaret Koskinen and Louise Wallenberg pointed out to me that the young boy's Stockholm dialect is out of place in the part of rural Sweden where the events in the film are meant to take place.[10] More generally, many of the lines have a characteristically Bergmanian poetic quality. This may be taken as one of the virtues of the film, but it does not square with the ambition of making a fiction that closely resembles "everyday reality."

Another exception to the film's literal realist quality is one of the film's most striking and effective sequences. As Tomas waits for Jonas in the sacristy, he reads a letter that Märta has given him. When Tomas begins to read, Bergman cuts to a lengthy shot in which Ingrid Thulin, in the role of Märta, addresses herself directly to the camera and unblinkingly delivers the lines from the handwritten letter. As Märta is obviously not present in the sacristy at this moment, we are not supposed to imagine that it is literally true in the fiction that Märta faces Tomas or anyone else while speaking the text of her letter out loud. We need not even imagine that she has ever actually spoken the text at all. Nor is it literally true in the fiction that this is what Tomas imagines as he reads the letter. This aspect of the film is clearly to be taken as an expressive stylization. It is as if the director is overtly showing us a sequence depicting a state of affairs that is only *counterfactually* true in the fiction: this is how Märta *would have* presented her thoughts directly to Tomas *had she had* the courage and the opportunity to do so, *which she did not*. One way to appreciate Bergman's adoption of this counterfactual strategy is in terms of the overarching goal of expression: an enhanced expressivity and emotive impact are achieved at the cost of loosening the constraints of a literal form of realism. Given that this is what happens in the letter-reading scene, reflective spectators might ask whether Bergman has not done the same in the scene where Tomas and Jonas apparently meet. Once the spectator observes the temporal inconsistency entailed by the realist reading of their exchange, the possibility of a non-realist reading may readily come to mind.

There is some additional relevant evidence, but it is inconclusive. When Tomas visits Jonas's wife and informs her that her husband has killed himself, he claims to have had the conversation: "I spoke to him, but there was so little I could do," he says. She replies with "I'm sure you did what you could, sir."[11] (These lines are in both the script and the film.) If the conversation was only a dream and Tomas afterward figured this out, then he is lying to her. Why would he do that? The motivation for this lie could be benign: perhaps he did not want her to know that one of her husband's last actions was breaking the promise he made to her about having a conversation with the pastor. If, on the other hand, the conversation actually took place, Tomas is not lying to the fisherman's wife, but he does conceal the fact that he failed to say anything that might have had even a remote chance of persuading the fisherman not to take his own life. When the wife says she is sure he did what he could, the honest reply would have been to say that in fact he did not.

None of the above evidence and arguments gives us sufficient reason to rule in favor of either the dream or reality conjectures. That leaves us with the conclusion that the ambiguity remains unresolved in the film as a whole. And what is the nature of this ambiguity? This is a point where the reference to some kind of everyday realism is quite helpful. The story told by this film takes place in a world where people either have a conversation at a particular time and place or they have not; there is no third option. It follows that the ambiguity in Bergman's story has to be epistemic; in other words, there is uncertainty, not with regard to there being two possible but mutually exclusive options, but with regard to which one obtains, *where necessarily, one and only one of those options obtains*.

Who is it that suffers from the epistemic limitation of not knowing which option is correct? Bergman, in the first instance, because he somehow settled on conveying a story about a situation with two mutually exclusive options, without, however, reaching a decision as to which of them obtained in the story. As a result, all of his spectators or interpreters must also suffer from the epistemic limitation as well, since there is no decisive evidence pertaining to the relevant content of the work. This puts us in something of a quandary because if we think about the film's story along realist lines, *it has to be the case that either the conversation really happened or was only dreamt*. Yet the work is ambiguous because Bergman apparently made up his mind to hesitate between the two options (or at least did not decide between them), which means neither alternative can be known to be correct.

Some of David Bordwell's remarks about the role of ambiguity in art films are relevant here. Significant ambiguity in a cinematic narration, he observes, often calls attention to the performance of the implicit storyteller or author, who either lacks or withholds information about the story events.[12] Why, the spectator may well wonder, does the filmmaker fail to answer key questions about the story—questions that the story itself has been designed to raise? What reason could he or she have had for deeming that this part of the cinematic representation should remain unresolved?

One hypothesis that may come to mind in such a case is that the author thought that the issue under discussion did not really matter very much to the story he wanted to tell in this film. Narrative fictions are replete with trivial ambiguities and unanswered questions that are totally irrelevant to our appreciation of the story. Another idea is that leaving some important issue uncertain could add a certain complexity to the characterizations and story. It is often said that ambiguity can enhance the value of the work of art by making room for multiple interpretations and a depth of meaning.[13] Only highly conventional narratives answer all of the questions they raise, even when those questions are crucial to understanding the story events. A modernist narrative, it may be maintained, does not trivialize the problem of authentic representation and expression by having recourse to such a contrived storytelling convention.

These are familiar arguments in favor of the role of ambiguity within a modernist aesthetic. It remains to be shown, however, just how well these arguments apply to *The Communicants*. In raising this question, we do not wish to apply a standard that is wholly alien to Bergman's project. Here again something that Sjöman reports is useful. Expressing his satisfaction with the film, Bergman commented: "It hangs together. It's a complete unit. It's an adequate expression of something I have felt and experienced. It's an adequate expression of a vision."[14] Expressive adequacy and completion are indeed relevant standards to bring to bear on the film, and in what follows I shall make some remarks about how this film stands in relation to those standards.

Does the ambiguity matter? Consider once more in this regard the contrast between the two mutually exclusive scenarios. On the one scenario, Tomas has a chance to speak privately with Jonas and fails horribly to do his moral and professional duty, the only mitigating excuse being that his feverish condition has seriously weakened him and vitiated his judgment. Tomas might, for example, have spoken to Jonas about the gravity of leaving his pregnant wife alone with three children and another one on the way. As a Lutheran pastor, it was his duty to remind Jonas that suicide, like murder, was a mortal sin. The pastor might also have said things to calm Jonas's fear of nuclear warfare. We would do well to remember that Bergman's point of departure was an anecdote in which the pastor felt horribly guilty in an analogous situation. Compare these considerations now to what it would be appropriate to say if the conversation was only part of Tomas's feverish dream. No one is morally responsible for the content of a dream, so Tomas can hardly be blamed. Moreover, the fisherman failed to keep his promise to visit him and to discuss his suicidal thoughts. Tomas was anxiously waiting for Jonas, hoping to have a helpful conversation with the man. Yet Tomas never really got the chance to save Jonas, and certainly is not guilty or blameworthy for having said the wrong things, or of having failed to say the right things (Figure 3.1).

The upshot is that the ambiguity does matter to the story. If it remains unresolved, we are left hesitating between two strikingly different characterizations of Tomas, which in turn has implications for our understanding of other characters as well. Most importantly, we know that Märta knows whether Jonas spoke to Tomas in the sacristy. If he did, she could readily surmise that Tomas has failed the man miserably, since Jonas went out and shot himself immediately after the conversation. If Jonas never came to the sacristy, Märta would know that too.

Figure 3.1 Ambiguity on many levels in *Nattvardsgästerna/Winter Light* (1968).

If we accept the conclusion that the ambiguity remains unresolved, this has implications for how we might understand (and not be able to understand) other aspects of the film. I turn now to these matters.

The Communicants is often described as a film that deals with important religious topics, and many critics have tried to figure out what sort of religious or anti-religious stance Bergman might have been espousing, or at least expressing, through this film.[15] Sjöman reports that Bergman made the following comment to him during a pause in the shooting of *The Communicants*: "These guys who are to write about my films and haven't the vaguest idea of what they're all about. They haven't even read Luther's shorter catechism!"[16] This is not something a director would say if he were indifferent to how the religious themes in his work were understood by the audience. Bergman actually claims in this remark that the film is about something specific, and it is also implied that a critic can either have a good idea about this or not, and that knowledge of Lutheran doctrine is important in this regard.

As a matter of fact, critics, including those who know a great deal about protestant theology, have found it impossible to come to an agreement over the film's putative expression or endorsement of religious sentiments or convictions. Perhaps all informed parties might agree that there is no endorsement in this film of any sort of orthodox Lutheranism, but that is a rather broad and negative thesis that leaves a number of other options open.

Except for the fact that he is a pastor in the Church of Sweden, we are given little reason to attribute to Tomas what we might take to be the orthodox Lutheran credo, *or any other specific religious tenets*. Tomas says he suffers from God's silence, but he doesn't say anything about what he takes God's attributes to be; he does not say anything about the sources of revelation, the scriptures, or any other doctrinal matters. It does not help that a crucial scene in which he talks about his religion, and apparently denounces the illusion of God's existence, cannot be firmly identified as dream or reality. It is one thing for him to imagine, while dreaming, that he has only believed in an "echo-God" that becomes a monstrous, "spider-god" when confronted with reality. It is something else entirely for him actually to believe this to be true. Does he? We really are in no position to know. When Tomas leaves the sacristy he exclaims that he is "finally free." This seems to be the conclusion he takes away from his dream—or from the unsuccessful conversation with the fisherman—yet we have no way to say what might be meant by this. The most obvious reading is that he deems himself free of his former religious beliefs. Has he become an atheist, then? Again, Bergman has not provided us with sufficient evidence with which to work in trying to answer this question.

The longest conversation on a religious topic that definitely takes place in the story occurs when Algot, the sexton, briefly advances a conjecture about the nature of Jesus's suffering on the cross. Algot observes that when Jesus was on the cross he felt abandoned or forsaken by God and suffered horribly from God's silence. This mental suffering by far outweighed the physical agony he experienced on the cross, Algot reckons. Tomas nods silently as if in agreement with this supposedly insightful proposition.

With Bergman's remark about the shorter catechism in mind, we might want to compare Algot's ideas to Luther's thoughts about the crucifixion and the proper way for good Christians to meditate upon it. In a well-known sermon devoted to the matter, Luther places a lot of emphasis on depraved humanity's responsibility for the crucifixion; it is not God who makes Jesus suffer, but we sinners, Luther insists.[17] The crucifixion is a *voluntary* sacrifice whereby Jesus made justification possible for those believers upon whom God bestows grace. From a Lutheran perspective, Algot's rumination detaches the agony from the overarching story of the Fall, resurrection, and redemption. There is no emphasis in Algot's remarks on Christ's obedience to God, a point underscored by Luther. Perhaps I am missing something, but I do not see how a pastor trained in Lutheran theology would find any great insight in Algot's comments, yet in

Bergman's story, Tomas seems to do so.[18] It would seem that one reason, if not *the* reason, why Tomas nods in approval, is that Algot's mentioning of "God's silence" resonates with his own earlier complaint. It would also appear to be the case that Algot's remarks mysteriously inspire Tomas to go ahead with the liturgy even though there are no believers (with the exception of Algot) to participate in it. There is, however, another way to read this scene, to which I turn now.

We know that in searching for an ending to this story, Bergman drew upon an experience in which his father insisted that a communion service be performed in spite of the fact that the size of the congregation did not meet the minimal threshold as specified by the Church of Sweden. On several occasions when he discussed the film's ending, Bergman derived a kind of upbeat moral maxim from that episode. Bergman presents the "maxim" as "a rule [he, Bergman] was to follow from then on: irrespective of anything that happens to you in life, you hold your communion."[19]

Tomas lives up to that maxim and does his duty, Bergman seems to imply, by going on with the liturgy even though the church is almost empty. Although this could look like some sort of admirable existential leap of faith, we cannot be sure how or why this leap is taken by Tomas, or where it lands him. It is crucial to note here that the protestant liturgy is not successfully performed if the pastor does not actually believe in the relevant doctrinal tenets. Here we should recall Luther's emphasis on *faith*. So there is a very important sense in which Tomas may not really be "doing his duty" by saying the words and performing the required gestures: he does not really "hold his communion" if he is now "free" from his prior belief in the Christian deity.

There is some evidence suggesting that Bergman was persuaded, at least at one point during the making of the film, that Tomas is not to be taken as representing some new kind of faith. Consider in this regard the following exchange reported by Sjöman:

- "Any more objections?"
- "The end. One never feels that 'a new faith shows signs of life' in Thomas. He just goes in and holds the service."
- "Exactly. He's the pack donkey that keeps struggling on. Far too weak to be of any use in God's work. God cannot put any strength into him—but he can into Märta! It's Märta who takes over the struggle for faith in the end, do you see?"[20]

Sjöman has to admit that he does not in fact "see" this point. What the story events convey does not really point to what Bergman proposes in this conversational exchange. One has a *very* hard time trying to envision that God Almighty, the omnipotent Creator of the universe, was incapable of putting strength into Tomas, whereas He did find it within His power to give Tomas's unhappy lover a boost. What is there in the story that could prompt anyone to arrive at that theologically idiosyncratic line of thought? The viewer has no evidence there has been a divine intervention. And if he was merely speaking metaphorically, what was Bergman on about? Was Bergman himself, the "God-Author," who could not make Tomas a stronger character? As for Märta, she too would appear to be an unlikely figure with whom to associate a new religious orientation. The spectator has seen and heard Märta declare quite coolly that God does not exist. Her troubled emotional life has been consistently shown to us as being entirely centered around her unrequited romantic passion for the unappreciative and undeserving Tomas. This unhappy passion would seem to be the real reason why she comes to church services, where, as a self-declared atheist, she inappropriately takes communion and kneels as if in prayer. Does she really change her mind about God's existence in the course of the film? We are given insufficient grounds to believe that such a dramatic conversion has taken place. We know Märta still desperately wants Tomas to reciprocate her love. Her devotion to him is, as she blurts out in a flashback to some frenzied moments, mistaken by her as the very meaning and mission of her life. In the final scene we see that Märta falls to her knees in church and fervently gives voice to some wishes: "if only we could find safety and dare show each other tenderness; if only we had some truth to believe in; if only we could believe." Bergman cuts from a close-up of her in profile, uttering these lines, to a shot of Tomas, who is apparently trying to decide whether to go on with the liturgy. Bergman refers to this as Märta's "intercession" on Tomas's behalf. He mentioned this precisely at the moment when Sjöman resists the thought that it is Märta who is doing God's work. Bergman comments: "But what about her intercession. Right at the last?"[21]

Bergman's postulation of an "intercession" undertaken by Märta is puzzling. An intercession is a petitionary prayer in which what is requested from God includes the satisfaction of someone else's needs. Märta's phrases all take the form, "if only we could x." This falls well short of being the expression of a petitionary prayer; even less is it specifically an intercession on Tomas's behalf. Most importantly, unlike a prayer, her remarks are not an expression of faith in a deity to whom the request is addressed. If it truly was Bergman's final intention to have Märta represent some new kind of faith—or more feebly yet, a "struggle for faith"—the expression is neither adequate nor complete; it is, instead, woefully understated. Are we really supposed to imagine that God fulfills Märta's wish and grants her and Tomas a truth to believe in? At most there is the vaguest hint of some such thing, but the circumstances are far too sketchy for us to draw any firm conclusions. Note, for example, that for Jörn Donner, the upshot of the film is something totally remote from this conjecture about God's active intervention in the beliefs of Tomas and Märta. It is, instead, the proposition that "it is unimportant whether God exists or not."[22]

Where does all of this leave us with regard to the questions raised at the outset of this essay? *The Communicants* has many artistic virtues, but it also suffers from a kind of ambiguity that is in tension with other major features of the work's design. It would seem that the director opted for hesitation, in the sense of making up his mind not to decide between various possible branches in the world of the story. This hesitation fractures the work's characterization of Tomas and Märta; it also extends into the related religious thematics of the work, and effectively hampers Bergman's attempt to find a successful expression of a coherent "vision" in this film.

There is, however, a special kind of artistic value to be found in the ambiguity of *The Communicants*. Having changed his initial plan and shifted toward a scene that hesitates between fictional dream and fictional reality, Bergman discovered a device that he would go on to employ far more successfully in subsequent works, such as *Viskningar och rop/Cries and Whispers* (1972). In the latter film, Bergman resolutely backgrounds questions about what did and did not "really happen in the story," detaching such matters from the scenes' emotive valences, thereby heightening the work's musical and emotive qualities. There is, then, a sense in which *The Communicants* was a flawed but invaluable pivotal step on the path to Bergman's masterpieces of cinematic modernism.

Notes

1 Vilgot Sjöman, *L 136 diary with ingmar bergman*, trans. Alan Blair (Ann Arbor: Karoma, 1978), 39.
2 Ibid., 40.
3 Ibid., 76–7.
4 Ibid., 77. Sjöman's italics.
5 Examples include Peter Cowie in his remarks included in the Criterion Collection dvd of the film; Robin Wood, *Ingmar Bergman*, 2nd edn. Rev. (Detroit: Wayne State

University Press, 2013), 146–7; and Hubert I. Cohen, *Ingmar Bergman: The Art of Confession* (New York: Twayne, 1993), 188.

6 Discussion published in "Anteckningar från Bergmanveckan," *Filmkonst* 105 (2006): 24.

7 Robert H. Adams, "How Warm is the Cold, How Light the Darkness?," *The Christian Century* 81, no. 38 (1964): 1144–5; reprinted in *Ingmar Bergman: Essays in Criticism*, ed. Stuart M. Kaminsky (New York: Oxford University Press, 1975), 226–30, citation on page 228.

8 Frank Gado, *The Passion of Ingmar Bergman* (Durham, NC: Duke University Press, 1986), 287.

9 Egil Törnqvist, *Bergman's Muses: Aesthetic Versatility in Film, Theatre, Television and Radio* (Jefferson, NC and London: McFarland & Company), 61.

10 Personal communication, October 2019.

11 Ingmar Bergman, *Three Films by Ingmar Bergman*, trans. Paul Britten Austin (New York: Grove Press, 1970), 97.

12 David Bordwell, *Narration in the Fiction Film* (Madison: The University of Wisconsin Press, 1985).

13 For a sophisticated plea for certain types of artistic ambiguity, see Umberto Eco, *The Open Work*, trans. Anna Cancogni (Cambridge, MA: Harvard University Press, 1989). Eco does not claim that all ambiguities make a positive contribution to the artistic merit of a work, nor does he attempt to identify the conditions under which they do make such a contribution.

14 Cited in Sjöman, *L 136 diary with ingmar bergman*, 232.

15 See, for a start, Astrid Soderbergh Widding, "What Should we Believe?: Religious Motifs in Ingmar Bergman's Films," in *Ingmar Bergman Revisited: Performance, Cinema and the Arts*, ed. Maaret Koskinen (London and New York: Wallflower, 2008), 194–212.

16 Sjöman, *L 136 diary with ingmar bergman*, 117.

17 Martin Luther, "Eyn sermon von der Betrachtung des heyligen Leydens Christi," (1519); trans. "A Meditation on Christ's Passion," in *Martin Luther's Basic Theological Writings*, ed. Timothy F. Lull and William R. Russell (Minneapolis: Ausburg Fortress, 2012), 126–31.

18 This fact may not reveal anything about Ingmar Bergman's attitudes at the time of the making of *The Communicants*, but we know that he does not say anything along these lines concerning Christ's agony in the treatment he wrote in the early 1970s for a film on the topic. For a translation of that treatment and background, see Ingmar Bergman, *Il Vangelo secondo Bergman: storia di un capolavoro mancato*, ed. Pia Campeggiani and Andrea Panzavolta (Genoa: il melangolo, 2018). The emphasis here instead is on a conversation experienced by Rufus, a Roman centurion given the task of supervising the crucifixion (a character, by the way, for whom there is no scriptural basis).

19 Ingmar Bergman, *Images: My Life in Film*, trans. Marianne Ruuth (London: Faber & Faber, 1995), 274.
20 Sjöman, *L 136 diary with ingmar bergman*, 34–5.
21 Ibid., 35.
22 Jörn Donner, *Djävulens ansikte* (Lund: Aldus/Bonniers, 1962), 175–82; as cited by Söderbergh Widding, "What Should we Believe?," 95.

4

The Passion of Anna

The Wondrous Alchemy between Actors and Landscape, Interview with Atom Egoyan

Maaret Koskinen and Louise Wallenberg

When first planning the writing retreat on Fårö in the Spring of 2019, we reached out to a small number of internationally known filmmakers whom we knew had taken inspiration from Bergman's films in their own work. The first filmmaker we approached was Armenian-Canadian film director Atom Egoyan, whose film *Family Viewing* (1987) is still in Bergman's private collection of VHS tapes at Hammars on Fårö. Due to a hectic schedule finishing his film, *Guest of Honor* (2019), Egoyan was not able to attend the retreat in person. However, it was soon decided that we would meet through a digital format, and that we would talk to him about his long-term relation to Bergman's film work, focusing on one film in particular. To our joy, Egoyan chose *En passion/The Passion of Anna*, filmed on Fårö in 1969. The interview was conducted in February 2020 over Skype.

> **Atom Egoyan:** I was sorry I couldn't be there. I really was hoping that the schedule would work out, but I'm glad it went well. My dream is to visit at some point, to make the pilgrimage. I used to know the projectionist [at Fårö] who kept logs of all the films that Bergman was watching and he gave me this one page, which I have always treasured. I saw that Bergman had watched some of my films at his theater, and it just was very moving to think of that. There was an interview he once did with the national paper here in Canada; he had mentioned my work and I started to cry. I can't begin to express the gratitude I have for his extraordinary body of work and this acknowledgment of my career was quite overwhelming. I loved going back to an intense study of this one film, *The Passion of Anna*, which I think is one of the films that excites me the most for a number of reasons.

Maaret Koskinen: Can I just remind you of the year 2000 when you visited Queen's University and I happened to be there and we sat across from each other. I think I told you too that I found these papers in Bergman's archives, where I was working at this time, and sent the copy of it to you.

Atom: Of course, that's our connection! I remember vividly now. I was there to accept an honorary degree.

Maaret: Should we just start with why Bergman means a lot to you? Would you care to detail that a little bit in general before we start talking about *Passion*.

Atom: I'm somebody whose first passion was with theater and so I was very involved with drama at school. It was in the 70s when it was still possible to see Bergman's films in repertoire cinemas. There was one particular cinema in Victoria, where I was raised, and I remember feeling this extraordinary excitement that you could observe human beings with such focus, with such a degree of attention, and such clarity and honesty. I hadn't seen anything like these films: the relationship with the group of actors, the ability to explore all these different aspects of the human condition without formula, and defining this new language was just tremendously inspiring. It was unlike anyone else's work because of the connection to theater. I was able to understand that the camera could be an active participant in the exploration of the human condition—that it was able to involve itself in very intimate moments through close-ups and the specific gesture that the camera was making. It was a revelation and no other director I knew of was doing that so meticulously.

So that was really the first connection when I understood the possibilities that were revealed. I was able to see this theatrical element. This mastery of syntax of cinema and the ability to push it to the self-referential, as is the case of *Passion*, was incredibly invigorating. That is why I wanted to focus on this particular film (Figure 4.1).

I'm not suggesting that it's his masterwork, but a number of factors came into play during the making of this particular film that are really worth focusing on. The fact that he had four of his favorite actors with whom he worked so intensively and this concentrated drama in a landscape on this island that he really came to see as a kind of utopic playground for his own psyche—that to me creates in itself this amazing situation where he is working with the script that was never really formed. There were certain impulses and ideas that brought these four actors together, fused them into the landscape, and then created this extraordinary experiment. On top of that it seems to me that he locates himself in this film in a way that is quite unusual. We have the

Figure. 4.1 Bergman's quartet of actors in the film poster for *En Passion/The Passion of Anna* (1969).

Figure. 4.2 On the film set of *En passion/The Passion of Anna* (1969) with Erland Josephson as the cynical Elis and Liv Ullmann as Anna.

interviews [in the film] and we hear Bergman's voice and we also hear him at times rather impatiently sketching out the drama.

It's as though at that point he had finished his body of very private films and he tried to enter into a more political space. He received a lot of criticism for that, but whether or not he truly engaged with the political issues of the country at the time—he had made *Shame* [Skammen, 1968]—he was vulnerable to the criticism. What is remarkable is that not only does he then go back into himself and create this quite hermetic drama, but he uses the actual footage from *Shame* within the film. He incorporates it in a strange alchemy of the four actors and the landscape. The character played by Erland Josephson, Elis, is clearly a director, someone who creates his archive of emotion and behaviour, his own voice and his own material, by which I mean his own film. It's all brought together in this extraordinary experiment (Figure 4.2).

Maaret: It's interesting what you say about Erland Josephson, the architect who wants to be a photographer, and who is categorizing human emotions . . . Do you think he is sort of the mouthpiece of Bergman, or is it more that the character is a cynic?

Atom: I think he's an extreme version of Bergman's character cynical as Elis is. Elis seems quite detached. The film was originally called *The Passion*, not

The Passion of Anna, so it's looking at this idea of passion through these four characters. In Erland Josephson you have a person who actually seems to have lost passion even though he continues to do his work, that is to build cultural centers. At one point Anna [Liv Ullmann] interrogates him during the dinner scene, how is it that he can be creating this work, creating these structures for other people to celebrate their cultural impulses and yet be so detached and cynical about it? In a way Bergman is representing an extreme aspect of the human condition where we're seeing almost a scientific detached view of someone who is recording human behaviour without implicating himself. We see this in Josephson's performance, he is quite brilliant here, he is aware of this energy that's happening between his wife and Andreas [Max von Sydow], he can see it brewing but he's not stopping it and he's almost observing that as well. It's a kind of toxic situation.

Maaret: It makes me also think of what I think is a terrible scene, where Elis photographs Andreas and he sort of directs him. There's an odd kind of aggression involved in the sound of the camera going off all the time, and I seem to remember that that sequence follows right after the slaughtering of the lambs . . .

Atom: Yes.

Maaret: So there's this kind of connection to violence there, isn't there?

Atom: There is so much violence in the film. The film begins with the violence against the building, when Andreas is preparing the roof and then the pail falls. There is also the violence he feels towards these objects that seem to work against him. He gets on the bicycle, which works against him, but then it connects him to this neighbor who is accused of this violence, of these irrational sadistic acts against animals. There is a short scene of the dog hanging, and then the moments of repair—repair from violence, people trying to take some sort of solace in this almost orgiastic cruelty that you are seeing throughout the film even in small things.

And it's interesting because the camera feels very violent. For instance, the strange gestures that the camera is doing, violent sort of pans, which is very uncharacteristic of Bergman's work. From what I read about this, there seemed to be tremendous tension between Bergman and [cinematographer] Sven Nykvist. They previously made *All These Women* [För att inte tala om alla dessa kvinnor, 1964], which used color in a generic, traditional way. With *Passion*, they wanted to create something new, they wanted to have a feeling of black and white in color, but were very frustrated with the results and how long it was taking to light. You can feel the tensions in this film; you can feel his intimacies with these actors, while also pushing them to the extreme.

I think it was at this moment when he was ending the relationship with Liv Ullmann. So this investigation of the woman, this incredible five-minute close-up where she's telling her story—the fantasy of her family and the fantasy of how honest they were—brutally cuts to this letter that we already have seen. These are shocking cuts, when the camera is swishing across the surface of this letter, which involves the idea of the invocation of the nervous and physical breakdown and physical violence. It's almost as though he's creating a violence in the edit itself as a comment where you have this long close-up, where a character seems to be given the privilege of so much security, and then he rips that away. He is doing something remarkable and daring with the construction of the film: the construction of plot, the construction of these elements of unexpected cruelty, these accusations which lead to the suicide of his neighbor. And there is always a kind of primal sense not only of violence but also displacement, how things can get stuck, displaced, how they have to be repaired, how they have to be found—of trying to fit pieces into grooves they are not designed for. Going back to Elis, there is this beautiful room where everything is perfectly organized, which is in wild contrast to the emotions and feelings that are swirling around him.

Maaret: There is that violence and also the self-referentiality that you just mentioned—it's that strange clash or questioning, just like in *Persona*, of the means at hand, the artistic means at hand. Words, on the one hand, what people say, what people write in a letter, or for that matter what Liv Ullmann says in that long mesmerizing take of the close-up, and on the other hand, what people do. What we find out about characters, we only find out by chance, as opposed to so many other Bergman films. It seems to me that our knowledge of them is quite fragmentary, and it's also contradictory and in the prolongment of that is a questioning of the artistic means at hand. Words, images, what do they mean, how long can you take them, when do they become aggressive? And that's why it's so interesting too that the script was not finished, according to Bergman.

Atom: Right. What he is explicitly playing with here is the notion of a narrative contrivance. There is a moment where he quite daringly tells us that Andreas and Anna are living together in a relationship without passion, but that they seem to accommodate each other. That's a huge jump, you've had no preparation for this odd relationship to suddenly be at a place of complacency. And he has done something that I don't think I had ever seen before, the contrivance of the dramatic gesture. It's as if Ingmar Bergman himself is saying he could have prepared you for this in a traditional way—but no. Instead he is positing that now they are living in this type of relationship, and we're immediately aware of the fact that we believe it because we're told so by the director. This is how they are and we have to suspend our sense of any form of foundation for this action or decision because we haven't seen it up to that point in the film. We accept it because we're told to.

But then we see the consequence for these people who actually cannot stand each other in an act of violence that I think is unprecedented. Andreas takes the axe—he would have hit her if she hadn't moved. There's a switch as he then assaults her in a physical attack, which again is quite unprecedented. You really feel for Liv Ullmann, the actress who is suffering these blows. We're being taken to such extremes where the artist himself is playing out some sort of rage that he feels toward the actress. What are we in the middle of? And how are we implicated as viewers and as lovers of Bergman? I think this is a thing he is pushing. It's the end of the 1960s and it's the end of an extraordinary run of cinema. With this extraordinary involvement of the viewer he asks, how far are you prepared to go in terms of the trust you have placed in me as a creator?

There are also very aggressive scenes as in the first shot with the three suns. We know there is something strange about this primary source of light, that it's a manipulation. We also have the scene with Andreas and Eva [Bibi Andersson] where she is dancing to a jazz piece. And we're seeing this setting and it's going into this phase of being red, and then the whole scene is lit in this crazily theatrical way: it's bright red and it's as though we were in a darkroom with red light. We're seeing pictures being developed under this red light so that they won't be exposed and it's bringing that energy right into the filming. It's like we're shooting this scene and we'll be developing the stock as we see this relationship develop. It's volatile as is the chemical bath that this stock will be put into.

Then there is this very telling scene where we look outside a window and we see it's light, which doesn't make any sense. We've just seen a sunset scene and we're in this extended moment of sunset light, which is not natural. These are master craftspeople; every decision here is calculated; we're not seeing a mistake, we're seeing something that is intentional to displace our sense of reality and to shock us, an invitation to disbelieve. Bergman is acutely aware that even in the space of all of these aggressive devices, which should be disruptive, we will adhere to our suspension of disbelief because psychologically we are invested in these characters. It's a bold experiment; it's a little like the scene a bit later on with the conversation between Andreas and Anna where the background is completely black. It's as though we're in a theatrical space, there's no attempt to light the background. It's much like the interviews we've seen with the actors themselves reflecting on their characters. We're suddenly in a naturalist scene, but we're also aware that it's completely constructed. These are very unusual gestures that Bergman is making and in a way it's his most experimental work in terms of using the purportedly dramatic form. I can't think of anything where he has taken it as far as *Passion*.

Maaret: You are right about that, usually one talks about *Persona* [1966] in those terms, but that is an extremely planned deconstructive film as opposed to this one.

Atom: *Persona* starts off with this beautiful montage, which says this life, this is art, this is destruction—there is the moment when the film breaks down—it melts and gets stuck in the projector. But these are in a strange way external interceptions. *Persona* is my favourite film, but I would say *Passion* is a more extreme, more brave, and more reckless approach to narrative. *Persona* as you said is very planned. You can read the script of *Persona* and you can see all those decisions. They are made in the script, which is where he solves many of his problems. But, as he says, and I am quoting from *Images*: "The filming of *The Passion* took 45 days and was an ordeal and the screenplay had been written in a white heat, it was more a description of a series of moods in a traditional dramatic film sequence. Ordinarily I solved any anticipated technical problems immediately in the writing stage but here I chose to deal with the problems during filming."

It's interesting that he says that to some extent this decision was made because of a lack of time, but mostly that he felt the need to challenge himself. He had a 45-day shoot, which is a long period in terms of my work. I rarely have more than 25 days, so it seems like he had time. Again, though, there was this ability to challenge and to use the tensions on set and integrate them into the dramatic form. I don't know if there is a screenplay that includes the dream sequence using footage from *Shame*. What is the documentation of this script? I've looked for it but haven't found a working script of *Passion*.

Maaret: No, I don't think there is one. I haven't looked specifically for it at the archives but—as opposed to so many other things that Bergman has said about his work, what exists and what does not—it's hard to know for sure. But I could tell you that that during the year 2018—the centennial of Bergman's birth—there was a whole series of publishing of his work diaries. It's all still in Swedish, of course, and I just wanted to give you a little quote here, given the fact that I think it's in a way sad that this film—which I certainly and you certainly appreciate—was denigrated by Bergman himself afterwards. Whereas in the workbooks written at the time, he writes something to the effect that, and I quote: "I should not try to describe or put a light on these people from every vantage point, that would be really stupid. In fact that is the great thing about this: they step out from the dark, they give you a moment, something moves, and then they move into the darkness again." And then he adds sort of humorously: but something is missing, "we should light them as well, be a little bit more fun, dear Mr. Bergman," he tells himself.

Atom: That's so interesting. I feel when he talks about lighting these characters, these are four actors whom he loves no matter what their personal relationship might be at any given time. It's amazing, like the scene where we hear Anna having a nightmare in another room; we're just on Max von Sydow reacting to this and then follow these very long reaction shots. And the scene you mentioned when he's being photographed; he's really indulging in his love of these four people and the privilege of being with them in this space where he is able to also indulge in his love of the topography. You know the sequence where we see Erland Josephson and Max von Sydow, the window with the windmill in the background, what a composition . . . . And the use of this incredible shot where Max von Sydow is drunk and the camera is far overhead just following him through the woods as he's calling out his own name, "Andreas, Andreas," as though he is looking for himself . . .

You wish you were on the set that day, that you were able to understand the intimacy of the director's contact to these faces that he's explored so intensely over a body of work in this space where they are working as they are talking perhaps without a script about their motivation in these interview sequences which are also incorporated. He is asking questions about who they are and you hear them make incredible statements. In one of the first interviews Max von Sydow says that his character is trying to hide from the world, that he is trying to wipe out any means of expression and the hardest thing for an actor is to express lack of expression. That is interesting for what we then see is a multitude of expressions. If he's been given that directive by Bergman or if that is what he is asked to reflect on, it's certainly not what we see in the film,—but it's an interesting mission. The actors are wrestling with trying to form their characters at the same moment they're having to articulate the process and it's like we're also in the process. The characters are able to chart their space specifically as to where they are in the film at this particular point and one has the impression of being in the crucible of the artistic process as well. We see these four characters trying to understand who they are, being thrown into these wild improbable scenarios where suddenly they are in a relationship.

Maybe that was something that came to Bergman that day, we don't know. It's very different from *Persona* that way, since it was a thoroughly scripted film.

It's equally mysterious too at what point there is a structure to these decisions and at what point they are untethered and we're seeing scenes unfold as the camera is recording them. We can surmise that the scene around the dinner table when they are having that first communion is quite improvised. It feels unscripted when Elis is talking about the architectural project and Anna asks how he can do something without having a feeling for it. But maybe we're also dealing with the actress trying to understand where and how she is supposed to form herself without a set of directives. It's about people being left to their own devices after a rigorous understanding and working knowledge of formulas instituted by Bergman's own cinema over a number of years. Suddenly they are in this petri dish where there must be a series of choices that Bergman is making, but where he is also allowing them to interrupt the process with reflections of what their characters might mean. And that is shifting, it's not consistent . . . as you said earlier, there are so many paradoxes and contradictions between what they are saying and how they are behaving.

Maaret: There is that common theme, which of course runs through all of Bergman's films, and which I love about them, identities or masks—to get to the theatrical concept that you started with: that behind the mask is another mask and another mask. I mean, there are the actors trying to grapple with their characters, and then there is this impossibility of knowing and understanding others—and oneself. For example, when Elis shows the photograph of Eva to Andreas and says that "I took that photograph of her the very moment she had her worst migraine attack," and then he adds something to the effect that "I don't think I can in any way decipher or claim to know anything about the human condition, about any other individual at all," and here he says something very Bergmanesque, doesn't he?

Atom: Yes.

Maaret: And that is what *Persona* is all about too—the matter of floating identities. But this film *Passion* is made in such a totally different way, which I think is so invigorating.

Atom: Because these four actors are so comfortable in their skin, in their persona as people in Bergman's orbit. It's the reason they can reflect on this. Also they are in this location, in this space where they know Bergman is most comfortable, most inspired. Knowing they have this relationship with him, which by this point is substantial, they can posit these ideas. And yet on some level they know why they are there, they know what they are contributing to.

You said that Bergman kind of rejected the film; maybe it was because it didn't have the same emotional coherence as much of his work and he reacted to the criticism. We know how vulnerable he was to criticism so maybe the volley of charges at that point in his career made him see this film as the embodiment of what was said: that it was the most self-indulgent work he could imagine. He indulged himself in shooting without a script and felt impatient with how these characters end up. And yet there is an anger and rage, which is generated in the body of the work. Maybe what he was shocked by—and again it's conjecture, which I hesitate to do—was what he was able to summon without any real plan. We have a character who is prepared to senselessly massacre the woman he is in a relationship with—who Bergman was in a relationship with. I've heard comments that Liv Ullmann was asking for forgiveness; in the middle of the most abusive relationship, this is so disturbing.

To me, this film is a pure expression of Id. It's an Id-based film: it's completely impulsive. There is a sense of form because these actors are at the peak of their craft so it's almost impossible to put a camera on them without feeling that there is intention. But we're divorced from dramaturgy and we're really looking at a series of impulses here: what does it mean to fall drunk on the floor of your room and have a dog lick you and bring you to some sense of your own humanity; what does it mean to find the same dog hanging from a tree with no explanation; how long does that last; what does that lead to? And in the middle of this we have Elis with his archives recording faces but without any effect on his own artistic joy. He feels like somebody who is completely detached. I can understand why Bergman would react to this project with alarm when we see the film in its final form. But as someone who is involved in the process himself, I cannot help but be completely overwhelmed by the proposal.

Maaret: Now this might be gossip, but I seem to have heard from somewhere that the interviews with the actors commenting on their characters are written by Bergman. Possibly together with the actors—and that the only one who really speaks from her heart is Bibi Andersson. What would your take be on that? If indeed that was the case.

Atom: She is the one who is most concerned about her character's direction. She is hoping that the character will be saved and says she hopes the character is not suicidal. It's also the only interview that ends with an incredible fade to white. The light that comes up on her at the end suggests there is some kind of salvation. Yet another interesting thing about the film is it's devoid of religion; moreover, there is an explicit discussion of the absence of God. Yet we see Andreas go to the house of the man who has committed suicide. He approaches the bed and places his hand on him in a way that is very tender and there is a transference. At that point the light from outside brightens, there is an incredible burst of light, and then there is a close-up of Andreas with this religious iconographic image behind him. It's curious that in her interview Bibi Andersson talks about this as though she is not sure what is going to be decided for this character. Is the suicide something Bergman is going to throw at her as an action and that she is trying to defend herself from? His decision might be made. Or is she talking about a future that might be beyond the film?

As I said, all boundaries have been kind of extinguished here, we're cutting in real scenes from another film. We're bringing in the end of *Shame* so the parameters of the film itself have also been exploded. If Bergman can bring in films that have one idea and lead to one place and intersect them into the dream of a character in this work, then surely Bibi Andersson hopes that she doesn't meet the suicide she is talking about. It's exploded open, we're not sure where the boundaries are and again it's divorced from any kind of dramatic formula. The central mystery is not solved. This man is accused of being a sadistic animal serial killer, he commits suicide and of course at the end we realize he's not the demon as the killing continues. We have the scene with the burning barn so we know the mystery is not solved. We have the bit of evidence in the letter that Andreas finds in her purse and we also have the letter, which says the community is going to kill the neighbor, thrown with a rock into his place, which leads to his suicide. We have all these violent interventions with letters as means of communication. They are moments of possible intention, which don't come to satisfying fruition or conclusion.

Maaret: At the same time it seems to me that there is no other Bergman film where this kind of violence shoots through everything, yet which is sort of punctuated by these moments of tenderness. Like the light flooding over the man in the suicide scene. But also between Andreas and Anna there are these moments at the end where their faces emanate from the black and they actually try to set up some kind of dialogue, some kind of communication. I think it's Andreas who says something like, "I am humiliated but so are so many other people, everybody lives with humiliation, and we're forced to do that." It's so wonderfully phrased, and it's so tender.

Atom: There is also the question of compassion and empathy as with the moment when Andreas and Anna watch the newsreel footage on television with the burning monk and the images of Vietnam, also used in *Persona*. It's an extraordinary moment of violence that they are watching and they are strangely detached from it. Suddenly we hear something hit the window; it's a bird, and they go outside. After seeing the execution of this human being, they are looking at this bird, which has been hurt by crashing into a window.

They make the decision to end its life and bash its head with a rock and bloody their hands. Then when they are washing the blood off their hands together in the sink, they have this really strange conversation where Anna asks, "could the bird have been saved?" And then there is the mysterious point of "why was the bird flying alone at night?" It's not answered. And then when they are playing chess, suddenly Anna takes the chessboard and wipes it clean. This is another violent action—and then right from that we go to the interview with Bibi Andersson. There is this incredible sequence of events where our sense of proportion in terms of what should be an act of empathy or compassion is questioned. No resolution is given and we're shocked or confused by what we should be feeling in terms of our identification with these characters. I suppose the question is whether all of these characters are unhinged at some level. Is Bergman saying we have to like these characters? I would say no, but rather we're completely fascinated by where and how far they are into their state of mental deterioration and its cause. What's causing Anna to be completely delusional about the relationship she had and the family she came from? The letter is the proof of the inherent physical violence, it's a breakout. And we see Andreas breaking down through the film. In that final shot there is that materiality; Bergman uses an optical zoom, he's making us zoom into the actual frame of film so we're seeing the granular structure breaking . . . it's all about the notion of deterioration and also the question of the materialization of how we form and identify character. Every time I watch this film it just provokes so many issues in me, I think it's both inspiring and terrifying.

Maaret: Inspiring and terrifying, yeah. Just to wrap this up, because you've really given us a lot of fantastic stuff. First of all, can we get back to the beginning, and that key term that you mentioned, that besides the actors there is the landscape, inner but also a physical landscape? Is there something about that island landscape that you were thinking of when you brought that up as a kind of an entryway into talking about this film?

Atom: Yes, it's knowing what that landscape meant to Bergman, knowing how transformative that space was for him, seeing how it has been used for films before this, and then seeing it in color for the first time and knowing that he was trying to depict this landscape which had predominantly been photographed in black and white. He was trying to hold onto this notion of black and white through color and you do feel that there is something about the color. It's not just the shock of seeing Bergman working with color on such an intimate drama for the first time, even now there is a strange tone of color in that first scene of the sheep and the sound of the bells. We haven't even talked about the sound work, that too was quite remarkable—the sound of the bells on the sheep, the sound of the clock that's ticking over the letter, the sound of foghorns. You think that these must have been elemental sounds for Bergman, the island sounds that he was focused on and exaggerated. It becomes part of the construction of the film in an impressionistic way. These are natural sounds which are heightened. That is the way I feel about the color as well, that there is a shock to the color and it's used graphically. I know that Bergman writes that he and Sven Nykvist argued often about this and they were not happy with the result, but I would like to know what those conversations were. I don't know if there is any record of that in the working diaries, but it's a remarkable moment in a filmmaker's trajectory to use color in this way when he is so identified with black and white imagery. It must be a part of the alchemy of what we're feeling, but there's something very violent in this gesture to naturalism because up until that point the black and white had been a naturalist element for Bergman.

Maaret: Exactly. When Ang Lee was over at the Fårö Island in 2006 with James Schamus, he was asked by the journalists "Mr. Lee how is it now to be on the island that you admire so much?," and he just answered "well, I'm still surprised the landscape is not in black and white!"

Atom: There you go. And maybe it was shocking to Bergman to see the seasonal shifts in the dailies. It's these things in Liv Ullmann's interview, the red hat she's wearing; it's crazy red and it kind of anticipates the fire that we're about to see in the next scene and the red again of the room with Andreas and Eva. I really do like this notion of developing in a darkroom because there is something magical and unexpected about the transformations. We're prepared, we're asked for acceptance as if Bergman says that when he gives you this red room or when he says that this relationship was formed, he is asking you to react as a viewer and say, no, this is not acceptable. But we trust these actors and this is what I think we're talking about really. I think it is a triumph of this quartet of actors working in the most concentrated space. And let us not underestimate Erik Hell who had worked with Bergman earlier; this is the person who plays the neighbor who commits suicide.

This is to me what we're celebrating with this film. It's not just the creativity of the director but also the extraordinary resourcefulness. That's an important word because these actors are being left to their resources. One has the impression, and the interviews make that clear, that they are being asked to defend themselves without a blueprint. And they arrive at something as arresting as this film is. It's not coherent but it's certainly arresting and demands our attention. These actors are so fine, they have found a place; they are the core. We were talking before about the masks, these layers, and what defines identity. At some moment you feel with each of these actors you have some access to their core and that cuts through all of the plot points and all of the things that Bergman has thrown at them. And maybe this is why the interviews were so important because even if they were co-scripted by Bergman, we're given an invitation to think that this is at the core of who these people are above and beyond the roles that they are being asked to play.

Louise Wallenberg: We may not like the characters, but we love the actors, right?

Atom: That is beautifully put. That's what I think Bergman was betting on. That's what he felt and that's what we feel. And he also loves Sven Nykvist, and he loves this landscape. It's as if he's asking how far he can go with just the feeling of compassion, interest, and love he feels towards these primary elements of his creative process. What happens if he puts the characters through the most extreme tests and sees what emerges, sees what he's left with and so we have passion. It's important to use as the singular word, which is the title. It's not really about Anna, it's about the concept of where and what passion is.

5

Scenes from on and off the Set

Ingmar Bergman, Power, and MeToo

Maaret Koskinen

In January of 2018, in the midst of the centenary festivities commemorating the birth year of Ingmar Bergman, British newspaper *The Guardian* published an article with the telling title "Hard-hitting film takes aim at Ingmar Bergman's flawed way with women." It was an interview on an upcoming documentary, *Bergman - ett år, ett liv/Bergman: A Year in a Life* (2018) (later that year screened at the Cannes Film Festival), which, it was announced, "is to examine the sexual relationships in which the Swedish film director engaged with almost all of his actresses, and detail his shortcomings as a husband and father."[1]

The film's director, Jane Magnusson, was reported as saying that "she hoped Bergman admirers would be more willing to acknowledge the great director's flaws after last year's revelations about the systematic sexual exploitation of actresses by Hollywood producer Harvey Weinstein." Because, she noted, Bergman "did have a tremendous amount of women, and a lot of them were dependent on him—they were his actresses—and in Sweden no one has looked at that seriously." For, she added, the fact that "neither [Liv] Ullmann, [Bibi] Andersson, nor indeed any of the other actresses in Bergman's films have ever publicly accused him of sexual misconduct does not mean that he is blameless." On the contrary, she concluded, "That's the nature of being a man with a lot of power. If you're an actress and he dumps you after a year, and you're angry and denounce him, then you're out of a job, and that for me is what #Me Too is about."[2]

At the same time, however, Jane Magnusson is reported as being "keen to credit Bergman for the unusually powerful and intelligent roles he created for his actresses. 'He has these amazing female characters in a lot of his films, and we have to thank him for that, because he was quite alone in casting in that way.'"[3]

To be sure, one senses quite a bit of ambivalence here. And as this phenomenon of "pro-cons" has hovered around Bergman all throughout his long career—regarding not only the reception of his films but also his private life and, not least, his position of power in the Swedish film industry—let us make an attempt at mapping out some of this in more detail.

Fact versus Fiction—Another Round

Let it first be said, however, that once Magnusson's film premiered, it did not seem as sensational as *Guardian* had set out, which, in hindsight, makes the article seem more like part of the PR-buzz that is always set in motion before a premiere. Nonetheless, the film did put forth certain problematic issues on the table, and unsurprisingly the film did create a debate in Sweden. For instance, in an article called "Was Bergman a Rapist?" in the Swedish daily *Svenska Dagbladet*, Jannike Åhlund, chair of the Bergman Centre, voiced her misgivings about the way that Magnusson's film at times posited easy parallels between Bergman's life and fictional work.[4] In particular she refers to a text that was omitted from the published version of Bergman's autobiography *Laterna magica/The Magic Lantern* (1987), as this omission is presented in the film as if it was a journalistic scoop, intimating that the event described in it had taken place in actuality, while also suggesting that it had been "censored." This omitted text reads as follows:

> Some twenty years earlier I was living together with a woman a few years older but a lot more experienced than me. We live in an airless one room apartment and had been quarrelling a couple of days, all to the irritation, alternatively entertainment of our neighbors. We are both exhausted, upset and beside ourselves with jealousy. She stands there naked and badly beaten in the middle of a pool of sunshine, and strikes at me with a kitchen knife. I swing at her with a stool and it hits her. She loses the knife and falls. Her face becomes discolored and she moves, twitching. A brief pleasure, a streak of freedom. I realize that I'm strangling her that I'm hitting her head against the floor that I've penetrated her, and that she wants me to kill her and that I'm on my way to fulfilling her wish. (My translation)[5]

No doubt this passage oozes of aggression—a violent brawl involving a knife, and an attempt at strangulation, which culminates in rape. But is this text in some sense "true," and has it been "censored"? As for the first assumption,

Jannike Åhlund writes, taking it on face value is highly problematic, as Bergman's (so-called) autobiography *The Magic Lantern* is more autofiction than an attempt at writing fact-based memoirs. Here I would have to agree, as this has been delved into by numerous scholars, including myself. Take, for instance, the opening of the book—"When I was born in 1918, my mother had Spanish influenza. I was in a bad way and was baptized as a precaution at the hospital." This is definitely a forceful opening: drastic, dramatic—and totally false. He was not frail, and there was no emergency baptism.[6] As fiction, however, it is very effective. How can it not be, as little infant Ingmar has a near-death experience at the very entrance into life—what can be more Bergmanesque?

In this context it is also worth pointing that the omitted passage conflates with a scene described in Bergman's unpublished short story "Puzzlet föreställer Eros" (The puzzle represents Eros) dated 1946, later turned into the film *Kvinna utan ansikte/Woman without a Face* (1947), directed by Olof Molander. In fact there are many other such passages in *The Magic Lantern*, where pure fiction has entered the stage. Another example is Bergman's description of visiting his mother's room after she had died. Claiming, first, that he hardly remembers what really took place in that room, his description is nonetheless both lengthy and full of concrete details—which most of all reads like a transcript of a scene from the beginning of Bergman's film *Beröringen/The Touch* (1971).[7] In other words, when Bergman sat down to write his autobiography in the mid-1980s, it seems that his own previous scripts and films came to mesh quite freely with memories of certain life events—all according to the formula "when memory does not suffice, fiction will have to do." Or, as Bergman himself put it in a conversation with me: "*The Magic Lantern* is the only book I've written with any literary pretensions whatsoever."[8]

As for the alleged censorship of the omitted passage, and that it had been kept from the public eye, this is not true either—quite simply because, as Jannike Åhlund points out in her article, that I myself had published it in its entirety over a decade earlier in the book *I begynnelsen var ordet* ("In the beginning was the word"), which was a study of the young Bergman as (literary) author. In fact, as I at that time had been given free access to his (then) private archive, full of unpublished scripts, it was not more than right that Bergman got to read my book manuscript before print—and although claiming that he was "shocked," as he found it to be "an autopsy, a close-up of a relative that I'd rather not to be acquainted with," he did not want to change a word.[9]

Gossip as Viable Object of Study—A Theoretical Aside

Another point that Jannike Åhlund makes in her article is that "many, perhaps even most of the characters, in [Bergman's work] are self-projections."[10] Self-projection is precisely what Linda Rugg has taken a closer look at in her book *Self-Projection: The Director's Image in Art Cinema*, arguing that in film this can take several shapes.[11] For instance, and as any Bergman buff knows, he did not only appear, Hitchcock-like, in a number of cameos in his early films, but also in the later films acting as a ghost-like presence in the shape of voice-over.[12] It goes without saying, however, that it is mostly characters who tend to function as avatars for the director—and therefore also actors.

Erik Hedling for his part, sees no problem in connecting Bergman's actors intimately to the director's private life. "As is well established," he writes in his review of Rugg's book, "Bergman had affairs with several of his leading women," mentioning Liv Ullmann, Harriet Andersson, and Bibi Andersson. All of them, he contends, "were duly represented in the films in ways that suggest their sexual relationships with the director." But then there is Ingrid Thulin, "who was married to one of Bergman's friends, Swedish Film Institute boss Harry Schein," and who has never been rumored of having an amorous liaison with the director. This, according to Hedling, is interesting, because her "representation differed from the others":

> After making her debut for Bergman as the highly attractive and wise daughter-in-law in *Smultronstället* (1957; *Wild Strawberries*), the representation of her became increasingly aggressive, from the unbearably repulsive woman who years after the clergyman/protagonist in *Nattvardsgästerna* (1963; *Winter Light*), the cancerous, alcoholic, jealous, and "masturbating" (a cinematic sensation at the time) sister in *Tystnaden* (1963; *The Silence*), the naked slut in *Vargtimmen* (1968; *The Hour of the Wolf*), to the shockingly self-castrating neurotic in *Viskningar och rop.* (1972; *Cries and Whispers*)[13]

While Hedling is arguably quite subjective as to what or who can be regarded as "unbearably repulsive," or for that matter be appointed "slut" (and not least by whom), he still has a point. For how was Thulin an "avatar" of Bergman's projections, he asks, intimating that Bergman's constant "ugly-fying" of this exceedingly beautiful actress, may have been deeply personal and perhaps even vindictive. But more important in this context is Hedling's point regarding the impact of an artist's "biographical legend," referring to the concept coined by the Russian literary theorist Tomashevsky. For, as Hedling notes, "[g]ossip or not, *these are definitely facts of the forceful biographical legend that has become Bergman's*: among other things, his legendary sex drive, his self-confessed and relentless womanizing, and his hypocondria"[14] (My emphasis).

Certainly the perception of Bergman's biographical legend as being characterized by the attributes enumerated by Hedling, is an established fact, at least in his native country. I myself have attempted to show, in an overview of Swedish newspaper articles ranging from the 1940s to the 1990s, the degree to which Bergman can be regarded in the context of star and celebrity studies, infused by gossip, rather than, as is so often the case internationally, "highbrow" auteurism.[15] In fact, this particular reputation of Bergman's has even resulted in a Swedish book with the titillating title (in translation) "Ingmar Bergman—a story about love, sex, and betrayal," by journalist Thomas Sjöberg. Unsurprisingly, in Sweden the book has been accused of being overly gossipy, while the author himself was even barred from gaining access to the Ingmar Bergman Foundation archive.[16]

True, Sjöberg is in no way burdened by methodological or theoretical considerations. However, and just as Hedling points out, his book does bring up on the table the fact that gossip can be a viable object of study. This is of course precisely what Pierre Bourdieu too suggested—that in any study of power relations, it is theoretically a perfectly legitimate enterprise to delve into what might be defined as gossip, speculation, and conjecture.[17] Important in this context is not least Bourdieu's notion of gossip encompassing both formal and informal power structures, and how the two are entwined. For instance in Ingmar Bergman's case, one cannot, as Hedling intimates, overlook his close friendship with Harry Schein, who was not only Ingrid Thulin's husband but more importantly the founder of the Swedish Film Institute, and the state-supported system of film production, of which Bergman arguably was not only the foremost exponent but also beneficiary. In other words, between these two men there existed precisely the kind of informal bond that Bourdieu put his finger on, which in fact also resulted in the exercise of real power.[18]

As for Bergman's rise to power, it had become evident by the early 1960s. It is a sign of the times that it was then that Bo Widerberg, a then young up-and-coming Swedish film director (later internationally best known for his Cannes-winning *Elvira Madigan*, 1967), wrote a much-cited newspaper article, which amounted to no less than an outright attack on Bergman, and the power he had started to sway. True enough, at this time Bergman was indeed winner of two recent Oscars (for *Jungfrukällan/The Virgin Spring* (1960) and *Såsom i en spegel/ Through a Glass darkly* (1961)), which according to Widerberg, was a problem in itself, as his films kept spreading a mythologizing and non-realistic view of Sweden. Bergman was, in Widerberg's infamous phrase, "our spiritual Dalecarlia horse in the world," referring to a wooden, best-selling tourist souvenir.[19] But worse, he claimed, this was also why there was no funding left for younger film directors, like Widerberg himself.

Although outbursts such as Widerberg's in part can be regarded as a classic Oedipal "father murder" that any young generation sets in motion in order to enter the public stage, he did have a point. After all, at this time, Bergman had not only won international fame but also, as mentioned, had access to generous funds from the SFI, led by his close friend Schein—on top of it having recently been appointed both artistic head at Svensk Filmindustri, Sweden's largest film production company, *and* Head of the Royal Dramatic Theatre. In other words, already fairly early in Bergman's career, himself not yet in his mid forties, the main issues in his native country revolved around his alleged and/or real influence and power. True enough, from this point on, debates regarding his power in the film industry as well as cultural life at large would become staple fodder, up until as late as Bergman's swan song, *Fanny and Alexander* (1982), which, characteristically, stirred debate for being the most expensive Swedish film production to date.[20]

Andecdotal Evidence I: Colleagues and Co-Workers

There is no doubt, then, that Bergman reached a position in Swedish cultural life from which he was able to wield considerable power. Thus there is good reason to believe that this spilled over onto individual relationships as well, be it with actors, co-workers, or colleagues.

This is indeed the case, at least judging from the constant trickle of gossip and anecdotes in, for instance, interviews and published biographies. One term that keeps occurring in these publications, as well as in public parlance, is the term "demon director," so often in fact that it has become cliché. While the term seems to emanate from the 1940s, and Bergman's legendary outbursts of anger attributed (both by colleagues and Bergman himself) to youth, inexperience, and a generally nervous disposition, one might expect that this would have changed with increasing fame and professional success. However, various manifestations, for instance the infamous so-called "pedagogical outbursts," both in the theater and film sets seem to have reoccurred through the decades (see Katinka Faragó and Linus Thunström's contributions in this book).

In the 1950s, Gösta Ekman (1939–2017), who later became a much-appreciated actor and comedian, served as the director's assistant during the shoot of *Smultronstället/ Wild Strawberries* (1957). In his memoirs published in 2010, Ekman recalls that Bergman was abnormally interested in the personal affairs of his co-workers, and even describes his curiosity as "exceptional, and his need for control as abnormal." In a letter to a friend he wrote: "I'm in love, and he doesn't approve. He's really weird. I don't like him. Not because he's weird but because he tries to hurt you if you don't go along with [his] dictatorship. I can't explain it, but he does everything to ruin what's between me and Maud." The young woman referred to is Maud Hansson, who played the girl who was burnt on a stake in *Det sjunde inseglet/The Seventh Seal* (1957). She too had noted that Bergman pried into people's love lives, and also that he tried to own "his" actors, and that when they acted in other films, Bergman was "jealous." Although, she added, his scripts were psychologically penetrating and insightful, as a person Bergman was "crazy." At the time "I thought that great artists were great people as well. Ingmar Bergman was not."[21]

And so, after a year in Bergman's shadow, Gösta Ekman decided to quit. "I felt I couldn't stand it any longer. There was something unsound, and I didn't want to sink deeper into it." When Bergman asked why he wanted to quit, Ekman sarcastically answered there was no point in telling why, as "Bergman knows everything anyway"—at which point Bergman became "so hellishly angry that he threw something at me." Here Ekman also cites Marianne Höök, who in 1962 wrote one of the first truly insightful books on Bergman, because she too had noted that he enjoyed exercising power: "He tests his surroundings and gets reaffirmed that he can catch and makes people 'his' (his what? his ally? his admirer? dependent?) out of almost anyone."[22]

Even cinematographer Sven Nykvist, longtime and valued collaborator from 1960 up until the 1980s, became object of Bergman's wrath and irrational demands. In his autobiography *Vördnad för ljuset* (*Reverence for the Light*) Nykvist remembers that during the shoot of *The Silence* in the early 1960s, he needed to visit his mother, who was dying of cancer. "'Don't you dare leaving in the midst of the shoot! If you do, you might as well leave forever, you devil!', Ingmar shouted. 'If you call me devil in this situation, then I really won't come back', I said, and left." Later, Nykvist writes, Bergman did apologize, "but I'll never forget what he said. It was so typical of him: 'You should know, Sven, that

Figure 5.1 Bergman to Nykvist: "Don't you dare leave in the midst of the shoot!" Here in harmonious times, on the shoot of *From the Life of the Marionettes.*

the most important thing is what remains. What still lives on the white screen'" (Figure 5.1).²³

Even as late as in the 1990s, one finds telling incidents of this need for control, and even professional jealousy toward colleagues outside of Bergman's immediate sphere. A prime example is film and theater director Suzanne Osten (b. 1944), who since the 1970s has built an extraordinary career, having directed a number of films, and established a theater stage of her own (Klarateatern in Stockholm).

In the early 2000s, after having read in the papers about my involvement in the beginnings of the Bergman Foundation archive, she sent me a letter that she had received from Bergman, which she requested be added to the archive. His letter was in response to her having sent him the script for what was to become her second film, *Bröderna Mozart/The Mozart Brothers* (1986). She did this "with hope," she writes, since previously Bergman had declared how much he had liked her first film, *Mamma* ("Mother," 1982). But his response was not what she had hoped for, as in a letter, dated May 29, 1985, he declared that the script was cynical, heartless, and even "elitist" (ironically, Osten's film turned out to be a popular hit). "Anything Bergman said at the time," she wrote to me, "had incredible weight," and because it had taken her five years after her first film to scrape together funds for making *The Mozart Brothers*, and, on top of it, the shoot was about to start the week after she received Bergman's response, she hid his letter "deep down in a drawer," adding: "I was simply afraid that people in the film industry would find out the kind of shit I was making."

But Suzanne Osten's encounters with Bergman do not end there. For the same year that her film *Skyddsängeln/The Guardian Angel* (1990) was one of the nominees of the European Film Awards (at the time called the Felix award), Bergman happened to be the head of the jury.[24] Her film had been nominated in no less than seven categories, for best film, best scriptwriter, best cinematographer, best actor, best actress, and best-supporting actress.[25] Based on this, the whole production team, as well as most of the actors, flew to Glasgow, confident of receiving at least one prize, as "it was statistically assured," Osten writes in her letter. But they received none at all—due to Bergman, who nobody in the jury dared go against, she found out later. Once back in Stockholm she requested to have a meeting with him, at which he declared that the film was "bad," and that the hand camera was "too shaky" ("quite comical" these days, Osten comments).

However, in the press Bergman claimed that it would have been wrong to vote for "his own countrymen"—not heeding the fact, Osten writes, that "the previous year the Polish head of the jury had voted for his countryman Krzysztof Kieslowski's *A Short Film About Killing* (1988), which bought him a newfound independence." True enough, Kieslowski went on to make several major co-productions with France, such as *The Double Life of Véronique* (1991). In her own case, however, the result of Bergman's intervention was that a large French distribution company, which had shown great interest in the film at the Cannes Festival, dropped it. "What's so sad," Osten writes in her letter, is that "often he has told of how happy he became when he won his Cannes award [in 1956], because that's when his real freedom as a filmmaker began." It is strange, she adds, to think that "this truly great director could not find it within himself to be generous in a similarly crucial situation for me."

"Jealousy is a term I'd use," she put it later in a mail (dated August 24, 2010), which, she added, "also had to do with my ability to create an ensemble of actors, and he hated that—he simply did not want any competitors." That is spot on. Suzanne Osten was a real competitor, having founded her own stage with actors who liked to return to work in her projects (just as he once enjoyed), and with a film career as well.

One last example worth mentioning in this context revolves around a novelist. While authors of literature normally do not belong to the category of co-workers in the film industry, sometimes some of them can be counted into a director's circle (one example is Swedish novelist and playwright Per Olov Enquist (1934–2020), whose works Bergman staged both for the theater and television). In 2006 the Swedish author Alexander Ahndoril (b. 1967) published a novel called *Regissören*, which was translated in 2008 as *The Director, Ingmar Bergman Imagined—As Son, as Priest, as Visionary Filmmaker*. As is made clear by the British subtitle, the author utilizes the director's name and persona as a fictional character, while weaving a story about events taking place during the shoot of Bergman's feature *Nattvardsgästerna/The Communicants* (also *Winter Light*, 1963). At the same time Ahndoril made good use of the factual material that already existed about this shoot, not least the television documentary made by Vilgot Sjöman in 1962 for Swedish public television, as well as Sjöman's reportage book (see Paisley Livingston's chapter), while also employing articles in popular print media, including reportages and lush photographs in Swedish women's magazines on Bergman and then-wife Käbi Laretei's domestic life.[26]

The novel is quite complex and poetic, and as such good literature. Interestingly, it seems that Bergman himself thought so too—at least initially. For as Ahndoril has recounted himself, his manuscript had been sent to Bergman, upon which he phoned Ahndoril, and they had a pleasant conversation. But, then, after publication, in an interview broadcast on Swedish public television, Bergman launched a fierce attack on Ahndoril, calling the novel an "affront" as well as "humiliating" and "disgusting," and was particularly upset that his (then) wife Käbi Laretei at one point in the book was described as being naked—after which he pretends not to remember Ahndoril's name. "Now, what *is* the young man's name? It sounds a bit like some medicine—Sobril?" (which is the name for what in English is known as Xanax).[27]

Bergman's turnabout was no doubt due to a loss of power—that now, suddenly, he found that he was playing a role in someone else's script, as if overtaken by a fictional avatar. It was not he who controlled and directed his own image anymore, as had been his want. The issue here was an age old one—the negotiability and contingency of biographical truth.

In a certain sense, then, Alexander Ahndoril's case is not unlike Suzanne Osten's. For even though she was a well-established artist in Sweden, in her case Bergman did his best (or worst) to quench her international career in its bud—just as he now attempted to undermine a relatively young author's literary career. Still Ahndoril arguably ended up getting the last word, since he, together with his wife, became the internationally (extremely) best-selling author-duo under the pseudonym Lars Kepler.

Anecdotal Evidence II: Actors

As already intimated, perhaps the most important exercise of Bergman's power concerns his relation with actors. If nothing else, it is a fact that for at least fifty years, between the early 1950s to the early 2000s, he had access to several generations of the foremost actors in Sweden in both film and in the theater, among them Bibi Andersson, Harriet Andersson, Ingrid Thulin, Gunnel Lindblom, Gunnar Björnstrand, and Max von Sydow, and later, from the 1980s up until the early 2000, Pernilla August, Lena Olin, and Peter Stormare. Indeed, the actors in the older generation were often referred to as the "Bergman troupe," having been formed already during his successful sojourn as artistic director of Malmö City Theater, 1952–8, at the same time as they acted in his films. For all intents and purposes, then, Bergman also functioned as employer.

Perhaps it is no wonder, then, that Bergman grew to harbor a sense of ownership and privileged access to certain actors for his own projects, as was seen already in the case of Ekman-Hansson, and that lasted to the end of his career. For instance, when Bergman wanted the young actor Thommy Berggren to play the role of the waiter in *Tystnaden/The Silence* (1963), a conflict immediately brewed as Berggren instead chose to act in the aforementioned up-and-coming director Bo Widerberg's film *Kvarteret korpen/Raven's End* (1963). In fact, there was a conflict in a double sense, as by this time Widerberg had already launched his attack against Bergman being "our Dalecarlia horse in the world," and as Thommy Berggren very well could have acted in both films (not least since his intended role in *The Silence* was small), but instead actively chose to join Widerberg's film only.[28] It was not a bad choice, given that *Kvarteret korpen* turned out to be a canonical film in Swedish film history, announcing the entrance of a younger filmmaking generation influenced by the French New Wave.

Another telling case is Gunnar Björnstrand, who arguably was Bergman's first leading man, playing an important role in *The Seventh Seal*, while being the male lead in films such as *Kvinnors väntan/Waiting Women* (1952), *En lektion i kärlek/A Lesson in Love* (1954), *Kvinnodröm/Dreams* (1955), *Såsom i en spegel/ Through a Glass Darkly* (1961), and *Nattvardsgästerna/The Communicants* (also *Winter Light*, 1963). His case is well documented, as his wife, Lillie Björnstrand, in 1975 published an insightful book on Gunnar Björnstrand's acting career, which includes firsthand observations about her husband's and Bergman's relationship. And like so many before her, she is deeply ambivalent about Bergman—at times admiring, at other times angry and frustrated. "Ingmar always had a hard time for spouses—of both sexes," she writes, and then goes on to confirm the reoccurring theme of professional jealousy. "Most of all he'd like to 'own' his actors, and Gunnar he made sure to possess to such an extent that both family, relatives and friends felt neglected."[29] But, she adds, Bergman

> has been endowed with such a variety of personal qualities, and with so much of each sort that it seems not quite human. A violent sense of humor, which masks deep streaks of anxiety and melancholy. A sensitivity and intuition so distinct, second to none [. . .] in addition a strong sense of tenderness, which wells forth in parts and abruptly, and which makes his actors, male and female, do anything for him. But it's a tenderness that just as quickly may change into chilly distance [. . .], which makes many of his co-workers insecure, even overly devoted. So that those people in the margins often have feeling of finding themselves in a quagmire. But Gunnar was his favorite, so he was spared [. . .] if Ingmar happened to be difficult, Gunnar just said—"listen Ingmar, just watch out for my memoirs, which I will call 'I was Ingmar Bergman's maid.'"[30]

This is a beautiful and clear-sighted passage. Nonetheless, there is a problematic incident, which Lillie Björnstrand makes sure to include in her book. It is regarding the shoot of *The Communicants*, in which the Lutheran minister, acted by Gunnar Björnstrand, is supposed to be afflicted with a severe cold. At the beginning of the shoot, Björnstrand felt in perfect health. But then the staff doctor of the film company (SF) informed him that Bergman had decided that he should undergo an extensive health check, supposedly because of his demanding role—the result of which, the same doctor soon informed him, showed that he had "extremely" high blood pressure. This threw Björnstrand into deep despair, and his wife writes: "Up until the very first rehearsal I tried to convince him that that this was an exaggeration by the doctor, and a totally un-psychological and reprehensible treatment—an attempt at scaring the hell out of someone."[31] Finally, Björnstrand sought a second medical opinion—and found out that his blood pressure was fine.

Lillie Björnstrand remained convinced that the whole thing had been a cruel ruse, an attempt on Bergman's part at manipulating the actor to seem less robust, and so fit the role better. In any case, she concludes, "and so the long work companionship between Ingmar and Gunnar ended abruptly." For even though Björnstrand later got parts in for instance *Skammen/Shame* (1968) and *Riten/The Rite* (1969), "those good times when they had worked together as friends and equals were definitely gone."[32]

Max von Sydow, who had already appeared as lead in *The Seventh Seal*, *Ansiktet/The Magician* (1958), and *The Virgin Spring* (1960), continued to solidify his function as Bergman's leading man from the mid-1960s on, in films like *Vargtimmen/Hour of the Wolf* (1968), *Skammen/Shame* (1968), *En passion/The Passion of Anna* (1969), and *Beröringen/The Touch* (1971). Unsurprisingly, he was often, particularly internationally, referred to as Bergman's mouthpiece. For instance, when von Sydow received the 2006 Donostia Award at San Sebastián, the world's largest Spanish-speaking film festival—up until then, the only Swede in the illustrious list of awardees, encompassing everyone from Gregory Peck to Judi Dench. Still, after a several decades-long international career, von Sydow found that the motivation cited "el alter ego de Bergman"—something that the actor did not agree with: "I'm not an ounce more Mr. Bergman's alter ego than many of his other actors, the women included."[33] One can sense a streak of irritation here, as well as an attempt at distancing himself from Bergman. For while it is undeniable that the director had been an important influence in launching von Sydow's international career (it was, after all, thanks to his roles in *The Seventh Seal* and *The Virgin Spring* that he was cast as Jesus in *The Greatest Story Ever Told*, George Stevens, 1965), he may have sensed a risk of forever remaining in debt, and so, the risk of being hauled back.

Regardless, there is no doubt that Bergman could make or break careers. Nowhere is this clearer than in the case of female actors associated with Bergman's films. He was after all instrumental in launching the international careers of Bibi Andersson, Ingrid Thulin, and Liv Ullmann. This is especially true in the latter case, given Ullmann's role in *Scener ur ett äktenskap/Scenes from a Marriage* (1973) which became a huge hit in the United States. In fact she was twice nominated for Broadway's Tony Awards, as well as nominated twice for an Oscar, while also winning the New York Film Critics' Award for Best Actress no less than three times.[34]

On the other hand, one should add that it was not only the actors who rode on Bergman's wave as auteur, but, conversely, the director too who benefited from their star value. It is significant that when Bergman made a dark and difficult film like *The Silence*, it was built on a script where the protagonists originally had been two men, one of them elderly—but who in later versions became two young women.[35] This obviously allowed Bergman to cast a beautiful and voluptuous actress like Gunnel Lindblom, whom he proceeded to dress in designer clothing, alternately show in various stages of undress (for the actress' reaction to this, see further below). Arguably, then, it was not only women actors who profited from being in Bergman's films, he too profited, on a very basic level—in raising interest for his films abroad, and in helping getting them distributed. It was very much a mutual affair between consenting adults, if you will.

Perhaps this two-way deal, and the importance of star value, is no more evident than in the case of Harriet Andersson, and her importance for *Sommaren med Monika/Summer with Monika* (1953). For by now it is somewhat of a cliché to refer to the impact that her few seconds of nudity had internationally—on other film directors like Francois Truffaut (the movie poster of Andersson in *The 400 Blows*, 1959), or the changing of the film's title in the United States (*Monika—the story of a bad girl*) or, for that matter, the inordinate sales in various countries in South America.[36]

It is not by chance that the interviewer who helped write Harriet Andersson's memoirs insists on lingering on the shoot of *Summer with Monika*, as this was her first film with Bergman. And Harriet Andersson is game, for this humorous lady is one who knows how to spin a tale. "All rumor aside," she comments, "the man did have an incredible charisma—otherwise all of us [women] wouldn't have jumped into bed with him or more importantly have lived with him." But, she hastens to add, in her case, "it wasn't because I thought that I would get lots of roles—that didn't even occur to me. By the way, he hardly became kinder to me when shooting films after we had become an item, on the contrary—he became more harsh probably exactly because of it."[37]

But, the interviewer insists, what about the fact that she was so young, only nineteen, whereas Bergman was almost twice her age, when they became "an item," as she puts it. Here she is adamant about setting the record straight, as many have taken for granted that it was Bergman who "seduced" her—this putatively young, impressionable woman. Quite the opposite she claims, both in her autobiography, and as late as in a radio program in 2017, the very year of MeToo—"*I seduced him! I decided to kiss him.*"[38] The other thing she wants to set the record straight about is that she did not get the role of Monika as a result of already having slept with Bergman. "When it happened [on the island where the film was shot], all contracts had already been signed."[39]

But she too, just like Gunnar Björnstrand, is deeply ambivalent about Bergman. While "there were lots of [exaggerated] myths circulating about him," on the set

> he could really explode. I've been exposed to this too. And one doesn't always understand why. [. . .] It's like a predator, a hawk, or a cheetah, or a hyena. When they detect a heard of animals, they unfailingly focus in on the weakest [. . .] Ingmar sees this instantly—people who cannot defend themselves.

She even goes as far as calling such incidents "a public execution [. . .] One wonders if he does this only to show that he has that kind of power, and that he can say whatever without anyone daring to contradict him."[40]

Gunnel Lindblom, for her part, always had a friendly and professional relationship with Bergman (he produced her first two films as director in his production company Cinematograph). But she also has a story to tell, and in a way that is highly relevant to MeToo, in this case regarding nudity and the power relation between director and actress. She wrote about it in an article that I have cited elsewhere, but which is worth citing *in extenso*, and reflecting upon retroactively in light of MeToo.[41]

> In the old days, Ingmar's temper was [. . .] volcanic. He used to refer to anyone who didn't throw furniture around as "inhibited". [. . .] Well, once he became terribly angry at me. God knows if he has ever really forgiven me.
> It was during the filming of *The Silence*. There were complicated, atrociously difficult love scenes [. . .] in the hotel room bed. Birger Malmsten and I were completely exhausted. But it had apparently worked well. [. . .] Anyway, in I went again, ready for the next scene. The floodlights had been moved in seconds flat. Ingmar met me near the lights and gave me a peculiar look.
> "What's that you're wearing?"
> "A slip."
> "Did you intend to wear it in bed?"
> "Don't you like it, Ingmar?"
> "No! You're supposed to be naked. In the script, it says Anna is supposed to be NAKED."

That ice-cold look, those penetrating dark eyes. Marika Vos [the film's costume designer] and Sven Nykvist [cinematographer] had vanished behind a cabinet. They didn't like it when a hurricane was brewing.

I was trembling badly, hoping it didn't show. Ingmar's outburst didn't materialize. But it will be a long time before I forget the glowing rage in his eyes and the contempt in his voice:

"So what do we do now?!"

"You'll have to find a stand-in, Ingmar."

Why he didn't kill me, I'll never know . . .

A little later, as I lay there in the bed with my slip on, I heard Ingmar whisper loudly to our make-up man, "What is so f---ing *important* about those hellish goddamned cursed globs of fat?!" I looked down at my breasts, which were rather small, and felt rather foolish.

Well, why *was* it so important? A couple of years later I felt I had been unforgivably stupid and prudish. But at the time, I had only one thought in my head: "It's OK to turn my soul inside out, but I want to keep my clothes on."

After that I wasn't in any more films [by Bergman] until *Scenes from a Marriage*. But perhaps there were other reasons.[42]

One senses a strong ambivalence here, and also that there is much unsaid. First of all, as this was written in hindsight in the late 1980s, Lindblom seems to think that she was prudish, and that later, in more liberal times, she has come to change her mind about nudity. But then there is her first intuitive response, which in the light of MeToo is most understandable—and which she stuck with, in the end. For in the nude takes of the film there is indeed a body double in Lindblom's role. In addition one could note that it was never discussed whether Lindblom's male colleague should be dressed or naked in bed. This was obviously, and tellingly, not an issue.

So, for all the humor of this piece, one gets the sense of Lindblom's strong personal and professional integrity, but also a sense of rage, as if kept under a lid. If nothing else, there is the ending regarding the fact that for many years she was not offered roles by Bergman—something that speaks multitudes of the asymmetrical power relations between actor and director (see Wallenberg's contribution in this book).

Late Style, and A Lion in Winter

But when predators, as Harriet Andersson so drastically (albeit metaphorically), put it, get older, their bite may not be as forceful. This seems to have been the case in relation to the casting for *Fanny och Alexander/Fanny and Alexander* (1982/3), designated to become Bergman's swan song. For here the role of the children's mother Emilie (in film acted by then-31-year-old Ewa Fröling) was actually written with Liv Ullmann in mind. If nothing else, this is clear from a scene in the published script where Emilie at one point walks around talking to herself: "It's a May evening and here I am alone talking to myself and I'll be forty-one next week."[43] It is clear from the shooting script too, in which Bergman has drawn a thick, angry line over "forty one years old," adding, in handwriting, "thirty six," thus coming at least a bit closer to actress Fröling's real age. But perhaps the most telling sign is a handwritten addition in the shooting script, in the scene where Emilie is supposed to pick up a photo of her mother, which reads "The photo of her mother (Liv in Whispers!)."[44] This scribble not only confirms that Ullmann was intended for the role of Emilie, but also that the director imagined including a still photo in the film that would have functioned as an elegant allusion to one of his earlier films with the actress, *Viskningar och rop/Cries and Whispers* (1972).

The fact that Liv Ullmann turned down the role of Emilie was obviously a major disappointment for Bergman. This has been corroborated by Ullmann herself, who in the interview has related that when Bergman found out, his answer was: "Liv, nu har du förlorat din förstfödslorätt" ("now you have lost the privileges of the firstborn")—the meaning of which obviously was that she would not necessarily be his first choice at castings in the future.[45] Bergman must surely have experienced a similar disappointment when Max von Sydow, who he had in mind for the role of Bishop Vergerus, the children's evil stepfather, turned it down. This is clear from the script, as here the bishop is described as "a tall, broad-shouldered man with a large bony face"—a description that captures von Sydow's "bony" look perfectly, but hardly fits the actor who finally took on the role.[46]

It is no wonder that Bergman found the presence of these two actors essential for *Fanny and Alexander*. Part of the reason is no doubt that in this film we see an artist who in old age, as Jan Holmberg has pointed out, is an example of what Edward Said wrote in his article "On late style," discussing artists who in old age "repeat, reinterpret, return and revise" well-known territory.[47] But another reason is that actors like Liv Ullmann and Max von Sydow obviously would have been bankable names (not least internationally) in a prestigious production such as this, because of their status as certified auteur-stars. For it goes without saying that these particular actors would have added a specific *aura* to this production, including a whole field of those associations that these two actors had accumulated over time, through their combined "ready-mades"—not least in previous Bergman films in which they had acted together, like *Hour of the Wolf*, *Shame*, and *The Passion of Anna*.

That mutual affair between consenting adults, which had served Bergman so well for so long, seems to have come to the end of its tether.

Conclusion

Generally speaking, there has always been a good amount of Bergman-bashing in Sweden, both on a fairly sleazy tabloid level and in more putatively sophisticated circles. This overview, which has focused on the negative, problematic, and, at the very least, ambiguous, could be accused of having done the same.

At the same time, it must be said that it is hard, even if one tried, to outweigh the other end of the scale—that is, the beneficial influence, structurally as well as individually, that Bergman has had, as artist, as agent in the film industry as well as in the theater, and in Swedish culture at large. If nothing else, it would be hard to neglect the overwhelmingly positive evidence on Bergman's professionalism, offered, literally for decades, by actors and co-workers, and even by those critical of Bergman—including those in this overview.

But such as it is, this anecdotal overview could possibly be seen as one reason for a more encompassing and in-depth historical study of the Swedish film industry, with a view toward issues such as the degree of dependency of actors on the director, the asymmetrical power relation between director and actress, including potential sexual repercussions in their wake, job opportunities, and other instances of power relations which may have come to the detriment of (specifically) female actors and co-workers, as well as a multitude of minutiae—salaries, contractual wordings, casting issues, and so on. It goes without saying that such a study best be undertaken by researchers who are able to historicize. That would entail looking at, for instance, MeToo in the context of a particular Zeitgeist, and in the varying conditions of production in the Swedish film industry over time, and perhaps even whether the very concept of MeToo is a useful tool when looking in the rear-view mirror. Or conversely, that it is always relevant, to one degree or another—that MeToo structurally is revealed as having been a constant, structural, and endemic problem in the Swedish (or any) film industry.

As for Ingmar Bergman specifically, it is easy to conclude that there are no excuses for some of his behavior. And even if he probably is the last one in need of defense, there still seems to lie some redemption in the fact that all of the actresses who were involved in personal relationships with Bergman continued to work with him after their breakups. To mention a few—Harriet Andersson as the female lead in *Through a Glass Darkly*, Bibi Andersson in *Persona*, Liv Ullmann in *Scenes from a Marriage*, and classical pianist Käbi Laretei in *Fanny and Alexander*. The same was the case with Gunnar Björnstrand, who, as we have seen, had a serious falling out with Bergman in *The Communicants*, but who accepted the important part as theater director in *Fanny and Alexander*. And if redemption is too strong a word, at least this illustrates Bergman's adherence to what he told Sven Nykvist after their altercation—that the most important thing is what remains on the white screen. Indeed, it seems that work came before private life, at any cost—probably at times, at too high a cost, to the detriment of other values.

Finally, one may also note that those women actors who are still around, most of them with firsthand experience of working with Bergman in the theater, all seem quite respectful, when interviewed both after his death in 2007, as well as in the midst of the 2017 MeToo events. These include actors such as Lena Endre (b. 1955), who worked with Bergman in the theater as well as his last productions for Swedish public television, and Marie Göranzon (b. 1942), grand old lady of the Royal Dramatic Theatre in Stockholm, who worked alongside Bergman for over three decades. Although the latter enumerates quite a few related incidents at the theater involving male actors, and acidly remarks on the recurring turf wars among male directors (including Bergman), she clearly keeps him in high esteem.[48] Known for her straightforward honesty, she would certainly have said more, had there been reasons for it—by that time having nothing to lose.

Then again, most of the actors in the theater worked with the older Bergman, which reasonably will give different results when compared to, for instance, on a film set in the 1950s. Which is just another way of saying that no man is a monolith—or, as Bergman, sometimes his own best critic, put it on the sleeve of that book about his younger self: "this is a close up of a relative that I'd rather not to be acquainted with."

Notes

1   Richard Orange, "Hard-Hitting Film Takes Aim at Ingmar Bergman's Flawed Way with Women," *The Observer*, January 6, 2018. https://www.theguardian.com/film /2018/jan/06/ingmar-bergman-beauty-beast-flawed-way-with-women-great-art.

2   Ibid.
3   Ibid.
4   Jannike Åhlund, "Var Bergman en våldtäktsman?," *Svenska Dagbladet*, April 17, 2019.
5   All translations are mine, unless otherwise stated.
6   Ingmar Bergman, *The Magic Lantern: An Autobiography* (New York: Penguin Books, 1989), 1, translation Joan Tate. If one is to believe his father Erik Bergman, the baby was baptized in a customary manner on August 19 in the summer home of Erik's mother-in-law in Dalecarlia. This is corroborated by his wife Karin, who wrote "No one came to our house *Våroms* in Duvnäs as early as Ingmar. He arrived when he was only fourteen days old, and there he was baptized on an August evening at sunset in the corner of the living room." See the volume of correspondence compiled and commented by Birgit Linton-Malmfors, *Den dubbla verkligheten: Karin och Erik Bergman I dagböcker och brev 1907-1936* [Dual Reality: Karin and Erik Bergman in Diaries and Letters 1907-1936] (Stockholm: Carlssons, 1992), 87 and 89. In other words, Karin Bergman did not contract the Spanish flu while she was pregnant, but several months after the child's birth, and baby Ingmar could hardly have suffered through the illness already at birth.
7   See my *I begynnelsen var ordet. Ingmar Bergman och hans tidiga författarskap* [In the Beginning was the Word. Ingmar Bergman's Early Writings] (Stockholm: Wahlström & Widstrand, 2002), 203-6.
8   In a telephone conversation, September 14, 2005.
9   Cited on the sleeve of Koskinen, *I begynnelsen var ordet*. For a more detailed presentation the beginnings of the archive, see my "Au commencement était le Verbe. Les écrits de jeunesse d'Ingmar Bergman," *Positif* 497/498 (July-August 2002): 17-22, and "From Short Story to Film to Autobiography. Intermedial Variations in Ingmar Bergman's Writings and Films," *Film International* 1, no. 1 (2003): 5-11.
10 Åhlund, "Var Bergman en våldtäktsman?".
11 Linda Rugg, *Self-Projection: The Director's Image in Art Cinema* (Minneapolis and London: University of Minnesota Press, 2014).
12 Arne Lunde, "Ingmar's Hitchcockian Cameos: Early Bergman as Auteur Inside the Swedish Studio System," *Journal of Scandinavian Cinema* 8, no. 1 (2018): 19-33.
13 Erik Hedling, *Scandinavian Studies* 87, no. 2 (2015): 301-2, https://doi.org/10.5406/scanstud.87.2.0299.
14 Ibid., 300.
15 "From Erotic Icon to Clan Chief: The Auteur as Star," in *Stellar Encounters: Stardom in Popular European Cinema*, ed. Tytti Soila (New Barnet: John Libbey Publishing Ltd, 2009), 81-9. Similar findings were confirmed in a later study based on big

data; see Jono Van Belle, *Scenes From an Audience. The Auteur and the Film Text in Audience Experiences: Ingmar Bergman—A Case Study*, doctoral dissertation (Stockholm University/University of Ghent, 2019).

16 *Ingmar Bergman—en berättelse om kärlek, sex och svek* (Stockholm: Lind & Co, 2013).

17 Pierre Bourdieu, *The Field of Cultural Production* (Cambridge: Polity Press, [1972]) 1993).

18 While this kind of power normally is subject to corruption, it may also work in beneficial ways. One example is how Bergman and Schein colluded in lifting the Swedish film censorship regulations, as Schein had direct access to the relevant ministries in the government at the time. See my chapter "P(owe)R, Sex, and Mad Men Swedish Style," in *Swedish Cinema and the Sexual Revolution: Critical Essays*, ed. Mariah Larsson and Elisabet Björklund (Jefferson, NC: McFarland & Co, 2016), 153–67.

19 Bo Widerberg, "Vår andes dalahäst i världen" [Our soul's Dalecarlia horse in the world], originally in a series of articles in Swedish daily *Expressen*, January 8, 10, 13, 14, 1962. Reprinted in Bo Widerberg, *Visionen i svensk film* [The Vision for Swedish Film] (Stockholm: Bonniers, 1962).

20 Maaret Koskinen and Mats Rohdin, *Fanny and Alexander. Ur Ingmar Bergmans arkiv och hemliga gömmor* [From Ingmar Bergman's Archive and Secret Hideaways] (Stockholm: Wahlström & Widstrand, 2005), 26–8.

21 Gösta Ekman, *Farbrorn som inte vill va' stor* [The uncle who wouldn't grow up] (Stockholm: Leopard förlag, 2010), 110–11.

22 Ibid., 110 and 112.

23 Sven Nykvist and Bengt Forslund, *Vördnad för ljuset. Om film och människor* [In reverence of the light: On films and people] (Stockholm: Albert Bonniers Förlag, 1997), 94.

24 After Bergman's death, she revealed this story publicly, the first time on June 27, 2012, at the "Bergman week," which takes place each year on Fårö island.

25 "The Guardian Angel," European Film Awards homepage, https://europeanfilmawards.eu/en_EN/film/the-guardian-angel.5249.

26 "Multiple Adaptation Processes: The Case of Alexander Ahndoril's *The Director* and its Predecessors in Feature Film, Television Documentary and Popular Print Media," *Journal of Scandinavian Cinema* 5, no. 1 (2015): 35–47.

27 In the television program "Babel," on Swedish National public service channel SVT2 September 12, 2006.

28 In conversation in the fall of 2007 with Mårten Blomkvist, longtime film critic at the daily *Dagens Nyheter*, as well as son-in-law of Bo Widerberg.

29 Lillie Björnstrand, *Inte bara applåder* [Not only applause] (Stockholm: Tiden, 1975), 144.

30 Ibid., 145–6.

31 Ibid., 180–1.
32 Ibid., 187.
33 Jan Lumholdt, "Filmskolan special no. 9: Max von Sydow," *Ingmar* 4 (2006): 66–71.
34 "Reception, Circulation, Desire: Liv Ullmann and the Transnational Journeys of a Scandinavian Actress," *The Journal of Transnational American Studies* 7 (2016): 1, https://escholarship.org/uc/item/09h5b6m1.
35 *Ingmar Bergman's The Silence: Pictures in the Typewriter, Writings on the Screen* (Seattle: University of Washington Press/Copenhagen: Museum Tusculanum Press, 2010), 55.
36 Birgitta Steene, *Ingmar Bergman: A Reference Guide* (Amsterdam: Amsterdam University Press, 2005), 887.
37 *Harriet Andersson. Samtal med Jan Lumholdt* (Stockholm: Alfabeta, 2005), 45.
38 Ibid., 43. Also in radio program "Sommar" on SR, Swedish public radio channel P1. https://sverigesradio.se/avsnitt/909821.
39 Ibid., 46.
40 Ibid., 71.
41 Koskinen, *Ingmar Bergman's* The Silence, 62–3.
42 Gunnel Lindblom, "Confessions of a Bergman Co-worker," in *Ingmar Bergman. An Artist's Journey. In Stage, On Screen, In Print*, ed. Roger Oliver (New York: Arcade Publishing, 1995), 62. Originally published in Swedish as "I skuggan av en vulkan" [In the shadow of a volcano] in *Chaplin* (film magazine) 30 (1988): 2–3, 100–3.
43 Ingmar Bergman, *Fanny and Alexander*, trans. Alain Blair (London: Penguin Books, 1989 [1982]), 213.
44 Shooting script "Fanny och Alexander," dated Fårö Sunday July 8, 1979, 285 pages. On the blank back of p. 279 (opposite p. 280) one finds, in handwriting, "the photo of her mother (Liv in Whispers!)," accompanied by a directorial note to the actor: "picks up photo of mother."
45 Olof Brundin, "Vi levde med en mur omkring oss" [We lived with a wall around us], *Aftonbladet* (Sunday section) June 14, 1998, 6.
46 Bergman, *The Magic Lantern*, 88.
47 Jan Holmberg, *Författaren Ingmar Bergman* [Bergman the author] (Stockholm: Norstedts, 2018), 247.
48 Marie Göranzon, *Vrålstark & skiträdd*. [Superstrong & scared shitless] (Stockholm: Norstedts 2017), 142–3, and 209–12.

/ 6

For Good or for Bad?

Bergman's Ambivalent Influence—Some Observations

Linus Tunström

There's a slightly musty smell. It cannot be easy to keep the 1970s interior with wall-to-wall carpeting fresh in the damp Gotland climate. We are a small, devout company unlocking and switching on the lights at the small cinema in Dämba. The entry door leads straight into the projection booth, where the first thing we encounter is the great old 35-millimeter-Ernemann cinema projector, aimed through the glass into the room. After a few days here we've made ourselves at home. We ignore the cinema projector and turn to the easier-to-use DVD player alongside. I take on the job of starting the machines and finding the switches to light up the room. The lamps are weak and are mainly focused on the tapestry with motifs out of Mozart's opera *The Magic Flute*, covering the one wall, so they aren't much help to the older people in the group who are anxiously fumbling to avoid falling down the stairs. At last, everyone has found a seat and sunk down in the remarkably wide armchairs.

There are a number of unwritten rules, obedience of which is closely monitored by those of our little company who, so to speak, were here "when it all happened"; who were here in this room when it came to the crunch, in the presence of the Master. For example, never ever sitting in Ingmar's own armchair here in the cinema. This mix of respect, bordering on veneration, and a living artistic environment, meant to be used, is somewhat of a paradox. We all pitch in to get the films rolling. Today it's my turn and I've selected the day's Bergman title for collective viewing and subsequent discussion. In addition to contributing to the group discussion, I hope to find something inspirational for a few of my own projects that I'm struggling to blow life in. That's my personal task during this little visit.

Figure 6.1 From Linus Tunström's theater production of *Fanny and Alexander* at Uppsala City Theater in 2012. Photographer: Micke Sandström.

I hope that these days will lead to a breakthrough. That the input of good films and interesting discussions will lend inspiration, the environment and nature focus, and in addition, that perhaps some mystical presence of Bergman's spirit will contribute magical energy to get everything going. Otherwise, life continues as usual in a slightly unfocused, fragmentary way around me. I have a thousand small obligations and an overshadowing desire I've never really come to grips with. The obligations are all over the place, including preparing my two upcoming theater shows, trying to decide on wall colors and which lamps to buy as part of a planned home renovation, navigating relationships and parenthood, the always neglected tango dancing, theater premieres, belated birthday gifts involving people taking me out to restaurants, and feedback I promised on others' work. My overwhelming desire is to write. To formulate something that is not only interesting and touching, but also has something to say. The rest I all barely manage, if at the last minute. The writing is not going as well. This little trip to Farö has been like a mirage since I'd been invited a few months ago. Here it will happen! And now that I'm here . . . Still no deliverance has come, but on the other hand I've barely had the time to sit down alone at a desk. Besides, only two days have passed of the week I carved out outside of my everyday Stockholm existence, so there's no need to despair just yet.

Our little company roaming Bergman Country comprises, in addition to myself, academics from across the Atlantic as well as firsthand witnesses, old colleagues of Ingmar's. Some prominent international filmmakers were also supposed to have been present, but they've become variously indisposed and canceled on short notice. Our stays here overlap; some leave while others arrive; our quarters are scattered about, and we take turns eating dinner and having our post-film conversations in the different buildings of the Bergman Empire.

The night before I had, after spending my first night at Hammars (the main building and Bergman's private residence), installed myself in the so-called Writing Cottage, which became available when one of our group returned to their academic post in the United States. The cottage is right at the edge of the forest, before you get to the shore, and is reached by taking a pitch-dark October path from the rain-destroyed gravel road a bit higher up. Glimpses of the full moon could be seen through the dense trunks and enticed me to take a closer look. When I passed through the small gate in the low stonewall demarcating the property from the beach, I noticed that it was broken. As if it had been damaged by some wild animal. That wasn't the case earlier that day. Although I wouldn't describe myself as afraid of the dark, it gave me a slight shiver.

Half-lying in the hypnotic moonshine on the beach's characteristic flat stone slabs, the broken gate seemed apt. This attempted intrusion, someone or something that wants to tear down the walls protecting the cottage against the wilderness, was like a sign of some kind of psychic process. Like demons that are concrete manifestations of the shadowy parts of the psyche. A bit like in Bergman's film *Vargtimmen/Hour of the Wolf* (1968), when the scary little child attacks Max von Sydow. Those scary vampiric neighbors—half human and half wild animal.

Both the projects I'm struggling with have similar elements. Repressed feelings, experiences, and needs that take physical form and overpower the protagonists. What I love about genre films, like thrillers and horror, is that they through the story, the exaggeration, and the archetypes can tell us things about psychological processes in an entertaining and directly physical way. The scariest thing is often that which moves in your own psyche, which you cannot really get a look at, except perhaps for a peripheral glimpse, from the corner of your eye.

These faint shudders bode well. That seems logical here. Particularly since one of the rational academics and her ultrarational husband told us how their front door had opened; they heard steps and the faucets were opened to a spray in the kitchen while they were sleeping upstairs at Dämba, the old private Bergman residence. This entire ghostly Bergman Country is charged with the tensions and paradoxes of the past, between reverence and impudence, between aggression and generosity, between anxiety and a free flow.

And now I'm sitting in one of the wide armchairs of the private cinema. Like a scrap collector, I keep one eye on the lookout for treasures and collector's items, which I can take with me to my own unfinished projects, while I'm with the other eye trying to do my best to watch the first film I had chosen,

Såsom i en spegel/Through a Glass Darkly (1961), without a predetermined attitude. Just observing neutrally what I see, without evaluating it.

I've had dealings with Bergman before. Partly through direct contact, at the age of twenty at the Royal Dramatic Theater when I participated in his staging of Shakespeare's *A Winter's Tale*, and then twenty-five years later, after his death, when I directed his *Fanny och Alexander/Fanny and Alexander* (1982/3) for the stage. This was the first Bergman film I had seen, at the cinema with my mother, on a cold Christmas day when I was twelve.

When I became the director of Uppsala City Theater, I knew that I wanted to stage it, that it should "come home" to Uppsala [where the story of *Fanny and Alexander* takes place]. I wanted to free it, both from nostalgia and false reverence, and try to release the homage to the irrational embedded in the story. And perhaps also liberate the piece from its connection to the Royal Dramatic Theater.

I had spent a few of my first fumbling directing years in the Royal Dramatic Theater's gilded rooms and experienced a strange mixture of fear and self-solemnity that risked transforming charged plays into good, yet boring, theater. This is a time I would not be without, because it gave me something to brace myself against as I blaze my own path. And this period came back to me when I started working on *Fanny and Alexander*.

It was in the 1990s, and I had only directed a few plays. I was about to come in from the cold and become a part of "The House," as everyone at the Royal Dramatic Theater called their workplace. According to old acting school custom, I would stay there a while to soak up the knowledge and traditions saturating the walls, and eventually direct something. The formal title that allowed me entrance to the Master's rehearsals of *A Winter's Tale* was that of "figurant," which was a bit better than an extra but below the rank of actor. The hierarchy was clearly visible in the staff canteen: each of the three mentioned categories always sat at a different table and the lead actors or "stars" usually appropriated a fourth table.

Some rejoinders are stuck in my head. A few months earlier as a student I had walked around in the building to "soak up and learn." A lighting master had shown me the technical control room for the main stage and with reverence in his voice described how when

> Ingmar directs you are always a bit scared; you shape up, everyone is on tiptoes and does their best. The main stage is difficult. When a less experienced director comes you wonder how it will go. You wait a bit and see if they'll manage. Some directors are too nice, you know. Then nothing gets done. Then you almost want things to go wrong.

The rehearsals were on. I heard him dethrone Donya Feuer, the choreographer, in front of all of us, because of how worthless her work was, and saw her grit her teeth because she tried to project discipline and authority in front of us figurants. I observed how Ingmar somewhat violently dragged a 75-year-old Gösta Prüzelius up and down the stage stairs, impatient that he did not understand the staging quickly enough, and then winking to Börje [Ahlstedt] as if they shared sadistic pleasure in seeing their colleague so rattled. By the way, this sadism later led to an uncontrolled Börje cracking Prüsse's ribs during one performance, because the only one who could have curbed Börje's aggression–turned stage energy had declined that responsibility.

Often in the mornings, before we started the day's work in Rehearsal Hall 1, Ingmar sat for a while in a chair in the foyer outside and the actors gathered around him, like a family portrait. Or a bit like naptime at a kindergarten when everyone wants to lie down closest to the teacher; a moment of pleasant, familiar chitchat with the hierarchies and battle for a moment of the Master's attention just below the surface. Another day I was still sitting on stage during a break between rehearsals. The lights were down for the moment and cloaked in half-darkness on the middle of the stage, Ingmar and Pernilla [August née Wallgren] remained on the scenography couch to have a quiet chat. Pernilla, then relatively new at the theater, asked if there were many "ghosts in the walls" there at the main stage. Ingmar chuckled: "Yes, you better believe that. Many ghosts. It's gruesome. And the young directors who come here sense it. They can't handle it, you know. They are broken by it." I reacted to his slanting of the subject a bit away from Pernilla's original question and his slightly raised voice and pricked up my ears—it actually felt as if he had wanted me specifically to hear. I later described the scene to an older colleague who was of the opinion that Ingmar kept an eye on all the directors, even if they were young, and if I had heard this it was because he had wanted me to; he wanted to send some kind of message.

Later in the process, we had a large rehearsal of the opening scene. All participants, the stars, actors, figurants, and extras, around thirty people, were to come on stage in a large movement. A powerful "stop" came from the house. "You there, young Tunström." I was standing right at the back and thought myself invisible in this giant scene. "I've told you to smile and be glad when coming on stage. You look as if you find this boring. Do you think it's boring?" "No, absolutely not, I was thinking of something private," I tried, embarrassed about being the reason for stopping the entire machinery. "Never take the private with you on stage," he said sharply. Then his tone changed and became more philosophical:

"What we're doing is writing on water. There now—and then gone, so incredibly fragile. So if I see anyone yawning or lost in their thoughts I am afflicted by such a damn sense of futility that I just want to cancel the whole thing." Everyone was quiet; nobody wanted to cause Ingmar Bergman's anxiety to compel him to cancel his big production. (Yet the fear of yawning on stage induced everyone to think of nothing else and a veritable yawning epidemic broke out.)

After the rehearsal Ingmar Bergman grabbed me, placed a typically stern, fatherly hand on my neck, using the same hand he had used to steer Prüsse's head movements like a marionette when he was showing the staging—and the same hand he described Carl Axel Dymling (then CEO of SF, Svensk Filmindustri) as laying on his neck during the shooting of *Kris/Crisis* (1946) in *Laterna Magica* (*The Magic Lantern*; 1987): "Listen, young Tunström. I apologize for being a bit harsh toward you just now. But you can never take the private out on stage. That applies to me too. If I were to take my private rage into the study that would be a mortal sin." Suddenly he winked conspiratorially: "But the pedagogical rage should not be discounted, you see!" I realized that he was actually giving me a lesson in directing, and that was quite nice, in its way. We were in the first full-dress rehearsal on stage. Suddenly Ingmar interrupted everything:

"Who has sewn this jacket?"
Silence. Everyone was holding their breath.
"I asked, who has sewn this costume?"
A man entered.
"I am head of costumes."
"I didn't ask for you, I asked who has sewn this costume."

Further silence. The poor tailor was fetched. He stood center stage, and the head of costumes watched uncomfortably while Ingmar dressed him down. I wondered if this is "the pedagogical rage" he had talked about. It seemed private. But perhaps this was calculated theater. Giving the whole theater a dose of fear so that everyone shaped up. I remember being scared. Not by the actual scolding, but by the fact that such strongarming was needed to get respect; that the whole job, the entire theater, the whole "House" required fear. I thought that I never would succeed as a director myself, because I was gutless and afraid of conflicts, not unrestrained enough.

* * *

Like all good pieces, *Fanny and Alexander* has many threads, many ways in. One of these is control versus freedom, play and fantasy as a rebellious strength. The directing is complex. Of course it demands clear leadership to give the actors who are exposed to meeting the public some security. But freedom from fear is a must if these actions, scenes, and situations, which really involve fantasy and playfulness and release these energies in the company, are to be created. The belief in right and wrong, that a genius has all the answers, and will release them from the actors through violent manipulations, usually does not encourage play.

If something new is to be born involving the collective, you must all together dare to expose yourselves to the emptiness, to not knowing; not just a personal but also a collective courage to dare to fail is required. This is a matter of taste, of course, but for many years I experienced an artistic crisis at the Royal Dramatic Theater, especially at the main stage; often you saw productions that were well crafted but rigid and lacking in fantasy, predictable—something which I understood as the result of fear. The fear that arises when you have something to lose. When you think that you are at the top of the pyramid, the true guardian of an antiquated notion of quality. And this fear of losing demanded a counterforce: the fear an authoritarian genius dad could put into a company and technical staff so that they would manage the job. "The House" was built on fear.

This system was not created by Ingmar Bergman; he inherited it and was great at navigating it. And it was a different time. But I knew that this was not how I could or wanted to lead and work. Neither as director nor as boss. And I remember the work on *Fanny and Alexander* at Uppsala City Theater as a happy time. Entering Bergman's text, his images and longing, and trying to let the rebellion of fantasy and play against the fear be more than just a verbal pronouncement by some of the characters, so that it actually takes shape on the stage and permeates the whole.

We gave a guest performance in Bogota at one of the world's largest drama festivals, Festival de Teatro Iberoamericano. When Columbian intellectuals, whose worldview is borne both out of the country's tradition of magic realism and the immense violent conflicts of the recent past, saw our show as an analogy of the dangers of fascism and of how fantasy resists repression, I saw this as recognition that we in some moments together succeeded in giving the things moving in Bergman's text a life of their own. Maybe Ingmar's text was rich exactly because of this paradoxical, and probably subconscious, inner field of tension between repression and terror infused with a longing for irrational fantasy. They say that if you want to write a good story you need to write about that which you don't want others to know about you. If you want to write a great story you must write about that which you do not want to know about yourself.

This is precisely what I struggle with. I know that I have to visit my own dark sides, my repressions and tensions, to be able to write. And I cannot grasp hold of these. I watch *Såsom i en spegel* and try to see what it tells me; if I can find something to pinch. I'm slightly gratified when I notice that I can identify shortcomings. It's not really alive; it's like a little construction. On the other hand, the "real" is not always the truest.

Bergman wrestles with whether it is possible to forgive crippling father figures. The dad in *Såsom i en spegel* is so bad at loving his daughter; he has let her down, used her as material for his art rather than seeing *her* when she was at her lowest. Presumably Ingmar is working through his own guilt, through having done exactly the same. Having used his children as material; turning his mind to his writing pad to vampire-like jot down his observations instead of turning to the child with comfort when something happens. But this guilt does not seem to be deep seated—or perhaps his ability to deal with it is just not that well developed. It stays at an idea, presented a bit flauntingly. No stronger pain gets through the screen. And after the daughter is taken to an asylum the son speaks to his father and forgives him. The price is not particularly high. Yes, there is a tender moment when the son tells his father, "You are speaking to me, for the first time." I am also touched. Still, it somehow feels mendacious that they are reconciled there. Or it is painfully, revealingly true at a deeper level, because reconciliation is a bit mendacious; the flaunting of his feelings of guilt is an uncomfortable truth about himself that he reveals and that precisely therefore makes the reconciliation interesting, even if it is not really moving.

But it is not always wholly clear who is the hurt child and who is the parent of the internal roles staged in one's art. I remember a day during the period when I was a figurant in *A Winter's Tale* at the Royal Dramatic Theater, before I became a parent myself, when I had some errand at the dramaturgy office and saw Ingmar through a half open door sitting there with the then-chief dramaturgist Ulla Åberg. He saw me and beckoned. I sat down on the chair facing the desk. He asked what I was working on, directing-wise; which projects I had going. I told him that I was preparing a theatrical production of my father's novel *Juloratoriet* [*The Christmas Oratorio*; 1983 by Göran Tunström]. He immediately leant forward in his armchair. "Brave. It is hard to take on your dad's work. There may be blood. Blood. My boy filmed one of my texts, you know. He had misinterpreted the end and we had a heated argument about that. Blood was about to be spilled. But he came to his senses." We spoke a bit more and he wished me luck. I later heard the same story from a different side: his son Daniel was going to film Ingmar's short story "Söndagsbarn" [*Sunday's Children*; 1992, dir. by Daniel Bergman]. When Ingmar read the film adaptation he reacted to the unrelenting ending between a strict, absent father and the son that was himself as he wrote the story. But then, with his own son about to film the story, new associations arose and these were not too flattering to him. He was not that enamored. He demanded that Daniel change the ending and threatened to disown him if he did not obey. It became a matter of principle for Daniel, of standing up to his father and finding his own identity. It was a stalemate. In the end Daniel yielded, made the required changes, and pleased his dad. I don't know if this is the whole truth; I've just heard a secondhand version of the event.

Later we watched *Viskningar och rop/Cries and Whispers* (1972) and *Ur marionetternas liv/From the Lives of the Marionettes* (1980). The slight release I felt from my own shortcomings when I saw *Såsom i en spegel* melt away when I watch the former again. I recognize storytelling techniques and visual motifs that agree with my own needs and preferences. Unforeseen time jumps, intricately embedded flashbacks, meta-narrative levels. Dead bodies remind the living of something unprocessed, unresolved; openings for some kind of irrational terror. So psychotic and secret. Fascinating that it was made at all. Both films are fascinating in their portrayals of bourgeois environments, during different eras and in different costumes. Couples devote themselves to some perverse malice, in many ways completely incomprehensible. I wonder if anyone identifies with it anyway? Men who hate women. People who repress their impulses and become captives. A stale, claustrophobic world. Everything is sexualized, but this is a strange, crammed, unrealized sexuality. There are many small, subservient housewives, submissive bourgeoise women, some of whom are about to explode and want to escape. I don't know if it is good, but the implementation is consistent. Did Bergman truly experience the real world in this way, or was he just a dramatist looking for maximum effect and, perhaps inspired by Strindberg, aggrandized and exaggerated? Should the films be regarded as a true reflection of Bergman's social class and sexual relations? Or were they rather an amplified fantasy about the dark sides of the psyche?

I want to understand, to get some kind of key to where he had found his material.

* * *

"Do we have to dissect everything?" The question comes when we sit at Hammars, after the overwhelming deluge of inner repression and the inability to communicate, trying to make sense of our experience. One of Ingmar's old colleagues seems to think that we are irreverent when we do not solely want to pay tribute to his genius. I am fascinated by this veneration, a bit paradoxical as it is. Bergman himself was audacious. He sought, or in any case represented, a modern, fresh attitude to the works he tackled. This was particularly clear at the theater, because there you often deal with previously staged pieces, "classics" that must always be updated. Just the other day we saw a documentary on the dress rehearsals of Bergman's legendary TV theater production of Mozart's *The Magic Flute*. There sat he, intoning like a university lecturer, making claims about Mozart, dissecting and pulling apart. So I think of course we may dissect him, albeit at a small scale.

He sat there, aloft on the silver screen, quite literally on a high chair on stage facing the singers and orchestra, holding forth on *The Magic Flute* as if presenting well-packaged nuggets of truth. This is obviously a role he had created and played to unite an unwieldy team in their purpose. And besides, he was certainly aware of the documentary filmmaker immortalizing the moment for public consumption. So of course the situation demands a certain degree of power, authority, and seduction. Yet, I miss some kind of crack, an admission of the uncertainty I imagine he, like me and most artists, felt. But perhaps there was no room for that at the time. He would perhaps claim that revealing his doubt would entail shirking his responsibility, if ever so slightly. That it is the director's role to take on the entire burden of the father figure. To know all, see all.

It's almost possible to see this assembling of *The Magic Flute* as an anthropological time capsule, a Brechtian scene, in which we watch people from another society, a different culture, a different time, like, yet unlike our own, allowing structures they are unaware of to appear clearly. He directs the women in their tight 1970s-colored sweaters: "Be a little more aggressive." They giggle and answer "OK, sure." A little moment that captures most of it. Liberating someone else, but within their own limits. He gives them permission, encourages them to let go and show themselves, but completely within the framework set by his authoritarian manner, together with the Zeitgeist and their social class. And none of them seem to notice these frames which now, when we watch them thirty years later, seem significantly clearer than the aggression he wanted to release in them. Bergman describes the entrance of the Queen of the Night: "She must come in, singing, furious, blazing—and showing a hell of a cleavage." The women, still in their everyday clothes, listen gracefully. They are pert. This is the discrete charm of the bourgeoisie. A repressed, toned down, yet present sexuality. Which the powerful men on screen clearly don't have to engage in. Instead the men wear old-man's cardigans and are brilliant.

I should feel unburdened by being able to watch him with some distance. Instead the recognizable feeling of self-loathing comparison creeps up on me. This is a different type of demon, less productive. Bergman himself is perhaps the demon. He mocks me. Just touching on the thought of measuring myself against his enormous productivity makes me feel sick to the stomach and ready to give in.

I stagger down to the Writing Cottage that evening again, overwhelmed by the psychic pressure Bergman creates. All the muddledness, all the contradictions, all the paradoxes: his power, boundlessness, childishness, sharpness, ruthlessness, the inner compulsion, the enormous productivity he managed. His way of consciously or subconsciously converting his inner figures into action. His psyche spills over, forces its way onto the blank sheet of paper and later onto the screen. Sometime by design, and not always great, but always interesting at some level. I stare at my own blank pages. I can opine and think and theorize about Bergman, but in the end I have to approach my shadow sides and set them alight, so that the characters run out on to the page in panic. I'll clearly not solve the blind spots in my own projects right now. This is also not the time my creative constipation becomes a free flow.

7

Jacobi's Burden

"Jewish" Figurations in *Fanny och Alexander*

Jonathan Rozenkrantz

First released as a three-hour film in 1982, and then as a five-hour TV series the following year, Ingmar Bergman's *Fanny och Alexander/Fanny and Alexander* received almost unanimous acclaim from Swedish critics. The story revolves around two siblings whose idyllic childhood in a bohemian bourgeoise family is cut short by their father's death and their mother's marriage to an oppressive Lutheran bishop. The film pits an open-ended universe of magic and mystery against an ascetic and austere Lutheran prison, from which the children are eventually saved through a divine intervention called for by their Jewish "uncle Isak." The film can be read as a spiritual autofiction in which Bergman exorcises the demons of his own Lutheran upbringing.[1]

A Jewish hero at the center of a Swedish film was virtually unheard of in 1982. Up until the Second World War, "Jews" had routinely been represented as anti-Semitic caricatures; it has been estimated that a tenth of all Swedish films produced in the 1930s contained anti-Semitic elements.[2] After the war, Jewish characters disappeared almost entirely from the movie screens, as if Swedish filmmakers knew of no other way to depict Jews than as these caricatures—and deemed it easier to ignore them altogether.[3] Given these conditions, it is curious that Isak Jacobi's "Jewishness" was largely ignored by Swedish critics.[4] But it is perhaps more interesting that the few critics who paid closer attention proved to be highly critical. One observed that Bergman's framing of Jacobi's as a usurer "displays the cliché that has tragically marked the Jewish people."[5] Another went as far as to state that Jacobi's portrayal comes "dangerously close to hate speech. What other director would be allowed to draw such a caricature without being accused of racism?"[6]

The potential problems of Jacobi's portrayal have been somewhat overlooked by scholars.[7] For an artist who claims to have been a Nazi sympathizer in his youth, whose career began in an era when anti-Semitic caricatures were common, and whose work has occasionally touched on Jewish matters, the question of whether and how anti-Semitism might be reflected in Bergman's work deserves more attention than it has attracted.[8] It is hard to say why the issue tends to be avoided, while his claims regarding his own and his family's Nazi sympathies are often brushed aside.[9] But it is beyond the scope of this chapter to find out "the truth" about Bergman's political past (or its critical treatment). The aim is to study "Jewish" figurations in *Fanny and Alexander*, in their complex relation to the history of anti-Semitic stereotypes and their creative treatment. To do so, the chapter seeks to contextualize the processes through which Jacobi emerged not only in Bergman's mind, but through the body of the actor who played him, Erland Josephson.

A Prophet in a Profiteer's Pupa

Uppsala, September 17, 1981. Bergman's team, including 2 actors, 110 extras, and costume designer Marik Vos are gathered to shoot exteriors. Fyristorg has momentarily transformed into a 1907 market to provide a background for Alexander's walk home from school. Parking meters have been removed; gas lights substitute electric ones; small stands with fish, meat, and live chicken are surrounded by live horses and their carriages.[10] In the midst of it all: a slightly nervous Erland Josephson, about to shoot his first scene: a rumbling carriage ride.[11] In her 1984 book, *Dräkterna i dramat: mitt år med Fanny och Alexander*, Vos will describe this scenario:

> Experience of the day: a fantastic equipage. A great wagon with some sort of throne-like armchair mounted in the middle, harnessed to two enormous and highly temperamental Ardennes rumbling at full speed down the stone-paved slope behind the Uppsala Cathedral, and with Isak Jacobi—Erland Josephson—sitting in the armchair. He is composed, but tremendously pale. No wonder! "It is like the prophet Elijah," Ingmar whispers in my ear.[12]

In some spiritual feedback loop, Bergman marvels at his own creation, Isak Jacobi, whom he seems to rediscover through the mystical matrices of his own religious schooling. The "Jew, businessman," as Isak Jacobi is simply listed in

Fanny and Alexander's published screenplay, is transforming into a prophet before his maker's eyes—an Elijah, who ascended to Heaven in a whirlwind, riding a chariot of fire and horses of fire.[13] But while Bergman's association is qualified by the miracle that Jacobi has in store, saving the children from their stepfather by summoning a divine intervention, it is hardly toward heaven that this "Jew" rides. Despite its name, the Bishop's Manor is not a house of God but a house of hate, more so than anything against Jews like Jacobi. To rise as a prophet, he will first have to endure a double humiliation: enacting one of the most hated roles in the long-established anti-Semitic repertoire, the Shylock-type "Jewish usurer"—and to be punished for it. Composed, but tremendously pale. No wonder! (Figure 7.1)

As soon as Isak Jacobi arrives at the Bishop's Manor, under the false pretext of a business offer, his demeanor undergoes a drastic change. Received—reluctantly—by the bishop's sister, his mannerisms become at once submissive and superior, his discourse cunning under the guise of elderly confusion. As he stoops forward on his cane, announcing that "It's a matter of money, loads of money," whispering through a grin that he is willing to pay "almost any amount," his demeanor could be described as impish, where it not for the fact that it

Figure 7.1 Isak Jacobi enacting a stereotypical "Jewish usurer" in his encounter with Bishop Vergérus.

references a specific racial figuration: the historically persistent anti-Semitic stereotype of the "profiteer." Captured in profile, Jacobi's grimace and crooked pose remediates the catalogue of "Jewish" caricatures. The bishop's contempt remains better hidden than his sister's, up until the point where it does not. He launches a tirade of anti-Semitic slurs topped with a beating. Powered, it seems, by the pain and humiliation, Jacobi raises his fists to the sky and lets out a roar. His roar summons a white light. The white light heralds the magical act that will save the children from their prison ward stepfather. All along, the "Jewish usurer's" unannounced visit has been a rescue mission.

It is difficult to pinpoint the moment when Bergman blew life into Isak Jacobi, which is to say when the character became both a key player in *Fanny and Alexander*'s plot—and one of the most complex "Jewish" figurations in Swedish film: prophet in a profiteer's pupa, both a revival and subversion of anti-Semitic tropes, and a critique of their conditions. Early work notes suggest a figure far simpler than its final manifestation. The proto-Jacobi who appears in the September 27, 1978, workbook note—in an early synopsis for Bergman's project—is simply described as "the Jew Isak," a "curious collector" whose "toy store" contains "interesting and exciting things," and who lives on Fanny and Alexander's courtyard.[14] As scholars have noted, this "Jew Isak" is modeled on an earlier one.[15] In Bergman's 1946 play *Mig till skräck*, an old Isak, often referred to as "Juden," also "lives on the courtyard" where he "has a store with curious toys."[16]

What scholars tend to overlook is that Isak "lives in a hole in the ground" and is introduced sneaking on stage to the noise of knitting needles that "rattle like a truly hostile rattle snake."[17] Adding another layer to his already Nosferatic appearance, Bergman specifies that he is "a gigantic man with a huge overcoat that is very filthy." This filthy, sneaky "Jew's" first dialogue with grandmother concerns his and hers, which he frames as following: "I am dead. You are also dead or almost dead. Seventy-five percent. Let's say. (*Smiles.*)"[18] Sounding curiously similar to a bad business deal, as if "the Jew" was extracting percentage from grandmother's life, the dialogue thus frames Isak as a "procentare" ("percenter"), another word for usurer in Swedish.[19]

In his 1990 book *Bilder*, Bergman offers us another alarming source of inspiration. He cites two "godfathers" for *Fanny and Alexander*: E. T. A. Hoffmann and "naturally Dickens."[20] Why Dickens? "The bishop and his house. The Jew in the fantastic store. The children as victims." The fact that Dickens can be credited with the creation of one of the most infamous anti-Semitic stereotypes in literature, the child-abusing criminal Fagin in *Oliver Twist* (1838), raises some questions regarding Bergman's own chain of association: Dickens "the Jew" victimized children. Fagin happens to be one of the literary figures discussed by Marie Mulvey-Roberts in her study on the anti-Semitic association of vampires with Jews.[21] Dickens writes of Fagin: "The Jew sat watching in his old lair, with face so distorted and pale, and eyes so red and bloodshot, that he looked less like a man than some hideous phantom, moist from the grave, and worried by an evil spirit."[22] While Bergman's "Jew" in *Mig till skräck* is introduced with redeeming qualities (a "deep, dignified rabbinic voice," albeit to a "rattle snake" soundtrack), the allusions to the filthy underworld of the "Jewish" undead are there, and they return even more explicitly in the published screenplay for *Fanny and Alexander*. Isak Jacobi's introduction there is worth quoting at length, as it captures the ambiguous "effect" of his character, as well as its conditions:

> He is a lanky man with a stooping gait and large pale hands. He has a long beard, curls at his ears, black eyes, and a narrow white forehead. He wears a greasy hat with curved brim. His name is Isak Jacobi, and he dines with Helena Ekdahl every Thursday. Ester [Helena's parlour maid] says he is a dirty disgusting Jew, and she tells Alexander with relish that Isak Jacobi slaughters little children and drinks their blood. Alexander does not believe a word of it, but Ester's tales certainly add to the attraction of Isak's already mysterious person.[23]

The anti-Semitic association of Jews with vampires has a long tradition and is related both to the cultural stereotype of the "Jewish usurer" (a financial "bloodsucker") and to the Christian myth of "Jewish blood libel," that is, the accusation against Jews of practicing ritual murder on Christian children, the blood of whom is said to be baked into the *matzah* bread to be eaten on *Pesach*.[24] Bergman alludes to these conceptual conflations with a certain ambiguity—and not for the first time. In two of his stagings of August Strindberg's *The Ghost Sonata* (1941/1973), Bergman chose to provide the play's most odious character—a vampiric exploiter, former usurer, and killer of a young girl, who sucks the lifeblood of the people around him—with an unmistakably Jewish attribute: a *kippah* (a Jewish skullcap). In the 1973 version, Strindberg's "Old Man," now explicitly ethnified by Bergman as an "old Jew," also dons a stereotypical diamond ring.[25]

As for the published screenplay of *Fanny and Alexander*, the description of Jacobi's body—lanky, stooping gait, large pale hands, dirty garments—evokes not only anti-Semitic caricatures, but also brings a classic Nosferatu to mind.

Jacobi thus maintains something of the vampiric air of Bergman's 1946 "Jew Isak," albeit upgraded from a hole in the ground to a more spectacular lair. Meanwhile, his potential monstrosity is rendered explicit when Ester links him to the myth of blood libel, telling Alexander that the dirty Jew drinks the blood of little children. On the one hand, Alexander does not buy her anti-Semitic story. On the other, he does approve of it. This ambiguous "Jew effect" is enhanced by Isak's *milieu*—a mix of magic, mystery, dirt, and death:

> Fanny and Alexander like going to the Jew's shop. Amanda never goes; she says it smells nasty and that there is a rotting corpse in a back room. This is partly true. Isak Jacobi is the owner of a mummy, which rests in a glass case in the little inner room where he has collected his most precious possessions. [. . .] The shop premises extend into the building; there are several rooms with dirty, partly boarded-up windows covered with dusty hangings. On long shelves, on big tables, on the floor, and dangling from the ceiling are thousands of objects of the most varied kind. No one has ever heard of the Jew selling anything in his shop. Nor has anyone seen him buying anything. It is all a mystery.[26]

It is, indeed, all a mystery: Dickens as the inspiration for Bergman's own "Jew," his marking of Strindberg's "Old Man" as explicitly Jewish, his insistent association of vampires with Jews and vice versa, dating back at least to 1941 when Bergman first staged *The Ghost Sonata*. Evidently, *Fanny and Alexander* will end up scrambling the Dickensian dynamics, turning the "Jew" into the children's savior from their "Lutheran" stepfather and tormenter. Furthermore, Ester's tale does not make it into the film, nor does Jacobi's vampiric air. Instead, Bergman will render him not only the hero of the film, but one of its most endearing figures: tender old lover of Helena Ekdahl ("You were a sweet lover, like wild strawberries") and "uncle Isak" with the children—still a financial vampire, but one whose lair has become the children's safe heaven.[27] The point is thus neither to suggest that Bergman ever intended Jacobi to be a simple anti-Semitic caricature nor that the final product can be reduced to it. It is to show that Bergman's conception of this "Jew," which transformed along the way, emerged from the soil of anti-Semitic tradition.

Acting "Jewish" in the Shadow of Anti-Semitic Caricature

SVT/TV2, November 23, 1993. Göran Skytte introduces the guest of the week on his TV show *Skytte* (1990–3): Erland Josephson, "one of Sweden's most eminent and successful actors." Marc Chagall's *The Blue Fiddler* (1947) is hanging on the black studio wall, hinting at a latent question lingering over the conversation: Josephson's Jewish origins.[28] Forty-five minutes into the one-hour show, the question is finally addressed, albeit in a somewhat unorthodox manner. Like all guests, Josephson has been asked to bring with him a small object from home. As the camera zooms in, we see a small wooden figurine with large hooknose, thick lips, big feet, and the palms of his hands turned upward in a *who knows?* gesture. The figurine is thus a "Jewish" caricature of the typically racialized kind, the wooden rendition of the anti-Semitic cartoons that flooded Swedish culture in the first four decades of the twentieth century.[29] Dated to 1917, Josephson recalls finding it in a small junkshop in Southern Stockholm. The date for its acquisition is not specified, but the fact that the figure triggered his writing of the 1964 play *Doktor Meyers sista dagar* means that Josephson has carried this caricature with him for no less than three decades.[30]

A curious conversation ensues. Labeling the figurine "judegubbe," a mildly derogatory term that nonetheless neutralizes the extent to which the figure draws on anti-Semitic tropes, Skytte claims that Josephson has played "judegubbe" numerous times, asks how much of his ability to do so "comes from within," and exemplifies it with his portrayal of Isak Jacobi.[31] Blurring the line between being a Jew, playing a Jewish character, and enacting an anti-Semitic caricature, the conversation leaves out the very condition for such caricatures: anti-Semitism itself. Skytte's line of reasoning would seem to be insensitive, not so say offensive, where it not for the fact that Josephson seems to be entirely on board with it, apparently sharing Skytte's point of view. The conversation concludes with what could be read as an essentialist, not to say "race biologist" suggestion that Josephson's ability to play "Jewish" caricatures has been inherited genetically.[32] The question avoided by both interviewer and interviewee is whether and how the tradition of anti-Semitic caricature, rather than genetics, has affected Josephson's approach to playing Jewish characters. It is a surprising omission, given that this is a question that Josephson has personally wrestled with eloquently and in depth throughout his career, both as an author and a playwright.

Doktor Meyers sista dagar is only one in a series of works in which he explores the question of Swedish anti-Semitism and its effects on the Jewish self-image.[33] The play revolves around the old Jew Isak Meyer whose trauma of having lost his wife and son (presumably in the Holocaust) has rendered him suspicious, misanthropic, lonely, and extremely self-conscious. As a defense mechanism, he ironically and self-consciously slips in and out of the stereotypical role that he is expected to play, teasing out the anti-Semitism latent in the few Swedes that seek his attention. Meyer's survival strategy not only prefigures Jacobi's rescue tactics. Josephson will frame them both within the same discussion of how to act "Jewish" in the shadow of anti-Semitic caricature.

The focal point of Josephson's Jewish drama is a wooden figurine, the same one that he will bring with him to the *Skytte* interview three decades later. Meyer has found it in a small junk shop, becomes very attached to it, and through a kind of one-way dialogue reveals its meaning:

> You have held up well, ugly little poem you, you little nasty vision, dear little phantom with but one contour in the material world. [. . .] You frighten me, my love. [. . .] You, the one dignified memorial for a horrible crime. I like you much more than all those grand, pathetic monuments. [. . .] They should put *you* as a colossus on all of Europe's squares.[34]

In 1964, Josephson thus articulates the idea that anti-Semitism persists after the Holocaust, and that displaying old caricatures can serve as a reminder of this crime's ideological conditions. In its angry frankness, it differs from Josephson's later, more nuanced, but no less conflicted inner dialogue regarding the functions of such figurations and his own professional relation to them. By the 1993 *Skytte* interview, the question that concerns Josephson is rather: How can one free this caricature from the aggression aimed against it? How can one grant it a sense of dignity?

The question of dignity is at the heart of the "Jewish" figurations in *Fanny and Alexander*. What makes Isak Jacobi's enactment of the caricature and his subsequent humiliation bearable is the dignity that Bergman grants the character in the rest of the film. There is the subtle, but essential fact that "uncle Isak" is an integrated part of the Ekdahl family. Standing up against his own cinematic tradition, Bergman frees "the Jew" from the role of representing the Swede's negative other.[35] Instead, "Jewishness" here crystallizes an "Otherness" latent in the Ekdahl family itself, where the creative powers of art and magic come together.[36] The extent to which Bergman challenges the established racial dichotomy can be seen in the fact that Helena Ekdahl is identified as "née Mandelbaum" in the screenplay, which suggests that Fanny and Alexander's grandmother and the matriarch of the Ekdahl family also has Jewish roots. Then there is, more evidently, the dignity that awaits Jacobi as he is allowed to rise as a prophet in a scene to which we will return (Figure 7.2).

But the genealogy of Josephson's "judegubbe"—his own label for the stereotyped "Jew" under which he also categorizes Jacobi—might be best approached

Figure 7.2 Isak Jacobi and Helena Ekdahl as two old lovers sharing memories during Christmas night.

chronologically. In 1957, 34-year-old Josephson writes *En berättelse om herr Silberstein*. Prefiguring his 1964 Isak Meyer, Mr. Silberstein is also an old Jew who lost everything in the Holocaust and whose fear and suspicion of people trigger their latent anti-Semitism. In his 1995 autobiography *Vita sanningar*, Josephson recalls the creative process by which he took on the role of the author—as the actor that he was:

> I remember leaving my desk and studying myself in the mirror. I made grimaces that I described. I walked back and forth in the room for hours. I worked up a splendid feeling of abandonment. [...] I rehearsed before writing. I played. I came in touch with my fear by playing it. I sweated in my overcoat. I pulled down my hat to hide my gaze. I laughed covering my mouth to hide my rotten teeth. I was suddenly very afraid and very satisfied. The only thing that left me with a sense of security was that I told myself that I don't fit the part. Too young, too beautiful, too sociable. So silly were the expressions of my carefully packaged fear. Meanwhile, the book was full of it. I rejected the role. I didn't fit it. But I didn't doubt that I could write the book. I just didn't want to be identified with this figure.[37]

Half a lifetime later, Josephson is in Chicago promoting the novel's American edition. A young woman suggests that old Silberstein would be a fitting role for him. Josephson hesitates but soon finds himself in front of a mirror, making those grimaces again. Stooping gait, palms up, feet out. Short rocking steps over the floor. Acting out Silberstein triggers his memory of other roles: "That's how I did it in Fanny and Alexander. That's how I did the lawyer Rosenbaum."[38]

Josephson's performance as Jacobi is considerably more complex than the caricature whose weight has burdened him throughout his career. It suffices to look at the variety of roles that Jacobi embodies—gentle lover, safe grandfather figure, magician, prophet, each distinguishable through virtuous variations in Josephson's demeanor and delivery—to realize that Josephson's reduction of him to just another "judegubbe" is unfair.[39] In Josephson's mind, the multifaceted figure seems to be obscured by the shadow of the caricature that constitutes but one of its facets.

Josephson gets to the heart of his problem with this particular role in a 2009 interview in *Judisk Krönika*, given just a few years before his death. Having been asked whether he enjoys playing Jewish characters, he answers that he finds it amusing but that he had "concerns" with Jacobi. The crux of the matter is the cut that Bergman decided to make for *Fanny and Alexander*'s initial release as a three-hour theatrical feature. Read by Jacobi in his arguably most important scene (in a supposedly simultaneous translation from Hebrew), the "gospel of the fountain and the cloud" marks an essential moment for Jacobi's transmutation from "Jewish profiteer" to "Jewish prophet."[40] The fact that this gospel was written by Bergman himself adds to the implicit weight of the scene, as it aligns Jacobi's role with his own as the film's storyteller. Josephson makes a reference to this fact when he implies that he allowed himself to play Jacobi as a blatant caricature on the condition of the subsequent revelation that Jacobi is, in fact, "a tremendously thought-out storyteller."[41] In retrospect, his stereotypical demeanor at the Bishop's Manor can thus be read as a conscious meta-performance, a strategy to provoke the bishop's latent hatred. How important the monologue was for Josephson becomes evident in the 2009 interview, where he admits to having been angered by the decision to cut what he considered to be crucial for balancing what he felt to be an otherwise (consciously) stereotyped and clichéd performance.[42]

The Cross, the Hakenkreuz, and Bergman's Membrane

"Perhaps we are the same person. Perhaps we have no limits; perhaps we flow into each other, stream through each other, boundlessly and magnificently. You bear terrible thoughts; it is almost painful to be near you. At the same time it is enticing." It is night in the Jacobi household, the siblings have just been saved, and Isak's mysterious nephew Ismael has allowed Alexander into his confinement. In a 1979 work note, Bergman describes the androgynous character as "the idiot with the angelic face," but by the time that Stina Ekblad embodies him in the film's most mesmerizing performance, he has acquired otherworldly intelligence and a Luciferian air.[43] Holding Alexander in a soft, almost sensual, but chilling embrace, this angel of death—if an angel at all—channels the boy's innermost desire to free himself from his oppressor at any cost.

In a 1989 *Judisk Krönika* article, Freddie Rokem ponders the seemingly essential yet ambiguous function that "Jews" play for Alexander in Bergman's film. Rokem situates them within a struggle between two religious belief systems for the "young artist's soul": the bishop's "ascetic and vindictive Protestantism" against the Jacobi family's "life-affirming, almost magical Judaism."[44] The ambiguity of it all stems from the powers that "Judaism" is nonetheless granted within Bergman's spiritual scheme, and that cast a shadow of doubt over its morality. Consider the way that Bergman describes Jacobi's nephews in his 1979 work notes: "Both are timid and kind, one good, the other evil, carrying a cruelty but it isn't detectable at all. They are low-key and gentle, almost horribly fluttering. Very different, yet with something thoroughly evil in their look."[45] It is as if Bergman cannot decide whether the "Jewish" powers that the two nephews incarnate are good or evil (or perhaps beyond either), an ambiguity that extends to the whole "Jewish" world that Jacobi and his family represent. As Rokem observes, Bergman uses

> the demonic quality of the Jews to annihilate the destructive powers of Christianity and its authoritarian worldview, its hostility towards fantasy. [. . .] [Alexander] uses the demonic powers of Isak's "sick" nephew [. . .] to destroy his stepfather, the bishop and his family, in a sea of flames. This "revenge" is clearly based on what we have elsewhere learned about Ingmar Bergman's conflict with his own father. What is interesting is that Bergman uses a Jew to be able to project his wishful thinking about destruction. It is a frightening blow-up of the well-known image of a "pound of flesh," the symbol for Shylock's implacability.[46]

In his work notes, Bergman labels Ismael a "membrane for wishes" and the one that Alexander goes to "when he needs his awful assistance."[47] Insofar as Alexander's wishes are projections of Bergman's own, these sentences are enlightening for the function of "Judaism" in *Fanny and Alexander*. "Judaism," as imagined and desired by Bergman, is quite literally weaponized in his own spiritual struggle against what he perceives as his Lutheran repression. "I have to open up the spiritual world in which I once felt at home. I have to try to remember it so that it becomes concrete," he notes to himself in his workbook—in the midst of describing the Jacobi family.[48]

Bergman's spiritual struggle will culminate in a complex scheme at a particularly risky moment. *Fanny and Alexander* was released in December 1982, toward the end of a year that "saw the first major outburst of antisemitic sentiments within mainstream political culture" in postwar Sweden.[49] Triggered by the Lebanon war, Swedish media came to interpret and illustrate Israeli actions through a matrix of Christian anti-Jewish motives, with allusions to everything from "Christ-killing" to "Jewish blood libel," and the Christian notion of the Jew's "Old Testamental vindictiveness."[50] The juxtaposition of "an eye for an eye" with "turn the other cheek" had been reactivated in the political discourse of a secular country in which Jews had, just decades before, systematically been represented as morally inferior to Swedes. Such historical conditions place a burden on Bergman's "Jews" and the role that they are assigned in his own spiritual project. The fact that it is a "Jew" that both channels and compels Alexander to act out his revenge, and that the object of this revenge is a representative of the Christian church, evidently carries a thorny historical implication. But Bergman complicates these "Christian-Jewish" dynamics by adding an ideological variable, one whose autobiographical basis scholars have come to debate.

As Maaret Koskinen and Mats Rohdin argue in their book, *Fanny och Alexander: ur Ingmar Bergmans arkiv och hemliga gömmor*, there are implicit parallels between Bergman's portrayal of Vergérus's Lutheranism and Nazi ideals: from his declaration of values such as duteousness, purity, and asperity, to his proclamation of being a selfless slave to his office, not to mention his labeling of Jacobi as "vermin"—even *before* his outburst.[51] It is worth noting that these parallels went unnoticed by critics at the time. There is, for instance, only one Swedish review in the Swedish Film Institute's collection that mentions that Vergérus is an anti-Semite, however obvious his labeling of Jacobi as a "loathsome," "hook-nosed" "Jew-swine" makes it, and it is symptomatic that the critic reads it more as an appendage to a vilifying character portrait, than as a potentially political critique of a larger set of ideological circumstances.[52] That the latter is the case will become evident when Bergman first publishes his book *Laterna Magica* in 1987.[53]

Written a few years after *Fanny and Alexander*, Bergman's autobiography *The Magic Lantern* bears so many similarities with the film that it has been read as a source through which the film can be verified. As Jan Holmberg has shown, this is a risky endeavor since Bergman has proven to be an unreliable narrator who lets his autobiography be as colored by his fiction as the other way around.[54] This casts a shadow of doubt over any factual claim in the book that cannot be cross-checked, including some of those that concern the Bergman family's alleged Nazi sympathies. But the facticity of Bergman's autobiography is less relevant here, than the light that its sheds on its cinematic treatment, since both are parts of the same creative vision. And what is implied in *Fanny and Alexander* is so explicitly articulated in *The Magic Lantern* that it is difficult to read them together as anything but a carefully composed political statement.

Consider the way that the problem of Nazism is introduced a few pages into *The Magic Lantern*:

> Most of our upbringing was based on such concepts as sin, confession, punishment, forgiveness and grace, concrete factors in relationships between children and parents and God. There was an innate logic in all this which we accepted and thought we understood. This fact may well have contributed to our astonishing acceptance of Nazism.[55]

From the very first time that it is mentioned, the Bergman family's alleged Nazism is linked to its Lutheran beliefs. Lutheranism here becomes a condition for their adoption of Nazism. The ideological connection is then reinforced by Bergman's subsequent accounts for his stay in Nazi Germany in the 1930s (the locus of the debates on his Nazis sympathies, insofar as this is where he confesses to his former "love" for Hitler, his enthusiastic participation in a Nazi rally and his defensive Holocaust denial when first faced with evidence from the concentration camps).[56]

As a young exchange student, Bergman is placed with a pastor's family in Thüringen. While the son—who looks "cut out from a National Socialist propaganda broadsheet"—is the one who introduces Bergman to German anti-Semitism, the whole family worships Hitler to the point where they give Bergman Hitler's portrait as his birthday present.[57] If his own Lutheran family provided the conditions for his acceptance of Nazism, then another one is described as the catalyst for his conversion. The conflation of the two beliefs exceeds these home environments. Bergman follows his new friend to school. It happens to be a Religious education class. Instead of bibles, however, the desks are adorned with Hitler's *Mein Kampf*, the teacher reads *Der Stürmer*, and repeats the words *"von den Juden vergiftet"* ("poisoned by the Jews").[58] At Sunday morning services with the pastor's family, Bergman is surprised to see that the pastor preaches not from the gospels, but from *Mein Kampf*. Uniformed men in the church hall give Bergman ample opportunity to rehears his Hitler salute, which will come in handy during the climax of his stay: the exhilarating Nazi rally that he finally attends with the pastor's family. It should be evident by now that it is no coincidence that he points out that the church bells ring in Hitler's honor, heralding the parade—"both the gloomy Protestant and cheerful Catholic."[59]

A pattern emerges in Bergman's account of his experience in Nazi Germany. In his memory, the cross and the *Hakenkreuz* go hand in hand. If *The Magic Lantern* provides keys to unravel the spiritual scheme of *Fanny and Alexander*, it is not because of how it may help us verify Bergman's autofiction, but because it sheds light on the role assigned to clerical Christianity in the adult filmmaker's mind. It is from his treatment of a certain "Nazi-Lutheran" complex that his "Jewishness" and "Judaism" are derived; their role is to function as a symbolic counter-image. But the raised fists of a roaring old Shylock, the deadly embrace of his vengeful nephew, we have seen how these visions are conditioned by that which they sought to resist. Therein lies the tension of the "Jewish" figurations in *Fanny and Alexander*, a revenge fantasy that blurs the line between the representation of anti-Semitism and anti-Semitic representation. Granted its few references to Jewish culture, ritual, or scripture, it is safe to say that Bergman's film is ultimately less about Jewish matters than about Bergman himself.[60] By weaponizing "Jews" in his struggle with the burdens of his own past, he finds justification for his own revenge on his old demons.

Notes

1 For a succinct summary of Bergman's childhood years, see Birgitta Steene, *Ingmar Bergman: A Reference Guide* (Amsterdam: Amsterdam University Press, 2005), 23–33.
2 Rochelle Wright, *The Visible Wall: Jews and Other Ethnic Outsiders in Swedish Film* (Uppsala: Uppsala University, 1998), 3.
3 Between the end of the Second World War and a short-lived 1990s "Jewish renaissance," Jewish representation became remarkably rare in Swedish cinema.

Commenting on the "renaissance" in 1991, a Swedish journalist noted that a Swedish film about a Jewish family had been "an unthinkable project ten years ago," an observation that sheds light on the unique place that Isak Jacobi in *Fanny and Alexander* holds in the history of Swedish-Jewish cinematic representation. Mats Lundegård, "Svenska judar söker sina rotter," *Dagens Nyheter*, December 31, 1991. For a comprehensive study of Jewish representation in Swedish film (1930s–1990s), see Wright, *The Visible Wall*.

4 This conclusion is based on an analysis of the Swedish Film Institute's comprehensive collection of reviews.

5 Lena Öhrner, "Replik på [flash symbol] om Fanny och Alexander," *Södermanlands Nyheter*, April 14, 1983. Unless stated otherwise, all quotes from Swedish sources have been translated to English by the author of this chapter.

6 Anders Wennberg, "Förmår inte garvade recensenter ifrågasätta Bergmans storhet?," *Gefle Dagblad*, February 1983.

7 For an exception, see Wright, *The Visible Wall*, 233–47. Jewish figures in Bergman's films are discussed in Wright, *The Visible Wall*, 214–47.

8 Bergman's career as a stage director dates back to 1938. See Steene, *Ingmar Bergman*, 456–7. It is symptomatic that Steene's 1,150-page opus *Ingmar Bergman: A Reference Guide* mentions anti-Semitism only once, and not in relation to Bergman's work but to a petition that he signed in 1973. See Steene, *Ingmar Bergman*, 942–3.

9 The response to Bergman's Nazi "revelation" shows a tendency to defend him and his family by questioning the veracity of his account. Disregarding potential tensions between personal and political sympathies, the fact that the family housed a German-Jewish refugee, and that Bergman had a Jewish friend (Erland Josephson) is often held an argument against the possibility that he and/or his family also had Nazi sympathies. See Jan Holmberg quoted in Malin Ekman, "Överdrev sin kärlek till Hitler för konstens skull," *Svenska Dagbladet*, July 13, 2018; Jan Holmberg, *Författaren Ingmar Bergman* (Stockholm: Norstedts, 2018), 173; and Steene, *Ingmar Bergman*, 34; For a more substantial inquiry, see Peter Ohlin, "Bergman's Nazi Past," *Scandinavian Studies* 81, no. 4 (2009): 437–74.

10 Marik Vos, *Dräkterna i dramat: mitt år med Fanny och Alexander* (Stockholm: Norstedt, 1984), 96–8.

11 Elisabeth Sörenson, "Bergman vid Fyrisån—nästan på mormors Gata," *Svenska Dagbladet*, September 18, 1981.

12 Vos, *Dräkterna i dramat*, 98.

13 Ingmar Bergman, *Fanny and Alexander*, trans. Alan Blair (New York: Pantheon, 1983), 3. The Bible quote that Bergman likely has in mind reads: "As [Elijah and Elisha] were walking and conversing, behold!—a chariot of fire and horses of fire

[appeared] and separated between the two of them, and Elijah ascended to Heaven in a whirlwind." 2 Kings 2:11.

14 Ingmar Bergman, *Arbetsboken: 1975-2001* (Stockholm: Norstedts, 2018), 151.
15 See Maaret Koskinen and Mats Rohdin, *Fanny och Alexander: ur Ingmar Bergmans arkiv och hemliga gömmor* (Stockholm: Wahlström & Widstrand, 2005), 48.
16 Ingmar Bergman, *Moraliteter: tre pjäser* (Stockholm: Albert Bonniers Förlag, 1948), 198. For a discussion of said play, see Frank Gado, *The Passion of Ingmar Bergman* (Durham, NC: Duke University Press, 1986), 116–19. Bergman's capitalization of the "J" in "Juden" (i.e., "the Jew") is formally incorrect in Swedish and serves to emphasize Isak's "Jewishness" as his defining characteristic and function in the play.
17 Bergman, *Moraliteter: tre pjäser*, 198.
18 Ibid., 199.
19 The counting of percentage is a common trope in Swedish anti-Semitic tradition. On Swedish caricatures of Jews as usurers and antiques dealers (both of which happen to be Isak Jacobi's professions in *Fanny and Alexander*), see Lars M. Andersson, *En jude är en jude är en jude . . .: representationer av "juden" i svensk skämtpress omkring 1900–1930* (Lund: Nordic Academic Press, 2000), 259–69.
20 Ingmar Bergman, *Bilder* (Stockholm: Norstedt, 1990), 362.
21 Marie Mulvey-Roberts, *Dangerous Bodies: Historicising the Gothic Corporeal* (Manchester: Manchester University Press, 2016), 134.
22 Fagin's description in *Oliver Twist* quoted in ibid.
23 Bergman, *Fanny and Alexander*, 20–1.
24 For a detailed discussion on the anti-Semitic association of vampires with Jews, see the chapter "Nazis, Jews and *Nosferatu*," in Mulvey-Roberts, *Dangerous Bodies*, 129–78.
25 Egil Törnqvist, *Between Stage and Screen: Ingmar Bergman Directs* (Amsterdam: Amsterdam University Press, 1995), 39.
26 Bergman, *Fanny and Alexander*, 21.
27 Jacobi's function as a moneylender has been kept in the film, and Helena's son Carl (who owes Jacobi money) refers to him as a usurer. The screenplay renders his usury specific: "I pay forty-five percent interest," Carl says, "and if I'm not punctual he threatens to show the IOU to Mama." Bergman, *Fanny and Alexander*, 55.
28 One of the first Jewish families that were allowed to settle without conversion in Sweden in the late eighteenth century, the Josephson family has produced a number of prominent artists and cultural actors, including painter Ernst Josephson and actor Erland. For a history of Swedish Jewry, including notable members of the Josephson family, see Carl Henrik Carlsson, *Judarnas historia i Sverige* (Stockholm: Natur & Kultur, 2021).
29 As Andersson and Wright's major studies on anti-Semitic imagery have shown, anti-Semitism was "hegemonic" in Swedish society during the first three decades of

the twentieth century, which is to say during Bergman and Josephson's childhood and youth. Anti-Semitic cartoons were widely consumed until the 1930s, and such caricatures prevailed in cinema up until the Second World War. See Andersson, *En jude är en jude* . . . , 14; Wright, *The Visible Wall*, 1–68.

30 Erland Josephson, *Sanningslekar* (Stockholm: Bromberg, 1990), 177.
31 The term is not immediately translatable to English. The mildly derogatory ring to "-gubbe" in conjunction with "jude-" might best be captured by conflating the terms "old Jew" and "old geezer."
32 Swedish anti-Semitism has been largely influenced by the pseudo-scientific discipline of "race biology" (or "scientific racism"), championed by Swedish scholars and popularized through art, film, literature, and so on during the first half of the twentieth century and a significant force behind the discrimination of a number of minorities in Sweden, including Roma, Sami, Finns, and Tornedalians.
33 Erland Josephson, *Doktor Meyers sista dagar och Kandidat Nilssons första natt: två stycken* (Stockholm: Bonnier, 1964), 7–64. Other works written by Josephson on related themes include the novel *En berättelse om herr Silberstein* (Stockholm: Bonnier, 1957), translated to English as *A Story About Mr. Silberstein*, and the TV play *Benjamin* (Hans Abramson, 1960).
34 Josephson, *Doktor Meyers sista dagar*, 35–6.
35 On the racial-moral juxtaposition of "Jews" and "Swedes" in Swedish cinema, see Wright, *The Visible Wall*, 1–68.
36 Bergman, *Fanny and Alexander*, 3.
37 Erland Josephson, *Vita sanningar* (Stockholm: Bromberg, 1995), 108.
38 Ibid., 109.
39 Josephson would refer to Isak Jacobi as "judegubbe" throughout his career. See, for instance, *Sanningslekar*, 95; Josephson quoted in Michaela Lundell, "Jag vill veta vem jag är," *Judisk Krönika* 77, no. 2 (2009): 10.
40 Bergman's note on June 6, 1979, that Jacobi "takes on new dimensions" as it is he "who preaches the gospel about the fountain and the cloud" suggests two things: that the monologue was not written for Jacobi and that it makes a significant difference for his character that it has been assigned to him. Bergman, *Arbetsboken*, 180.
41 Josephson quoted in Michaela Lundell, "Jag vill veta vem jag är," *Judisk Krönika* 77, no. 2 (2009): 10.
42 Ibid.
43 Bergman, *Arbetsboken*, 180.
44 Freddie Rokem, "Bergmans Dibbuk," *Judisk Krönika* 57, no. 1 (1989): 17.
45 Bergman, *Arbetsboken*, 181.
46 Rokem, "Bergmans Dibbuk," 17.
47 Bergman, *Arbetsboken*, 179, 180.

48 Bergman, *Arbetsboken*, 180. Bergman seems to have held a spiritual longing for "Jewishness," as illustrated by rabbi Morton Narrowe, whom Bergman would consult on occasion. In 1994, the director asked the rabbi to make him an "honorary Jew," a title that does not exist in Judaism. Bergman's request, which was based on something that he had been told by his friend, Erland Josephson, suggests that Bergman's knowledge of Judaism was limited. Katharina Schmidt-Hirschfelder, "Odödlig Hedersjude?," *Judisk Krönika* 77, no. 2 (2009): 12–13.

49 Henrik Bachner, "Political Cultures of Denial? Antisemitism in Sweden and Scandinavia," in *Politics of Resentment: Antisemitism and Counter-Cosmopolitanism in the European Union*, ed. Lars Rensmann and Julius H. Schoeps (Leiden: Brill, 2011), 333.

50 On the Swedish response to the 1982 Lebanon War within a major study of Swedish postwar anti-Semitism, see Henrik Bachner, *Återkomsten: antisemitism i Sverige efter 1945* (Stockholm: Natur och Kultur, 1999), 371–452.

51 Koskinen and Rohdin, *Fanny och Alexander*, 146–53.

52 "Ingmar Bergman summerar sitt liv i en generöst myllrande gobeläng," *Nordvästra Skånes Tidningar*, December 19, 1982.

53 The book has been translated as *The Magic Lantern*, which is the version that will hitherto be referenced.

54 Holmberg, *Författaren Ingmar Bergman*, 163–83.

55 Ingmar Bergman, *The Magic Lantern: An Autobiography*, trans. Joan Tate (New York: Penguin books, 1989), 7–8.

56 Bergman, *The Magic Lantern*, 120–4.

57 Ibid., 120, 123.

58 Ibid., 120.

59 Ibid., 121–2.

60 Beyond Jacobi's *kippah* and a short dialogue possibility in Yiddish (albeit with a German accent that makes its *Yiddishkeit* difficult to discern), the film makes few references to actual Jewish cultural or religious practices.

8

Producing *The Magic Flute* (1975)

Conversation with Måns Reuterswärd and Katinka Faragó

Maaret Koskinen and Louise Wallenberg

As mentioned in the introduction to the chapter "Working with Bergman: Interview with Film and Television Producers Katinka Faragó and Måns Reuterswärd," we got the chance to interview them again during our writing retreat on Fårö, this time with a specific focus on their joint collaboration on Bergman's *Trollflöjten/The Magic Flute* (1975), as well as the behind-the-scenes documentary *Tystnad! Tagning! Trollflöjten!/Silence! Action! The Magic Flute!* (1975). Even better, after watching the documentary together in Bergman's private movie theater, we chose to include several of our guests at this retreat in the conversation, all of whom possess expertise in music, opera, and the theatre. Thus, besides the editors/interviewers and Måns Reuterswärd and Katinka Faragó, the discussion below includes Allan Havis, Paisley Livingston, and Linus Tunström. What do not translate into this transcribed version of our conversation, are the joyful outbursts of laughter that it evoked (Figure 8.1).

> **Louise Wallenberg**: We have just watched the behind-the-scenes documentary *Tystnad! Tagning! Trollflöjten!* and everyone is welcome to pose questions to its directors/producers Måns Reuterswärd and Katinka Faragó, regarding the process of making not only the film *Trollflöjten* but also of making the documentary. So could you say something initially about your roles as producers, directors, and consultants?
>
> **Katinka Faragó**: I wasn't in on the documentary until in the editing room, because I was mostly occupied in the studio. But I also want to point out that it was very generous of this man (pointing to her husband Måns) to put me in the credits, because I didn't do that much . . . I mean, Måns is the one who cut

Figure 8.1 Ingmar Bergman and conductor and musical director Eric Ericson instructing the orchestra during the film set of *The Magic Flute* (1975).

the film, really, while I sometimes said "no, no, no," or "yes, yes, yes," and "I don't know." Måns was fantastic.

Måns Reuterswärd: As the producer of the documentary, I had a rather simple task, because a documentary is first always captured by the cinematographer. In this case it was Jan-Hugo Norman [the cinematographer], whom I admire, and today, seeing the film again, I once more saw the skill of this man: he was always in the right place and in the right situation. My job starts when you've got all these hours of film, and you are sitting there scratching your head, wondering how to put it all together in order to tell the background story. That's why I asked Katinka to join me in the editing, so I think that in that sense we actually made the film together.

In the beginning Ingmar said that I have to be filming all the time, and that "I will sue you if you don't." So, at first he was very positive about us filming. But at some stage he became very angry, because he thought that the camera sound was disturbing the work with the music. For instance, we had some quarrels after he noticed that we were filming during Josh's [Josef Köstlinger's] solo. Josh was trying to sing this wonderful Pamina aria, and Ingmar came up to me and said: "don't you dare to film during this take." We still did so, and after this he wanted no disturbances on the set. But otherwise, he was very generous, and even helped us sometimes to get a take. For instance, I once saw him open a door, just when he was sitting talking with Josh about his Pamina aria, and Josh had some problems with nerves since he was so young. Jan-Hugo, the camera man, was nearby in the corridor, but the door to where Ingmar and Josh were sitting was almost closed—but then I saw Ingmar pushing up the door, so that the camera had free sight, which saved that scene.

Katinka: It is important to say that even if it was always playback in the film (they had sung everything in advance), the singers still sang for real in the takes as well. So, it wasn't fake that they were singing live, which is very important, because otherwise it would *look* fake.

Måns: Technically speaking we had long discussions about how we should record the sound. The most common technique when you make operas for television or film is playback, that is you do the singing first on one tape, and then you run the tape in studio while filming while the singers mime, which you then have to synchronize afterwards. But Ingmar hated it when you notice that the lips don't fit the sound, so we tried a lot of different ways of achieving this. "Sing back" is another way, and here you have the orchestra and the instruments recorded first as a background, and after this you sing in the film studio. Then you almost get the synchrony you want. But we had a big orchestra, so that was hard. We also tried something that we called "orchestra-back." Håkan Hagegård, who sang the Papageno-role, talked about it, and we tried it, but it didn't work: we agreed that it was a great idea but they couldn't get the whole orchestra synchronized. Because if you are shooting a film for, let's say, forty days, or a couple of weeks—while having singers on their top level, musically and also physically, all that time—it's not possible. Because there is always the risk that someone will say, "I'm sorry I can't sing today . . . ."

Katinka: Which was a joke, because every morning when we did the singing with the orchestra, somebody was sick, so we had to switch the daily schedule all the time. Even if Mr. Bergman had forced everyone to take flu shots and injections . . .

Maaret Koskinen: So, the myth is true . . .

Katinka: The myth is true—yeah. We all had flu shots. But for the singers it was actually very bad, because they had reactions against the shot. So, it was a big drama every morning. It was quite a circus!

Måns: Anyway—where we ended up in the playback issue was that we had a speech specialist helping us. When we see her in the documentary, she is in the midst of looking at the singers, watching their synchronizing. And she often had to tell Ingmar that it was not synchronized, and they had to do it all again until she was happy. So thanks to her and thanks to a wonderful sound editor, we managed to put this strange process in place. So I think we were very happy that we made a very good play back, given that it is very difficult.

Katinka: What was interesting too was that the singers always wanted to stand up and sing. And when Ingmar told them that they had to sit down and sing, they complained. So again he had to explain that they sang within a special shot, and that this is a *film*—so would you please sit down and sing! For instance, Ulrik Cold, who played Sarastro, wanted to stand up, and he was 2 meters 6 cm tall—so it would be a major visual difference if he was standing up or sitting down . . .

Måns: That is something that you see in the documentary—that if you want to do this kind of playback system, you have to know exactly how it's going to look in the camera. That's why you see Ingmar being so specific: here you sit down, here you walk, but you can't do so and so while singing. For instance, if there was to be a very intimate moment in a close-up, it had to be carefully prepared before starting to record the sound, in order to know how it was going to appear in the picture. Ingmar had a very detailed script, with every picture noted in the score, if the actor or singer should be sitting or standing or walking.

The interesting thing was also that Ingmar was trying to come close to the very first performance in Vienna. Mozart and Schikaneder wanted to write a popular opera, something different that would attract people to the theater. Today *The Magic Flute* would be a musical.

There is a scene in the opera where Tamino is going through three doors, with locks on each door. And then they could count every bar when he said, "now I have to go to this door, now I go to this door—tadamtadamtadam!" So Ingmar walked down his house at Hammars and that's how he figured out exactly how small the stage at Drottningholm was, or should be, because there were just 4–5 steps between the three doors. In fact, the small theater stage at Drottningholm was quite similar to the old Vienna theater where the opera was originally staged, at that time the typical kind of eighteenth-century theater, including all the drawbacks. So the whole concept was that he wanted to go back as much as possible to where Mozart and Schikaneder had their first performance.

Maaret: And therefore also to stage it for a modern audience? That is, taking the high-class or a high-arts opera genre down a few notches. That is why I gather that Eric Ericson [conductor and musical director] in the documentary says that "You have to understand what the singers are singing, otherwise there is no point."

Paisley Livingston: Do you know whether it was a new Swedish translation, or was that a fairly old Swedish translation of the old German one?

Måns: We had a new translation, which also was one of Ingmar's ideas—that we should make an opera for a new, young audience that hadn't been to the opera before. So we couldn't have the German version, because no one would understand it. The new translation was made by this wonderful and wise Swedish journalist and author Alf Henriksson. He wrote a very simple libretto, which was very funny actually, and musically also very possible to sing. But at the same time that's why people were shaking their heads when we tried to sell the film, because "what?—are you singing in Swedish?" It took a lot of time to get it translated, but once we had subtitling it was ok.

Also Ingmar's intention was very much to pick up singers that were younger and were good looking. It's a terribly difficult situation to find a "golden boy," both beautifully looking and singing beautifully. It almost doesn't exist. . . . In fact, there were so many new things with *The Magic Flute*: it was made for television, the little box, and it was made for "normal" people, as well as young people. This is why Ingmar really loved the idea of television, which goes directly into the homes, and in the middle of the hearts of families.

Paisley: Regarding the overture: if you make a filmed opera, the problem is what are you going to show while the symphony is playing the overture? Because in the actual opera performance, you are normally staring at a curtain. Here the solution was to show the audience, the images of the [Drottningholm] gardens, and so on. But is the audience shown during the overture—is it actually watching a performance? Because they are sitting and looking enraptured like they are enjoying something.

Måns: We had a show going on at this film studio at the Swedish Film Institute. We rigged up a kind of situation where people were sitting almost as uncomfortably on benches, as in the Drottningholm Theater. Ingmar said to me "you'll have to fix this," so that was on my shoulders. I had to fix all people of different kinds, which was very important. It should be all nationalities, all kinds, as well as young and old. It was supposed to be a kind of picture of humanity, in a way. Then we gathered about 20 people. Ingmar himself was in the audience as a cameo, and cinematographer Sven Nykvist was there too, while we ran the overture, and I told them: "Now you have to image yourselves sitting in the theater while you're watching the curtains going up. But it doesn't, so instead you will feel the music going into your minds" etc. . . .

Maaret: This sequence is really skilfully edited—the counter point between the images of the audience, and the music. If you had that kind of overture today, with the idea that Mozart's music, that is western music, is universal—that wouldn't work today, would it, especially not in American universities?

Måns: I don't know . . . Why not?

Maaret: I'm just saying that in today's atmosphere that wouldn't work, because you would be saying that Mozart is "good" for Inuit as well as people from a village in Africa—which was Bergman's idea.

Paisley: That play in general is very much based on Enlightenment ideology, which the whole story is about; is he a Prince, no he's a Mensch, an ordinary guy, so there is an appeal in Mozart to this idea of universal humanity. And so what Bergman did is appropriate at least to Mozart. It may not be appropriate to the world, but you can say that it has a kind of coherence and should be regarded within that. Because if you look at the libretto that Schikaneder wrote, there are lines in there that Bergman correctly took out, because they were verbally sexist statements made by Sarastro, who says women talk a lot but do little; he cut that line. So he had a concern for what he was going to present.

Maaret: Do you know when the overture came into being? Was the overture there in the beginning in Bergman's conception, or was it added after the shots of the faces? Because it could have been added afterwards.

Katinka: No, it was during the shooting. We were in the big studio, and I remember that they were in this little studio recording these people.

Måns: But I don't think the idea was fixed from the beginning. Ingmar was not clear about that, but during the shoot he came up to me and said—we have to do it this way! So I think it was an idea that came to him during the shooting, which I don't think he was prepared for at first. And the idea of "multi culture" shouldn't be misunderstood from today's perspective—it was an ideal at the time of how the world could look like. It makes me think of a wonderful photo book tour and an exhibition called "Family of Man" in the 1950s with photographs of old people around the world, all different, which made quite an impact when it came.

Linus Tunström: You said that Ingmar was very helpful, for instance when he opened the door for the photographer, so in a way he was also aware of what image he was presenting of himself and his work.

Måns: Of course.

Linus: Because as a young actor I was in a production by Ingmar of *A Winter's Tale* at the Royal Dramatic Theater. And what I saw was some very strong anger and aggression going on in the rehearsal process, which is also a famous side to Ingmar. So, I am curious—was there anything of this side here? Or was it different then, because there was a camera recording, or did you just choose to avoid it?

Måns: Of course, those kinds of situations occurred. But as I said earlier, we had a deal. But I had long discussions with Ingmar, for instance about a sequence in the documentary which he didn't want to include. There was no quarrel, but a discussion of how two worlds could meet and can't meet—music and film and the visual. After the shoot I realized how interesting those discussions between Eric Ericson and Ingmar Bergman were, and very revealing of the tremendous dissonance between those two worlds. Ingmar wanted the picture, the beautiful images, and he agreed that he didn't know all musical aspects. He was very fond of music but he was not a musician, while Eric Ericson was brought up in the music world, where every note matters, and everything is based on what you hear. But there was certainly a discussion between them, and at first I did include it in the documentary, but then Ingmar said that he didn't want this to be brought up, this dissonance between the two—Ingmar and the very famous Eric Ericson, who was loved by everyone. . . . I tried a couple of times to argue that this is interesting for the audience, and that this is how it looks—the competition between music and film. But he didn't agree, so in the end we took it out, also because we had this agreement, which I respected. I mean since he had the final cut.

Katinka: It was a deal. It was a deal with him.

Måns: Yeah. I remember another situation when [Finnish-Swedish writer/film producer] Jörn Donner was doing a documentary about Ingmar, and there was a quarrel between the two for four hours inside a room while we were waiting outside for them to agree. But Donner didn't accept, and he wasn't as nice as I was—so they were actually enemies for some time afterwards.

Still—what happened afterwards made me very sad. It was that some of these discussions came out to the press, just before the opening of the opera and the documentary was released. Someone talked to the press or the union, because at the time Ingmar Bergman was considered an enemy by them—they always wanted to get a hold on Ingmar. If journalists could find something on him then they could really hit him in the head with it—and they loved it, especially *Aftonbladet* (a Swedish tabloid). So I was so angry when I read that article a couple days after the premiere, and it was about censorship. "Ingmar Bergman censured the documentary about him," and they wrote at length about how the Swedish television corporation could agree to allow Bergman to censor himself in a documentary—a lot of blah blah blah. But that was actually nothing more than a misunderstanding of the agreement with the final cut. If a journalist doesn't understand that, and calls it censorship—that's a total mistake. I was so angry about it. Because if Ingmar wanted to "save" the image of himself, ok that's fine—but that's not the same as censorship.

Katinka: There was also another situation when Ingmar was not in favour, because everyone thought that *The Magic Flute* was too expensive, and that Swedish Television had spent so much money on him—"so what's so special about Ingmar?" This was of course more fodder for the newspapers.

Linus: You said it was expensive, and when I was watching it I was wondering how much did this cost—this immense time to record and rehearse, and the amount of people, and the technique . . . I wonder, if you were to translate it to a budget of today how much would it be?

Måns: We had a budget in 1974 of 3.5 million Swedish Kronor. Today it would probably be about 30 million, so about ten times as much.

Paisley: That's not a huge budget.

Måns: Also, the income of selling the opera was over 1 million plus. So it really didn't cost anything for Swedish Television, instead it paid off a lot of over-drawings by the news department. For instance, they had spent 1 million over budget, so *The Magic Flute* covered up their mess. So, the story is not as bad as everyone at the time wanted to think. Another rumour that circulated at the time was spread by the Swedish Television producers, who claimed that the money that Bergman spent was taken out of their budget, so that they couldn't make any programs. But that was a big lie—this money was not taken from other departments; every producer had exactly the same amount of money, and everyone could do what they wanted with it. This was just a mean rumour, but it was very hard to comment on it while it was all going on. But as a producer at this time it was hard to take, because I almost felt like being held responsible for the whole thing. Some people didn't say hello to me anymore, and even said that you are an enemy, and you are a thief that stole our money . . . that was terrible. But that's history, so let's forget about it.

Paisley: A question about your documentary, how many hours of footage did you have to use of the shooting for the total?

Katinka: You mean, how much footage did we have before we started the editing?

Måns: We had 20 hours or 25 hours. But we think this celluloid footage has been destroyed. At the time we had no digital cameras.

Katinka: We shot in 16 mm!

Allan Havis: I have another question. It seems like 1/3 of Sweden saw *The Magic Flute*. That is amazing statistics. It was that popular on Swedish TV.

Katinka: It was wonderful because they ran it on New Year's Day, January 1, 1975. I mean everybody was at home looking at television, so that was a good.

Måns: At that time the anniversary of fifty years of Swedish Radio and Television was celebrated, so there was a lot of promotion and of course interest from the press, and lots of talk about it in advance. But the most beautiful thing was when there was a question posed to young people about which was the best children's program they could remember, or that they would want to see again—and most young people voted for *The Magic Flute*! It proves that Ingmar was right from the beginning. It really hit the right audience, and that was the best review we could have had. Because it's a saga [fairy tale] and it's a poetry and it's a dream, as he said, or it's like Snow White with an evil queen, and everyone's happy. The kind of story that every child wants to hear.

Allan Havis: The famous critic for the *New Yorker Magazine* Pauline Kael was ecstatic about it.

Maaret: But other American reviewers, especially some musicologists really hated it. Allan, do you remember the reception?

Allan: On the whole the music purists found that it was compromised. It's equivalent to when Peter Brooke did *Carmen* at Lincoln Center—theater people loved it, and people that love opera hated it and found that it was too much a violation of the original opera.

Katinka: Yes, for instance the way Ingmar changed the story and cut out the Freemasons.

Paisley: There is a whole book about how to interpret that opera in the eighteenth-century context, and it's apparently loaded with secret symbolism that only a Mason can recognize. The person who wrote that book was himself a Mason. For example you have the three chords beat three times—that was a Masonic symbol. And the serpent that becomes a dragon and cut into three pieces at the beginning was another Masonic symbol. There is a limit to what I can say or remember, but it's chock full of it.

Katinka: It was big circus in the Swedish music world because he cut out the Freemasons and changed the story—you can't do that.

Maaret: So that means that he laid bare the essential stories of the mother, the daughter, and the family?

Allan: He highlighted what he thought was the most salient features of the story, and he lost some of the ambient symbolism, because it didn't translate.

Paisley: I remember an American critic calling it a soap opera version of Mozart because of the emphasis on the family drama, which was really a quarrel between a husband and wife, and now they are angry, fighting over the children.

Maaret: Yes, somebody wrote really sarcastically that "last time I checked Sarastro and the Queen of Night were not a couple in Djursholm [a posh Stockholm suburb]."

Måns: Ingmar also changed two scenes, because in the original the story is completely insane—Mozart and Schikaneder must have absolutely lost any sense of logic over the story telling.

Paisley: Yes, they had a problem with time; they were pressing to get it ready for review, so they were basically throwing it together. Mozart was scribbling the pieces and handing them over to the musicians as he went along, and they were trying to figure out what to play . . . it was really thrown together.

Måns: When Ingmar did the staging, Eric Ericson and the other musical artists shook their heads, and kept saying you can't do this, this is the key of F, and that means another key . . . And I shook my head and said what the hell, nobody cares, because the story was much easier to understand. Anyway he changed the story, and it makes much more sense and also makes the story end up in a good way, in musical heaven. But many couldn't accept it. I once talked to the most famous Italian conductor Carlo Maria Giulini, a wonderful old man, while working with him on another project, and I gave him the record of Bergman's version of *The Magic Flute*. He was so thankful—"thank you, thank you, thank you, very much"—but how could Bergman make these changes? It's such a rigid world.

Maaret: I have one question about the edit. What was cut out in the film, because the Queen of night never turned into a beetle, did she? Was that cut? Because that you could see in your documentary.

Måns: Yeah, that was cut, but it was a very short cut.

Katinka: Also, she never had the mask in the film.

Måns: No, I think it wasn't looking good and so it was taken away. Also we cut the entrance, when she came down on a kind of elevator [deux ex machina device]. You could hear her coming, and then there was a cut to Tamino—and in the next second she turns up behind him.

Allan: I have a very stupid question. One of the opera singers is smoking. I thought they were not supposed to smoke?

Katinka: They aren't, but they do.

Louise: That was the Queen, wasn't it?

Måns: I said to her, you have to stop smoking, and she just said yeah, yeah, yeah . . .

Katinka: In the film studio there was a big ashtray, a round thing in the middle, with very nice soft chairs around it, and in the studio we were all sitting and smoking there—and even Mr Bergman couldn't stop that.

Paisley: He never smoked.

Katinka: He did smoke, but he said he only smoked when he was young. And once he got very ill—but that's another story. And he drank too, and he "drank and drank," which is not true . . .

Måns: He didn't like the smoke but he accepted it anyway.

Katinka: But he couldn't do anything because it was accepted. It was a cancer party [kräftkalas]!

Maaret: I have one question about casting. Did you have more material in the documentary of people that were tried for the roles and were you part of that process?

Måns: All the casting was made by a team that traveled to all the Scandinavian countries.

Katinka: 130 people were cast or tried.

Måns: There was a lot; we were filming the whole autumn of 1973. Ingmar said that he wanted to pick out the final singers. He didn't want to have to cast by meeting them in person, and so we had a screening every week. They were asked to sing mostly something from *The Magic Flute*, and then Ingmar and Eric Ericson and we were sitting in a screening room. As mentioned, Ingmar wanted to see young people, but he also wanted singers that we couldn't look down their throats as they were singing. . . . Because opera singers open their mouth, they stand up, and make a big "to do." But then this wonderful young Tamino, who just graduated from music dramatic school, sang his wonderful aria while holding the portrait of Pamina in his hand. He was the first one who actually took the portrait in his hand, looking at it, while all the rest were singing straight into the camera—and Ingmar said "That's the boy!"

Katinka: They didn't care what they were singing about, even very well-established singers. They didn't look at the portrait—they looked at the camera.

Linus: This is not a question but more of a reflection looking from today's eyes, so it's possibly not relevant at all. But when I look at the gender relations I feel that in the 1960s most of the women singing are a little "bourgeois," wearing nice clothes, while Bergman seems like a big paternalistic father figure who says things like "when you come in the great entrance with your great décolletage" . . . That energy was fascinating because I really feel distant to it. In some way I feel like this is a really foreign time.

Måns: It doesn't look like it's made today, but then it doesn't look like it's made any particular time . . . to me it seems neutral.

Linus: I'm not talking about *The Magic Flute*, I'm speaking about the documentary, and the way the singers are behaving during the rehearsals, when they are rehearsing in their private clothes. The energy between them and the whole dynamic to me is very fascinating because I feel it's a foreign time when I see it.

Måns: It's interesting because it was 45 years ago, so we all have to put back our perspective a bit.

Paisley: It gave me a different perspective of Bergman because I haven't met him the way you have, or spent any time with him. But it gave me a perspective that I hadn't had before, of the strengths as well as weaknesses. The strength that I saw was how he had this minute imagination of everything that should happen, and the way he's moving people around and showing them "your hand should do this, you should do that." The imagination the guy had to think it all up. So when he sat listening to *The Magic Flute*, he imagined this incredible world that he wanted—and here we see him wrestling with people to get them to come somewhere near that. So that's what I would call his strength. But then there are these other things that I found a little bit appalling, for instance when he's giving a kind of lecture to the musicians. It's not technical musical advice, so what he is saying is completely of no help to them as musicians. Instead, it's some kind of series of metaphorical images, like when he says that this chorus sings "like it's made of wood." I'm sorry—if you're a singer there is no way that this will help you sing what you have to sing.

Katinka: But they loved it. Nobody had ever talked to them, just play.

Paisley: A conductor has a musical optical terminology that he can use to instruct musicians and to guide them one way or another—that's what the conductor does. Ingmar Bergman was not playing the role of the conductor, but gave rather philosophical, literary, and very high level of abstract descriptions about the music. In fact, in the scene in the beginning, where he gives one of those lectures, and he's talking about how it's intimate, and it's sensual and duh duh duh, if you look closely at the faces of some of those musicians, they're thinking "what am I going to do with this"—because there is no way they can translate the metaphors that he is offering them into the music.

Allan: But you can justify that he was saying to the musicians that, ultimately, we are watching a film, and giving you in a clumsy way how it will look as a film— not what is this going to sound like a piece of music. It was permissible.

Maaret: That is exactly why we called today's session, because what we're dealing with are all those transgressions, meetings, and conflicts between different media. I mean here we are talking about television, about opera, and film adaptations in all kinds of forms, for good and bad.

Allan: Let's just raise one other point. This is ultimately for television, which had a horrible sound system at the time, and it's about television in the 1970s. So you're going to hear a complete reduction of a wonderful orchestra and singers, and you are getting it on transistor radio . . .

Paisley: Unless you have a Bang and Olufsen!

Linus: But I think to speak in metaphors to people who maybe don't use them generally, is a fine line. I've seen directors do it, and I've seen as you say people say that this is of no use. But I think partly the magic is that they know it's Ingmar Bergman saying it, and that he takes the time to express his thought—of course that in itself is inspiring. I was working with dancers once, and most of the dancers were happy and just danced regardless. But there was one young dancer, and he was frustrated because I'm not a choreographer, I'm a theatre director. So he sat me down and said, "Linus you're shit at giving me choreography," and I was like "Aha, what do you want me to do?" "You have to give me images, you have to say that I am standing on burning fire, and I'm in a little box." So what he was saying was that since you can't give me the movements, you must find the metaphors that create my imagination. So, I think when Bergman says that the music seems "wooden"—it makes sense. I'm more reflecting on his lecture when he said that, "oh, we've come here just to be together a bit, to imagine a bit, and to fool around a bit . . ."

Maaret: But that was his psychology, wasn't it Katinka, quite often suggest that "oh, I'm so nervous"—and all that . . .

Katinka: People were nervous. If you know him at all, they were very nervous and afraid because of his reputation. He had a terrible reputation. Not so bad perhaps in the 1970s, but earlier. When I was hired I was very young, 17 years old, and when people at the studio found out that I was going to work with him, they told me that if he stares at you, stare back at him. And so, I met him in a corridor, which was very narrow, and he stared at me, and I stared back—and he started to laugh, and said "it's going to be ok." And it was ok for 30 years! But he did have a terrible reputation in the early years. He threw script girls and assistant cameramen out of the studio all of the time, they told me.

Linus: This may be just an anecdote that has nothing to do with this, but at 22 I was working at the Royal Dramatic Theater as some kind of extra in Bergman's production of *A Winter's Tale*. So, when it was found out that I was a director, and had directed one piece that was very successful, he started to approach me. He came in one day and he was doing some kind of gesture with his hands, and said "can you do this?" Everyone, he said, was doing it wrong, and he said "it's the right and the left brain, it's only directors that can do it—if you can do it, that's only because you are a director." And then one day, just when about 45 people were coming in on stage, he suddenly said "you you you you, young Tunström, behind there—you're yawning!" And I was like "uh, no." "But you looked like you were bored. Are you bored?" "No, I'm not bored," I said, "I was maybe just thinking of something private." And so he blurted out, "you should never bring the private onto stage!"

Katinka: Exactly.

Linus: He used this as a kind of pedagogical moment. So, I thought that perhaps it was ok, that once a week he will single out someone in the back, just to make a point so that we all know that I he can see everyone . . . Then he came to me a few rehearsals later, and he took this grip around me and said, "you see, young Tunström, I was a little bit harsh on you—but you know you should never bring the private to work. If I would bring the private into work, that too would be a mortal sin, if I would bring my anger for example. But the *pedagogical anger*—that's a different matter!" Then a few weeks later one poor tailor got this anger. There were like 1,000 costumes on stage, and Bergman looks at one costume and says "stop, who made this? Bring the guy who made it in here!" And as he was shouting, it was like the whole house was shaking.

Måns: I think he himself used the term "pedagogic outburst." He sometimes said that "today I am going to have a pedagogic outburst," so everyone knew that something was coming, just not when and where. But if you waited it came, and it was always something he really wanted to tell people, sometimes in a very stupid way how they should do or not do things . . .

Katinka: But it's also that he gave absolutely everything to his work.

Måns: Yes, but it was not always that pedagogic . . .

Katinka: Once he had an outburst on *Fanny and Alexander*, and he told me in the morning "today you watch, it's going to be something of a pedagogic outburst." Two hours later Ewa Fröling, the actress who played the children's mother, came up to the office crying and said that the atmosphere in the studio was terrible, and I said "take it easy, it'll take half an hour and then it's over." The reason was that Jan Malmsjö, one very great actor who played the Bishop in the film, was used to making films in bits and pieces. But this was a long, long, long take, and Jan wasn't prepared for this, so he didn't know his lines—and that was not good. . . . But he never made that mistake again, and he made a fantastic performance in the film.

Maaret: Since you who have such a long trajectory with Bergman, can you describe his development as a director, and your relationship within these productions? Is it possible to see what happened over the years, so to speak?

Katinka: Well, in *The Magic Flute* he wasn't a devil to me, and quite a few years he was nice to me. But in the beginning he was not always nice. But I didn't know my job well enough, and I was one who sometimes brought my private life into the studio. I could sit and cry for somebody, a guy or something, and he said "you can't do that, stop that"—and he was a monster sometimes. He always asked for your forgiveness, but of course not in front of the team but somewhere behind a bush. But it got better and better, also perhaps because I got older. And I started to understand some of these "pedagogical outbursts," which could be very practical from my point of view. If he had an argument with a woman actress, he very often turned to me and said something nasty to me—and I said "what did I do?" But it was more practical to get it out on me, than to have an actress who is crying and having to do a new makeup, which takes an hour. So it was more practical, and I understood that after some time. It's true! It was like that.

Allan: A surrogate victim?

Katinka: No, it was ok. Or perhaps it's that I am trying to forgive him—but I don't think so. The last ten years I really liked him because of the films we did. He employed me as producer in his company Cinematograph from New Year 1975, and in -76 came this terrible tax story, and he disappeared to Munich. He was supposed to be the producer, but I did everything at Cinematograph. I was alone, so it was the best school to be a producer. And at that point we became friends, and he respected that I did it alone. He called me every Sunday at home for those six years he was in Munich, and every time I had to throw my children out of the room, so they wouldn't make noise.

Louise: And how long were those phone calls?

Katinka: They could be 20 minutes or half an hour. We had to go through what happened and what had not happened, and so on. And when he was back in Sweden we would always have coffee and tea at Cinematograph at quarter to three, and so he sometimes came by taxi from the hospital [where Bergman had been admitted for depression after the so-called tax affair]. And he could say something like "oh, you fantastic women with your children, and you work and . . ." And I said "come on!!!" I was furious, because he never let you have those children in reality, they were something to keep in the shadows. So, when he was getting that pathetic, I had to say please, no, stop, because it was a pure lie. But I liked him, and I miss him. And I really respected him because he knew his trade; he *really* knew it and what was asked of him. So I'm sorry for this speech . . .

Maaret: But can I jump over to you, Linus, and dovetail with Katinka's experience and ask how does a younger director like yourself relate to Bergman and his ways of working? Given that you're in theater, and that you are now entering into film?

Linus: It's feels a bit presumptuous to speak for my generation. Well, I started in the theater to work at a so-called free group called Galeasen with director Richard Günther. He was ten years older than me and also had a very different way of working compared to Bergman. Because he was not in that sense prepared and intellectual, but he was forceful when he was directing, with huge intuition. So he used this very strong, emotional charge, and a little bit of violent atmosphere. So I saw this guy as my mentor when I started, and I was thinking do you have to be like that to be a director? Then at the Royal Dramatic Theater I was working in these Bergman productions. He was much more focused and prepared, but with the same kind of violent tension. For many years I was struggling with this role—do I have to be an all-knowing, repressive father figure, who can control everything? Or can I find a way to keep certain question marks and insecurities and search a path—but still keep the authority in the room, and not rid yourself of responsibility?

I remember once in the 1980s at the Royal Dramatic Theater a lighting technician showed me the light room, and he said—"you know when the new directors come here to work on the big stage, we often think they are not tough enough to make it on the big stage, and we sometimes watch and look at them fail. But you know when Ingmar comes we are afraid, so then we really work hard"! And you could see in a way that he liked this, and I thought that in one way I can understand it, that one respects a person who really knows what he wants. But there's a danger if I as a director need this fix of fear to do my own work properly. This is a double bind, because I also get angry if I am totally into something while someone else is not—then I will be very frustrated. So, what I saw in the 1980s was that the Royal Dramatic Theater was a house needing a very fearful, repressive father figure to function. But I think it's different now. I also think there are a lot of different aspects of this, because I also saw what a vital and charming and funny guy Bergman was when working.

Katinka: Apparently it seems like from all these stories that he was a little worse in the theater?
Louise: Than on the film set?
Katinka: He wasn't always such a charmer there either.

9

Metareference, Metalepsis, and Music in Liv Ullmann's and Ingmar Bergman's *Faithless*[1]

Alexis Luko

> It's hard. I have no words. I never talk about this. How can I talk about that which has no words? A person growing into another person. It's inexorable. Frightening. The process can't be halted. It's almost biology. David grows into Marianne. Marianne is frightened.
>
> Marianne to "Bergman" in
Trolösa/Faithless (2000)

This important scene is located at almost the midpoint of *Trolösa/Faithless* (2000), a film written by Ingmar Bergman and directed by Liv Ullmann. It features the words of a ghost named Marianne (played by Lena Endre) spoken to a character referred to rather unambiguously as "Bergman" (played by Erland Josephson).[2] Both characters take part in a larger meta-narrative in which "Bergman" is writing a screenplay about the painful memories of past infidelity. He calls upon Marianne as muse, to tell the story from her perspective. What ensues is a drawn-out confession, accessed through visual and narrative flashbacks, telling of an adulterous love triangle between Marianne, David (a writer played by Krister Henriksson), and Markus (a conductor played by Thomas Hanzon).[3]

Most provocative, is the power dynamic between "Bergman" and his muse, Marianne, and how it parallels comparable dynamics between pairs of characters in this and other Bergman films and real-life relationships between Ingmar Bergman and Liv Ullmann, in particular. These dynamics are grounded in different realities, which I will break down into "narrative circles" below. Bergman's screenplay and Ullman's direction play with different theories of metareference and metalepsis (defined below), to create multilayered cinematic magic.

Figure 9.1 Marianne (Lena Endre) and "Bergman" Erland Josephson in *Trolösa/Faithless* (2000).

In the scene referred to above, while Marianne reflects on the impossibility of expressing in words the complexities of love and identity, the plaintive tones of the third movement of Brahms's *Quartet in C minor, Opus 60* serves as backdrop. The text of this scene is eerily reminiscent of a scene in Bergman's *Vargtimmen/Hour of the Wolf* of 1968. In the latter, Liv Ullmann as Alma asks, "Is it true that a woman who lives a long time with a man eventually winds up being like that man? I mean, she loves him, and tries to think like him, and see like him? They say it can change a person." Throughout *Faithless*, metareference and self-reflexivity abound, on narrative, visual, and even sonic planes.

Indeed, one of the most powerful devices that Bergman and Ullmann use in this shared creative endeavor is music. At times, music is heard by characters in a scene. At other times it is only in a character's head or ambiguously sounding from off-screen. Music can break the rules, transgress the walls of different narratives, times, and realities, thus becoming an active force, almost like a character or like an object tossed between different narrative worlds. And in this slippery way, music is not to be trusted. At the same time, however, there is much that can be revealed about a film's meaning through music as a metaleptic agent.

Before going further, I'll reveal a little about how *Faithless* came about. Bergman apparently approached Ullmann with the screenplay and asked that she direct it. Ullmann had already directed *Enskilda samtal/Private Confessions* in 1996 (based on the turbulent relationship between Bergman's parents) with some guidance from Bergman. With *Faithless*, Bergman gave Ullmann control of all facets of direction, editing, and production. In an interview she has explained that he did not even indicate preferences for camera angles or blocking: "The exciting thing for [Bergman] was what I would put them in. And I even said to him, 'Should we discuss it?' And he said no, he thought it would be really exciting to see what images I would [come up with]."[4] Bergman only asked of Ullmann that she cast Lena Endre as Marianne and Erland Josephson as "Bergman."[5] He allegedly remained absent from the set with the exception of the final day of filming when he made a surprise appearance, hiding under the bed covers to surprise Endre.

Ullmann was Bergman's lover between 1965 and 1970. She was his close lifelong friend, and the leading actress in eleven of his feature films. Bergman famously referred to her as his "Stradivarius," a metaphor that is simultaneously complimentary and cringe inducingly belittling of Ullmann. She has admitted to such a symbiotic relationship with Bergman that, in interviews, she still refers to herself as his female counterpart. In *Persona*, she has claimed that she played the character of the mute actress, Elizabeth Vogler, by attempting to approximate the gestures and manners of Bergman himself.

> When I played Elisabeth Vogler . . . I just knew I was playing Ingmar. . . . I thought at that time, I will just watch Ingmar and I will try to act like him. In [*Faithless*]. . ., the character called Bergman is like the character he made into a woman and I played as Elisabeth Vogler. You can have great fun with this.[6]

And *fun* Ullmann had! Though Bergman was absent for the making of *Faithless*, his authorial presence is strongly felt—particularly in the soundtrack. The official title of his screenplay is *Trolösa. Partitur för en film* (*Faithless. Musical score for film*) and one of the main protagonists is a musician/conductor.[7] This gives Ullmann occasion to interweave flashback scenes featuring different private and public modes of diegetic musical listening—at an orchestral concert, in an opera house, at an intimate chamber music rehearsal, in a private context as a family listens to a record in their living room, and in Bergman's own beach-view music room where he listens to an LP to the accompaniment of the crashing waves of the Baltic Sea on the island of Fårö. Music is featured liberally throughout *Faithless*, including excerpts from the last movement of Bruckner's Symphony

No. 5,[8] the third movement of Brahms's Quartet in C minor Op. 60,[9] and two operas: *Backanterna* by Daniel Börtz with libretto by Bergman,[10] and Mozart's *Magic Flute*.[11]

I have argued elsewhere that Ingmar Bergman was a sonic auteur, a filmmaker who created distinctive soundscapes.[12] The soundtracks of his films are usually peppered with classical music excerpts, modernist non-diegetic musical cues that haunt from off-screen, hyperbolized sound effects of ticking clocks and church bells, and an eerie silence, void of ambient sound. In this chapter, I have three goals:

First, I peel back the layers of the proverbial onion and analyze the complex layers of the multiform narrative of *Faithless*, which draw together multiple biographical strands pertaining to infidelity (involving Ullmann and Bergman), and intertwine fictional and non-fictional characters, varied temporalities, and diverse ontologies. Second, I aim to reveal how the soundtrack (particularly music and voice) is used in *Faithless* to communicate between different narrative levels of the story. To this end, I project music through theories of metalepsis. I aim to demonstrate how music acts as a *metaleptic* agent and how it transgresses boundaries between different meta-narrative levels of the film. Bergman and Ullmann work with transgressions both in subject matter (e.g., infidelity and identity) and in the filmmaking itself, where a metaleptic agent—such as music—crosses boundaries of time and context. Third, I aim to reveal issues about *auteurship* in *Faithless*, particularly through the lens of music and sound. I am interested in how *Faithless* raises questions with respect to auteurism, its definition, and its limits. Questions like:

- What does it mean to project oneself as an auteur on the screen, particularly if one has relinquished directorial control of that projection?
- Where are the Bergmanian sonic trademarks in *Faithless*, moments where, through metareference, Liv Ullmann—whether purposefully or subconsciously—emulates or pays homage to Bergman?

In many ways, *Faithless* might be viewed as a cinematic experiment, a reflection on auteurism, the act of filmmaking, and a testament to how two people—Bergman and Ullmann—have truly grown into one another. It is a type of relationship that is as beautiful as it is monstrous, recalling the famous moment in Bergman's *Persona*, wherein the faces of the mute actress (Ullmann) and her talkative nurse (Bibi Andersson) join together as they assume the others' identity, fusing into one entity.

"So long Marianne"

Before exploring the soundtrack of *Faithless*, first, on the name and the identity of "Marianne," the female protagonist-ghost.[13] When Marianne first appears, the elderly Bergman (referred to as the "writer" in Bergman's first version of the screenplay) dreams her up as a muse and demands that she tell the story of her life with husband Markus, and lover, David.[14] Markus is a successful internationally acclaimed musician and orchestral conductor, while David is a local angst-ridden theater director whose reputation is tendentious at best. We witness both men at work—Markus during an inspired rehearsal of Brahms's *Quartet in C minor, opus 60*, and David directing an abysmal rehearsal of Strindberg's *Ett drömspel/A Dream Play*.

We eventually discover that David is actually a younger incarnation of the character "Bergman" (Ullmann's idea) and that the ghostly Marianne is serving as Bergman's metaphorical guide (like Dante's "Beatrice" or Strindberg's "Agnes") as he navigates the dark halls of his guilt-ridden past and attempts to come to terms with love, loss, and the deep pain of infidelity.[15]

The setting for "Bergman's" encounters with Marianne is allegedly a replica (created on stage at the Swedish State Television Company/SVT in Stockholm) of Ingmar Bergman's actual home office on the island of Fårö.[16] Ullmann has explained that, other than a picture of Strindberg on the wall, the furniture and decor in Bergman's study were created to look as close to the real thing as possible.[17] Oddly, Ullmann recently backtracked on this story, claiming that there was no SVT replica stage and that all these scenes were actually filmed in Bergman's study at Fårö.[18] Is this Ullmann's idea of playful deception?[19] Whatever the case, longshots of Josephson walking along the beach are definitely filmed at Bergman's property at Fårö and are featured at the opening, midpoint and close of the film, accompanied by a tune from Mozart's *Magic Flute*.[20]

"Marianne" is a name we have heard before. The Marianne of *Faithless* shares the same name with the protagonist of Bergman's *En lektion i kärlek/A Lesson in Love* (1954), *Scener ur ett äktenskap/Scenes from a Marriage* (1973), and his final film, *Saraband* (2003), the latter two featuring Liv Ullmann as Marianne. The fact that Ullmann played a "Marianne" in two Bergman films has prompted questions as to whether *Faithless* might contain reflections on Bergman and Ullmann's love affair (1965–70), but she has suggested in interview that the "Marianne" of *Faithless* may actually represent an individual (his mother Karin?) from "a story about faithlessness that had once affected him [Bergman] as a child."[21] In another interview, Ullmann presents a different story (an example of yet further playful storytelling?) revealing Marianne to actually represent Harriet Andersson, with whom Bergman fell in love while making *Sommaren med Monika/Summer with Monika*.[22]

Bergman's semi-autobiographical *Laterna Magica/The Magic Lantern* might hold the key to the "real" story as it depicts an affair with Gunvor *Marianne* Grut (married 1951–9) and a trip to Paris that bears many similarities with the plot of *Faithless*.[23] Bergman and Gunvor's affair resulted in a grueling divorce, due in part to the children involved from her previous marriage. Maaret Koskinen has uncovered references to Gunvor in Bergman's diaries and writings, demonstrating that he continued to be haunted by her memory throughout his life. One such entry that Koskinen posits was written just prior to the conception of *Faithless* reads: "Strong and strange dreams . . . Meeting with Gun in the land of the dead. Violent and unreal feelings. A whole film really. The things you carry around with you!?"[24]

To add another layer of complexity, there is a 25-minute film called *Dåså* that aired on Swedish television on October 6, 1987, and is credited to his daughter, Maria von Rosen.[25] Jan Holmberg has shown how Bergman was almost certainly the mastermind working behind the scenes on this short film. In the Bergman Archives, a short-typewritten script exists (F:093) of a mere twenty-two pages with Bergman's handwritten notes. The script is credited to "Ulrika Nordmark," a pseudonym of Ingmar Bergman and Maria [Elsa Ulrika] von Rosen.[26] *Dåså*'s plot is remarkably similar to that of *Faithless*, featuring two characters named David and Marianne who have an adulterous affair in Paris. *Dåså* predates *Faithless* by ten years and is assumed by Holmberg to be based on Bergman's own experiences, previously recounted in *Scenes from a Marriage*. Those familiar with the dysfunctional married couple, Marianne (played by Ullmann) and Johan (played by Josephson) in *Scenes from a Marriage* and *Saraband*, might recall that Josephson's character also takes a trip to Paris. Just one month before *Dåså* aired, Bergman released *Laterna Magica* where he admitted to cheating on his wife on a trip to Paris (recommending the third part of *Scenes from a Marriage* for the juicy details).[27]

But the plot thickens. Just five years before the release of *Dåså*, in 1982, while at Fårö, Maria von Rosen discovered (after a trip to Paris) at the age of twenty-two that she was not actually the daughter of Jan-Carl and Ingrid von Rosen but rather the illegitimate daughter of Ingmar Bergman. Born in 1959, Maria von Rosen came into the world the same year Bergman divorced Gun Grut and married Käbi Laretei. The mind reels at how Ingrid von Rosen (married to Bergman from 1971 until her death in 1995) and their daughter Maria von Rosen might figure into the fictional/non-fictional plot of *Faithless*. Is the nine-year-old Isabelle of *Faithless* an avatar for Maria von Rosen and Marianne an avatar for Ingrid von Rosen? As Ingmar said to 22-year-old Maria, "We didn't want you to carry such a big secret when you were little."[28]

But when we return to our original question—Who is Marianne?—we get no closer to a definitive answer. Whose story is being told? Ullmann's? Harriet Andersson's? Karin Bergman's? Laretei's? Grut's? Von Rosen's? But this is the beauty of Bergman. The deeper and deeper we dig for answers, the more he playfully pulls the rug out from under our feet. This is particularly poignant in a script like *Faithless*, the workbook of which Holmberg has characterized as "one of the most remarkable texts" of Bergman's oeuvre.[29]

Linda Rugg reminds us that in auteurist cinema, "metanarrative references to the . . . apparatus of filmmaking point to the presence of a director behind the scenes."[30] This is precisely what Ullmann teases us with at the outset of *Faithless* as she has the ghost-muse of Marianne appear from behind a film projector—a homage to *Persona*?) Who is in charge? "Bergman" (the writer) or Marianne (the oral storyteller)? Ingmar Bergman (writer of the screenplay) or Liv Ullmann (director of the film)? The fact that Marianne appears from behind the projector surely teases that she might be in a position of control and power. But the projector competes with the "Bergman"-character's notebook—the writer/thinker in his study who is apparently imagining everything that we see and hear on screen. In this way, creative protagonists meld with Bergman's own identity, suggestive of a self-conscious unmasking of the artist. As Marianne in *Faithless* says to Bergman: "I am you and you are you."

Defining Terms: Self-Reference, Metareference, Metalepsis, and Multiform Narrative

Before observing how music and sound function in *Faithless*, a cursory definition of some key interrelated terms is necessary—namely concepts of self-reference, metareference, and metalepsis. Self-reference, related to breaking the fourth wall, is when authors refer to themselves or their own work in the context of the work itself. Metareference is a type of self-reference that encourages the audience to reflect on the fact that they are viewing a fictional story. Metareference also typically invites reflection about the media involved. Examples of metareference in *Faithless* are scenes in which the character "Bergman" is engaged in writing the screenplay to the very film we are watching. In these scenes, actor Erland Josephson presumably holds the actual notebook (or a simulation of the notebook) in which Bergman wrote his film notes and screen plays. Other examples of metareference are the intertextual allusions throughout *Faithless* to other Bergman productions.

Metalepsis is a type of metareference, and because it is less understood, it warrants an extended definition.[31] Narratologist Gérard Genette originally coined the term *narrative metalepsis* in 1972 to refer to "paradoxical leaps across the *sacred* frontier between two worlds within a text: the level of representation and the level of what is represented."[32] Theories of metalepsis extending beyond the realm of narratology were few and far between until 2005, when Werner Wolf published an edited volume exploring theories of metareference in film, music, literature, photography, visual art, and theater.[33] According to Wolf, for *narrative metalepsis* to occur, the following four criteria need to be fulfilled:

a. The work must be a representation;
b. There must be a "stack of two hierarchical levels," which has the form of a sort of . . . story within a story . . . or any representation of a fictitious world within an artifact, via nested representation of other media, or the self-same media;
c. There must be a "transgression between, or a confusion and contamination of, the sub-worlds involved";
d. The transgression must be intentional.[34]

Metalepsis is a digressive technique that forces the viewer to reflect on the boundaries between different narrative worlds. Characters, objects, or, indeed,— music and sound—can transgress these boundaries, "contaminating" different levels. Levels are created by *multistrand* and *multiform* narratives—story structures that have been theorized by game and film theorists such as Janet Murray, Alison McMahan, Matthew Campora, and Stavros Halvatzis, among others.[35] As Halvatzis has explained, multistrand narratives involve a variety of distinct stories with different protagonists and are best exemplified in films such as *Crash* (Haggis, 2004), *Syriana* (Gaghan, 2005), and *Babel* (Iñárritu, 2006). Multiform narratives, on the other hand, feature one or more protagonists who move between different narrative worlds or ontological realities. Examples of multiform narratives can be found in art film, fantasy, and horror films, such as *Jacob's Ladder* (Lyne, 1990); *Eternal Sunshine of the Spotless Mind* (Gondry, 2004); and *Inception* (Nolan, 2010). Ullmann's and Bergman's *Faithless* fits the latter type of multiform narrative paradigm. As revealed below, characters—*and music*—transgress the boundaries of the different multiform layers. Such self-conscious digressions have the effect of forcing the auteur to the fore of the multiform narrative.

The Levels of Diegesis in Faithless

In *Faithless*, there are so many embedded stories within stories within stories in the multiform narrative structure, that the "Russian doll" effect is nothing short of dizzying. One way that Ullmann achieves metalepsis is through music, which she sets up to transgress boundaries between the various narrative levels. In her seminal book *Unheard Melodies*, Claudia Gorbman applies Gérard Genette's vocabulary to describe music embedded within a narrative (diegetic) and outside the narrative (non-diegetic).[36]

The limitations of this binary distinction are pronounced when conceptualizing the role of the soundtrack at a moment of metalepsis, where music transgresses boundaries between different diegetic and non-diegetic levels.[37] Film music theorist Robin Stilwell has a term to describe the actual transgressional space as a "fantastical gap," and Gorbman and Edward Branigan have names for one such *type* of transgression; while Gorbman uses the term *metadiegetic* to refer to music that reflects what is heard in the mind of an on-screen character, Branigan refers to "internal focalization."[38] For the present context, one of the more useful theories is put forth by Guido Heldt, who has identified "descending rhetorical metalepsis," whereby non-diegetic music enters the diegesis and characters sing or play their own non-diegetic motifs.[39] Campora has shown how metaleptic sound bridges have the ability to disrupt the boundaries between different ontologies or between real and imagined worlds.[40]

In order to understand how metaleptic transgressions occur between multiform narrative levels in *Faithless*, it is essential initially to identify these levels. Figure 9.2 attempts to represent the various "worlds" in *Faithless*, with the innermost first circle representing the main diegesis that focuses on the love triangle between Markus, Marianne, and David. The second circle represents the story of Isabelle, daughter to Markus and Marianne. Spotlighting Isabelle's story was Ullmann's idea.[41] According to Ullmann, Bergman was "very pleased that the child is now very much in the movie," and even wondered aloud, "[n]ow why didn't I think of that?"[42] The key here is that while Bergman perceived Marianne as victim, Ullmann saw the child as the helpless one as "she can't make choices."[43] The third circle is occupied by Marianne, the ghost narrator of the present, who is asked by "Bergman" to provide her version of those events surrounding a past extramarital affair. Metaleptic transgression, at the level of character, occurs most strongly with the "Bergman" and Marianne characters. Though his name is "Bergman" in the third narrative circle, he is ostensibly a representation of Bergman the director (fifth narrative circle), and simultaneously the character "David" (first narrative circle). As for Marianne—she is a ghost in the third narrative circle—recognized by the character "Bergman" as a creation of his own imagination and an extension of himself. When she tells "her" story about her affair with David, she flashbacks to the first narrative circle.

In the fourth narrative circle, we have the diegesis from the perspective of the character "Bergman," who is featured writing the screenplay to the very film we are watching. This undermines the authority of Marianne's narrative voice, forcing the viewer to question exactly whose story is being told.

The four outermost narrative circles (fifth to eighth) are extradiegetic (existing outside the film's diegesis) and relate to auteurist principles evident to initiated Bergman fans and scholars. These extradiegetic levels, though inaccessible to many viewers, nevertheless contribute significantly to the meaning of the film. The fifth narrative circle comprises Bergman's personal autobiography, which seeps into every aspect of his filmmaking and (as argued above) into the narrative of the film itself.[44] As is the case with auteurist cinema, autobiographical gestures throughout the film are palpable and no wonder, given that Bergman once described *Trolösa* as a passion drama he "experienced at close hand."[45]

The sixth narrative circle comprises Bergman's entire corpus of works—a narrative world that is familiar, created by a "director as recognizable author."[46] As pointed out by Linda Rugg, in auteurist cinema "there might be repetitions of aesthetic elements or narrative topoi or actual lines or scenes that lead viewers to recognize a directorial signature."[47] Here, the repetition from film to film of familiar names, characters, themes, objects, and music, generates a sense of a Bergmanian "universe" where every scenario feels familiar, as Bergman purposefully creates fluid boundaries between films.

The seventh narrative circle is Ullmann's autobiography. She has commented that, through her direction, she injects her own experience of both infidelity and love into the film. Furthermore, in several interviews she has made a point of reminding the public of what a distant and absent father Bergman was to their daughter Linn and to all of his children. This makes the scenes in which the Bergman-character stares at a photograph of a young girl all the more poignant. Ullmann has also made a point in interview, to incorporate her daughter into the film's mythology by explaining that the scenes in which the aging Bergman-character walks on the beach were inspired by Linn, who imagined that, after death, her father would dance on the waves.[48]

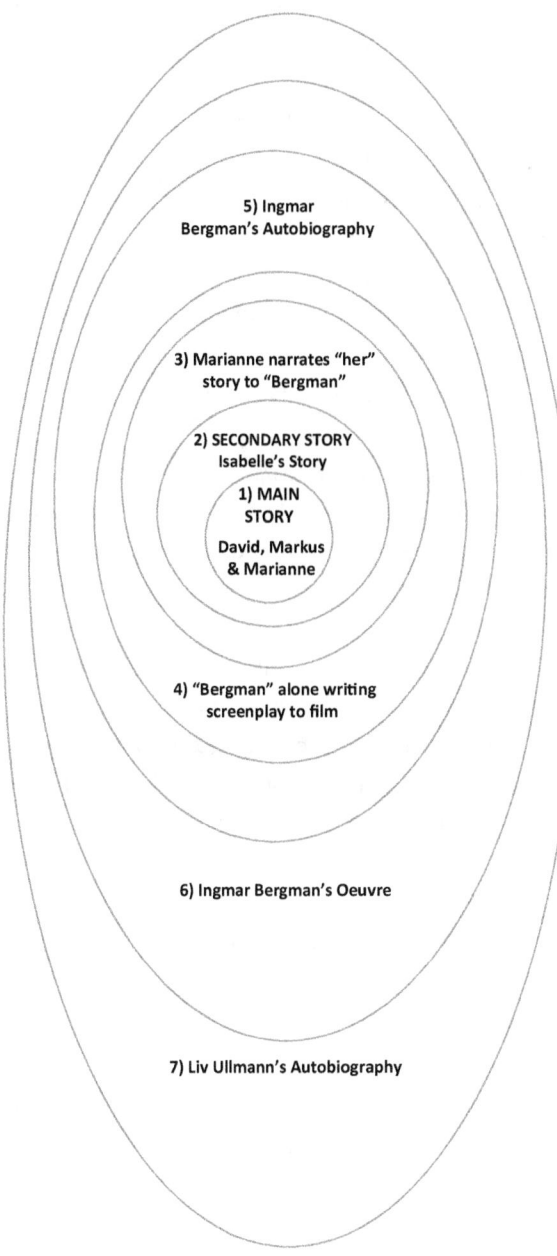

Figure 9.2 Diegetic and extradiegetic narrative circles of *Faithless*.

With all of these different worlds now identified, it does seem rather apt that Ullmann hangs the portrait of Strindberg in Bergman's office and Bergman chooses to reference Strindberg's *A Dream Play*. It was one of Bergman's favorite plays and one that is defined by metaleptic practice as objects and characters morph as dreams move fluidly into other dreams. As Strindberg notes in his preface: "The characters split, double, multiply, evaporate, condense, dissolve and merge. But one consciousness rules them all: the dreamer's."[49] How does music metaleptically participate in *Faithless*—a story so rich in metareference? The next section will address this.

Before launching into a deeper musical discussion of metalepsis, in addition to the metalevels diagramed above, I offer yet one further (Figure 9.3) depicting those worlds created by different pairs of lovers:

1. The world of Marianne and Markus, the married couple;
2. The secret world of Marianne and David's affair;
3. The even more secretive world of Markus and Margareta (not revealed until the end of the film).

Metalepsis roughly defines the physical and psychic experience of what constitutes infidelity itself—the jumping of one person from their story into another persons' story. There are three so-called *metaleptic agents* which jump between narrative worlds. Marianne's voice is one such metaleptic agent. The others are Isabelle and music itself (Figure 9.3).

Musical Metareference: Mutes, Screams, and Touch in Backanterna

Examples of musical metareference can be found in intertextual references to other Bergman productions—namely Mozart's *The Magic Flute* (directed for film in 1974) and *Backanterna* (an opera produced in 1991). First a few words about the lesser-known *Backanterna*, with its libretto by Ingmar Bergman himself, and music by Daniel Börtz.

Bergman based his libretto on a Swedish translation (by Östen Sjöstrand) of Euripides's *The Bacchae* but took some artistic liberties, transforming the

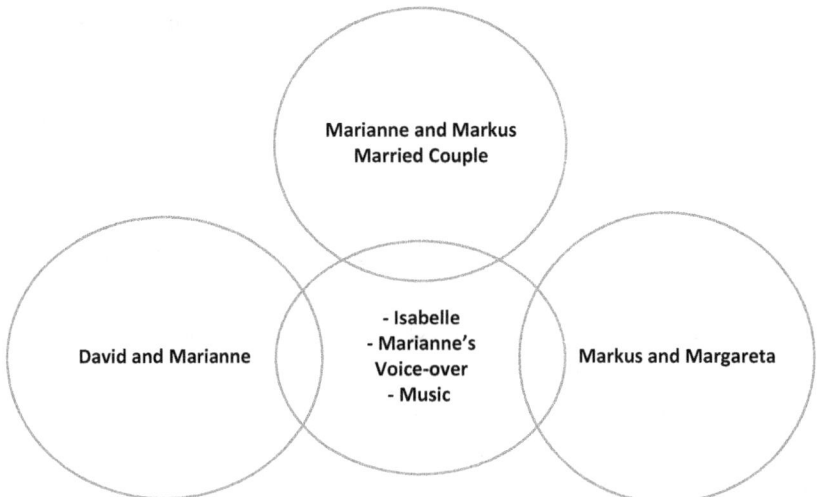

Figure 9.3 Love pairs in *Faithless*.

anonymous bacchae into more substantial characters, providing each woman with a backstory and, most significantly—a voice. Bergman also created a 14th baccha, named Talatta, a non-speaking dance role, performed at the premiere by another "Marianne"—this time, Marianne Orlando.[50] This mute baccha functioned as a doppelganger for Dionysus.

It is in the meta-world of *Faithless*, that some of the plot points of *Backanterna* are echoed. For example, the doppelganger-duo comprised of mute Talatta and Dionysus find their parallel in *Faithless* characters, Marianne and "Bergman" and similarly in mute Elisabeth Vogler and Nurse Alma of *Persona*. As with the bacchae, "Bergman" encourages Marianne to use her own voice to tell her side of her/their story of infidelity. The doppelganger and mute/voice themes play out at two additional levels, as two otherwise silent women are also given a voice to tell their story: first is a voice from beyond the grave of Bergman's deceased ex-wife, Gun Grut (if we are to believe that it is indeed Grut's voice that he is animating); second is the directorial voice of Ullmann, to whom Bergman hands the reins to tell *his* story, but, ostensibly, from *her* perspective. There, is of course irony here. The idea of a feminine voice might be considered a fallacy, as it is still Bergman putting words in the mouths of women. He is, after all, the author of the screenplay on which *Faithless* is based.[51]

The excerpt from *Backanterna* is found at a particularly climactic moment—the last ten minutes of the film, following a silent scream from "Bergman." The excerpt quotes a moment when all the bacchae come together: "What is all our wisdom? And what is the best thing that gods give us? Putting one's victorious hand on the head of an enemy in vengeance? No, [on] an eternal friend, that is the good."[52]

This topic of touching an enemy/friend typically figures at a climactic juncture in Bergman films, following a scream (often stylized through silence, close-up, or off-screen placement). Human touch, for Bergman, the act of reaching out and truly touching another human being (particularly one who acts as both friend and enemy), is a magical moment in his films, typically accompanied by music so as to emphasize the importance of wordlessness in authentic spiritual human interaction.

In interview, Ullmann has discussed how one of the major changes she made to the screenplay was to add a scene in which the old "Bergman" character of narrative circle three reaches out to tenderly touch the cheek of the young Bergman-character (David of narrative circle one).[53] Bergman was apparently uninterested in forgiveness as a theme in the script, but Ullmann got her way, forcing a brilliant meta-moment of loving touch for the auteur himself—and at

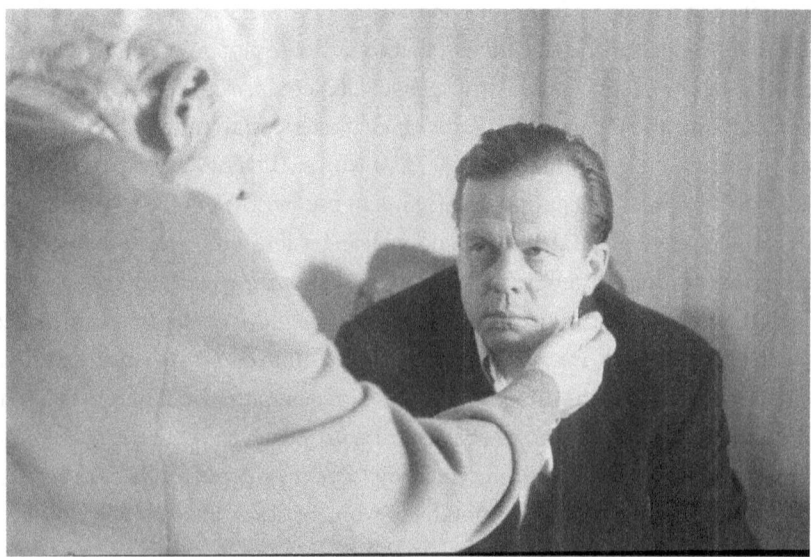

Figure 9.4 Meta-moment where "Bergman" (Erland Josephson) touches "David" (Krister Henriksson), a younger version of himself.

the same time, finding a way through *infidelity* to the script, to breath faith and forgiveness into her multiform narrative conception of the film (Figure 9.4).

The Voice as Metaleptic Agent

When we are first introduced to her, ghostly Marianne emerges from the ether in a way comparable to Rigmor, the clown, in *Larmar och gör sig till/In the Presence of a Clown* (1997) and Death in *Det sjunde inseglet/The Seventh Seal* (1957). At the beginning of Bergman's screenplay, Marianne is simply called "Voice"/"Rösten" and it is this "voice" that first suggests her own identity:

> **Voice**: Are you sitting there describing Marianne?
> **Bergman**: What do you know about Marianne?
> **Voice**: Not very much. Except that you and she had a stormy relationship for a few years. Is it Marianne?
> **Bergman**: It's definitely not Marianne, I promise. But you should have a name. Marianne is good? Marianne Vogler. You have retained your maiden name. Marianne Vogler. Actress.
> **Marianne**: So now I exist?
> **Bergman**: It might be a little strange if you think about it. A few hours ago you did not exist. Suddenly you are extremely present.[54]

This is a character imagined and made up by Bergman. He almost certainly hears her voice in his head—a metadiegetic sound. But, this is a voice that has its own autonomous presence. It does not carry the hallmarks of metadiegetic/imagined sound. In fact, Bergman's screenplay is written predominantly as a monologue for Marianne. Even the subtitle to his screenplay, "Faithless: Musical score for film," suggests that he is providing simply the soundtrack or—more precisely—the monologue track.[55]

Ullmann shot the screenplay in two versions. First, she filmed Marianne in Bergman's study, reciting her entire story. Then she shot the film again, this time providing visuals for the flashbacks.[56] Ullmann has joked in interview that most who watch the film do not even realize that it is mostly comprised of a continuous monologue. This means that Lena Endre's voice serves as a vital metaleptic agent, cutting through all narrative layers of the film.

In the shooting script, Ullmann indicates that Marianne's voice-overs are all to be recorded in the Bergman study, closely miked.[57] In this way, Marianne assumes what Michel Chion would characterize as an "I-Voice," a voice that has a "certain sound quality, a way of occupying space, a sense of proximity to the spectator's ear,"[58] and is "framed and recorded in a certain manner . . . resonating in us as if it were our own voice."[59] Bergman's authoritative i-voices are almost always prone to false or imaginative interpretations and the narrated stories, nested within other stories, call into question any semblance of narrative foundation—creating the ultimate postmodernist dilemma. Perhaps as an homage to Bergman, Ullmann manages to emulate exactly this sense of instability. The closely miked i-voice is intimate and the vocal timbre acquires a Barthian "grain" that includes the ambient sound that the space of Bergman's office affords. But, at the same time, Ullmann manages to destabilize the voice's authority by adding other sound effects such as cluster chords (a typical Bergmanian device to signal the realm of dream and imagination) making the viewer question whether the perceived i-voice is actually a meta-voice emanating from the mind of "Bergman."[60]

Metareference, Metalepsis, Magic Flutes, and Music Boxes

A major source of music in *Faithless* is Mozart's *The Magic Flute*. It was Bergman's favorite opera, one that he directed for Swedish television in 1974.[61] A Swedish television documentary about the making of *The Magic Flute* and an associated LP with personal liner notes by Bergman, reveal how connected he feels to Mozart's music and to Schikaneder's libretto.[62]

Bergman paid homage to *The Magic Flute* in his 1968 horror film, *Hour of the Wolf* in a haunting scene, where a group of ghosts gathers around a miniature stage to watch a *Magic Flute* puppet show performed by tiny flesh-and-blood human beings.[63] The non-ghost guests in the room are Ullmann (Alma) and Max von Sydow (Johan), a married couple who slowly fuse into one another as the wife pries more and more deeply into her artist-husband's diaries, revealing his private demons and darkest secrets of infidelity. Art, infidelity, and *The Magic Flute* resurface in *Faithless*, where Ullmann chooses light and cheerful instrumental versions of well-known *Magic Flute* arias—particularly those associated with magical musical instruments and music boxes in the opera.

Bergman loved music boxes, automated clock tunes, and mechanized music in general. This is manifest in the gorgeous and intricate examples of automatons and music boxes found in several of his films.[64] There is a difference for Bergman between music performed by live musicians and mechanical music. Mechanized motion, devoid of human intervention, is often suggestive of an omniscient hand at work—a magical presence capable of pushing the plot into new directions. In a Bergman film, where the auteur's voice is always present, the viewer is left wondering whether this is a magical hand from beyond the narrative— Bergman's hand? This is precisely the type of transgression that characterizes metalepsis.

The first *Magic Flute* melody of *Faithless* is the glockenspiel tune, "Das Klinget so herrlich!" / *That sounds so splendid* and helps to save the day when Pamina and Papageno are about to be ambushed by Monostatos. The magic tune essentially puts their enemies into an animated song-and-dance-state. They sing "Tralalalalala" as they twirl around, permitting Pamina and Papageno to escape.[65] The three women who present Tamino and Papageno with the magic musical bells that produce this tune explain that the music is capable of "transforming the passions of men, to render the melancholy joyful, the misogynist amorous." In other words, the magic bells deceive and render individuals temporarily oblivious to their true nature. Similarly, the so-called protection that *Das Klinget so herrlich* offers in *Faithless* is one of naïve self-deception. The tune is childish, ludic, and magically oblivious. It is first heard when David is visiting Marianne for dinner while Markus is away. As it sounds from off-screen, the camera pans over photographs that grace the walls of their home—of Markus, Marianne, and their daughter Isabelle. It continues to play, weaving a magical incantation, as an inebriated David asks Marianne, "Will you sleep with me?" Deception plays a role again when the tune plays in a scene of tenderness between David and Marianne, directly following David's outburst of physical violence spurred on by jealousy. Later, in one of the most pivotal scenes, the tune acts as a metaleptic agent, sounding as a flash-forward into the future, outside the narrative circle of Marianne and David. Reminiscent of *Persona*, Marianne the ghost, now with 20/20 hindsight, stares at her reflection and thinks about how her careless actions of the past affected her daughter. Isabelle's face appears and floats between the filmed and reflected images of Marianne. Marianne is now aware of her mask, her self-deception, and the damage she caused her daughter.

The second *Magic Flute* tune, *Ein Mädchen oder Weibchen*, is an aria from Act I, scene 3 and expresses Papageno the birdman's most fervent desire for a "girl or little wife." Tamino and Papageno, who are led in by priests for their three trials, are reminded they will be punished by the gods if they fail to remain silent. Oblivious to danger, Papageno immediately launches into his song. Deception is another theme associated with this tune as the music magically brings forth a false bride in the form of an old woman who then transforms into a beautiful young bird-woman before disappearing.

Ein Mädchen oder Weibchen	**Papageno's aria from *Die Zauberflöte***
Ein Mädchen oder Weibchen	A girl or a little wife
Wünscht Papageno sich	Wishes Papageno
O so ein sanftes Täubchen	O, such a soft little dove
Wär Seligkeit für mich.	Would be bliss for me.[66]

Ein Mädchen oder Weibchen is heard as a framing device at the opening and close to *Faithless*, where the old "Bergman" character walks along the non-fictional Bergman's beach-front Fårö property. In this narrative context, it is conceivable that Bergman will find his late-wife Ingrid through death; she died only a year before Ullmann made *Faithless*.

Ein Mädchen oder Weibchen resurfaces again during a flashback scene that tells us about the history of the music box when Marianne presents it as a gift to David while on their adulterous trip to Paris.[67] The lovers don white, with Marianne's hair scarf looking very much like a wedding veil. The couple stand opposite one another at what appears to be the Kiosque de L'Empereur in the Bois de Boulogne.[68] Clothing and setting, therefore, generate a sense of ceremony and ritual, but rather than an exchange of rings, it is mechanized music that is offered up as a symbol of love. The tune makes them smile. After all, the irony is not lost on them—both Marianne and David already have a "little husband" and "little wife."

As the pair listen to the music box, the music acts as a metaleptic agent. There is a flash-forward and the camera now focuses on the old "Bergman" character in his study listening to the same music box. The music, however, continues after he closes the box, suggesting it is metadiegetic and remembered music he/we are hearing rather than music of the moment.

Marianne later takes a turn to play with the same music box, after what she characterizes as "fumbling, aggressive sex" with David. She opens the curtains (a *Persona* reference?) in their Paris hotel room just before she opens the box. As in *Persona*, this moment signals a shift in power dynamic. Marianne is now in a position of dominance, made clear by David's self-deprecating banter: "If a person like you likes a person like me, I should be humbled."

There is no reference in Bergman's original screenplay to Mozart's *Magic Flute* or to music boxes. This is Ullmann's homage to Bergman and an example of musical metareference. One cannot help but think of *Det regnar på vår kärlek/It Rains on*

Our Love (1946), where another David-character finds a junk-music box on the ground.[69] "It sounds a bit off," he says to his lover Maggie. "We ought to keep it." Like the music box for these lovers on the margins of society, David and Marianne's music box acquires a pandora's box property—as a holder of memories and painful secrets.

Brahms as Agent of Metaleptic Transgression

Brahms's quartet Op. 60 is encoded with secrets, much like this film of infidelity.[70] Johannes Brahms had been a student and close friend of Robert Schumann and when Schumann was institutionalized after throwing himself into the Rhine, Brahms moved in on his best friend's wife, Clara Schumann. Opus 60 was composed as he attempted to work out his feelings for Clara. This is all the more palpable in the music itself, encoded with a musical motto for CLARA: C# -B-A-G#-A.[71] Besides his own feelings for Clara, Brahms revealed that he was also referencing Goethe's Werther, a romantic hero of unrequited love who takes his own life. To his publisher, Brahms asked, "On the cover you must have a picture, namely a head with a pistol to it. Now you can form some conception of the music!" The quartet itself, therefore, grapples with the same topics as the film. Markus and David, like Schumann and Brahms, are also best friends and there is a link between the history of the proposed score frontispiece and Markus's suicide.

Bergman's screenplay explicitly refers to the piece of music, but only once. In Ullmann's film, however, it functions as an organic thread throughout the narrative, heard eleven times, acting as an agent of metaleptic transgression as it transports the viewer and the characters of the film between layers of the multiform narrative. In this way, Ullmann aligns with the Bergmanian cinematic technique of repeating the same classical musical excerpt in multiple scenes, reminiscent of films such as *Saraband, Såsom i en spegel/Through A Glass Darkly* (1961), *Viskningar och rop/Cries and Whispers* (1973), *Ur marionetternas liv/ From the Life of the Marionettes* (1980), and *Nattvardsgästerna/Winter Light* (1963), which all feature musical repetition.[72] Music eases the transitions as the narrative shifts between levels, but also accrues ontological baggage upon each repetition, acquiring different ontological status for different characters, transforming as the film progresses, almost as if it is a living entity itself.

The first time we hear the quartet it is located in the third narrative circle, when the character "Bergman" implores the ghost of Marianne to answer his questions about the past. The next time, it is located as part of the main diegesis in the first narrative circle when Marianne and David sleep side by side. The two do nothing more than touch hands, but the Brahms quartet, which swells as non-diegetic accompaniment, suggests that there is an electric connection. The Brahms excerpt is also heard when Marianne waits in a hotel room in Paris for David to join her.

While the above examples are non-diegetic and associated with pre-infidelity scenes, in the next chain of scenes, there is a shift as a variety of characters from various narrative circles all experience the music diegetically. The character "Bergman" puts on an LP for Marianne (third narrative circle). He drops the needle haphazardly, coinciding with measure 28 of movement III of Op. 60 as Marianne reminisces about her ex-husband Markus. The music acts as metaleptic sound bridge, transporting Marianne (from the third narrative circle to the first narrative circle) to a memory of watching her husband rehearse the same piece of music with his quartet. We find out that Markus and the other musicians are rehearsing to make a recording of the quartet for an LP, probably the very same LP that "Bergman" and Marianne listen to in the first narrative circle.

In the quartet rehearsal flashback, the music underlines bonds and ruptures between pairs of characters in the rehearsal space. Marianne's voice-over suggests that she herself is unconnected to the music in a meaningful way. She acts more as an observer of other individuals' listening experiences.[73] When Marianne studies Isabelle listening, she immediately recognizes how immersed she is in the musical moment and how connected her daughter is to the music. She recognizes how Isabelle is clearly her father's daughter, sharing Markus's musical sensibilities. Then, a tight close-up on Markus suggests that Marianne is now focused on watching the listening experience of her husband. His is a face that depicts a man enraptured. As the music swells, through a voice-over, Marianne speaks jealously about how music is Markus's fundamental pleasure. The intimacy of the camerawork and the look of ecstasy on his face provide a glimmer of how deeply sensual this relationship actually is. Here, there is a subtle suggestion that it is the fault of music that there is distance between Marianne and her husband and daughter. Thus, music is being presented as perhaps the ultimate agent of infidelity in this film. This may also provide Marianne with a rationalization for cheating on Markus.

The quartet suddenly breaks off mid-phrase as Markus asks the cellist to sing her melody. Her sensuous singing creates a mysterious sense that there is something illicit about Markus's relationship with either the cellist or the music itself. Later in the film, the Brahms excerpt enters the second narrative circle, while Isabelle plays in her attic bedroom with her eerie menagerie of dolls, reciting stories about child-eating monsters. Marianne's voice-over asks, "Why such pain? Is this how we play?" Then, as Isabelle turns round and round (an important act as we shall see below), the Brahms excerpt is abstracted to merely the cellists' haunting vocalization from the rehearsal. Thanks to reverb and echo effects, the tune takes on a more ominous horror-tone, reminiscent of the lullaby in *Rosemary's Baby*.

The next time we hear the Brahms, the music transports us to the third narrative circle (from the introduction to this chapter) as Marianne speaks to "Bergman": "How can I talk about that which has no words. . . . A Person growing into another." Words fail her, but the music stands in for that which she cannot express.

Brahms is next heard in the fourth narrative circle linked to "Bergman," who is sitting alone at his desk. It transports us into a flashback revealing a dark secret, where Marianne discovers that she is not the only one cheating. Her husband Markus has been unfaithful with Margareta—the page turner who was present at the rehearsal.

To sum up, at first, the Brahms excerpt seems to serve as a special love signifier for David and Marianne as they become entwined in each other's lives. But, in fact, it ends up assuming a more active role, acting as a metaleptic agent, linking chains of characters on different narrative levels. We find out eventually, that it—along with Isabelle—held the key to this mystery all along. Isabelle, like the music, is able to metaleptically pass between the secret worlds of her mother and father. This explains her otherworldly personality. She lives on a plane with music.

Ullmann divulges that she "wanted to show that the child is . . . invisible for these people."[74] Ullmann also viewed the child as a trope in Bergman films—"represent[ing] a part of Ingmar . . . the child who was never loved or recognized."[75] Isabelle may very well be invisible to her parents, but like many of the mute characters in Bergman's films, she functions as an omniscient being.[76] Isabelle too, we find out, knew about the infidelity of her father. She even knew and, in fact, regularly socialized with her father's lover, Margareta. We see her in a flashback spinning around to the Brahms tune with Margareta, thus linking the faithless world of her father to the scene in her attic where she turns around and round to the disembodied voice of the cellist. The sighing figures of the Brahms quartet suddenly make sense in the context of Isabelle's pain. Indeed, though she has an apparent inability to act directly and effectively within the narrative, Isabelle powerfully affects our emotions and subversively affects her parents, and might be seen as a personification of music.

Conclusion

In interview, Ullmann has admitted:

> I saw myself as the woman who is asked to come into [Bergman's] work room and give images to his story. And he felt that these are images [he] cannot do himself, or [he didn't] want to do. [He] wanted a woman's images, her experiences. So he asked me to direct it. . . . So I've done it with tremendous love for him but also because it gave me a voice in someone else's script.[77]

Indeed, much has been made of the images that Ullmann gave to this film, but what is truly remarkable is the sonic world she provides. Though Bergman saw himself as providing the *Score for an Image-Medium*, it is undeniable that Ullmann played a huge role in helping to musicalize *Faithless* too.

After signing on to direct the film, Ullmann took a year to research Bergman's films as she "wanted *Faithless* to be a bit of an homage."[78] Musical homage abounds—from her use of *The Magic Flute* arias and the Brahms quartet, to her use of cluster chords to evoke a world of imagination, to her use of the closely miked i-voice of authority, to the use of the silent/mute omniscient character (Isabelle), to the use of a silent scream to connote a moment before a psychological breakthrough (Bergman).

Faithless provides countless examples of autobiographical, narrative, visual, and sonic metareference. Beyond musical metareferences to *Backanterna*, *The Magic Flute*, and the Brahms's quartet Op. 60, music also performs a metaleptic function, transgressing boundaries between the different narrative levels.

In my view, music is doing more than providing a smooth transition between flashback and flash-forward. It's doing more than simply acting as a common thread to bind together all the strands of stories. While our thoughts are poised, wavering in these in-between spaces, meta-moments are created as music takes on a ludic quality, jumping the fantastical gap between conscious and unconscious, transgresses between past and present between framing narratives and main narrative, between films, and, between autobiography and fiction. Perhaps most pertinent in the case of the consummate auteur, Ingmar Bergman, these meta-moments celebrate the creator, author, or "manager of metaleptic surprises."[79]

Ullmann's own conflicted sense of ownership and identity in the film has been expressed in various interviews:

> And afterwards, it's tough because if it goes well, it's a Bergman movie, and if it goes bad, I ruined his script. But still, it's a great privilege that you work with someone like that. So if [the public] likes it and says it's a Bergman movie, that's okay with me. . . . I do sometimes get tired of. . . . you know, I am not me. I am the muse of Ingmar, or he is my mentor. And you know, he has never been my mentor.[80]

And in another interview Ullmann states, "I was faithful, I didn't do things that I thought would be wrong against who he is," demonstrating that there were indeed constraints that Ullmann felt—constraints to please Bergman.[81] As he warned her, "When I gave it to you, I gave it to you with trust."[82]

The story that Ullmann has related about the battle for ownership before the film's release at Cannes, plays out like the ugly power struggle between Nurse Alma and Elisabeth Vogler in *Persona* for identity and artistic voice. Bergman had been unhappy with the scene in the film where Josephson walks on the beach, and he demanded that Ullmann remove it. In the end, Ullmann prevailed and her cut of the film is what exists today. In a meta-moment, Bergman "is featured in a similar scene in the documentary", *Bergman Island* (2006), where he walks along the beach. In an interesting twist, Ullmann takes pride today that this is an example of Bergman paying homage to *her*.[83]

As explained by Rugg, "[Auteur] directors often present an autobiographical connection, only to undo it, undermine it, complicate it."[84] By asking Ullmann to direct his screenplay, does Bergman solidify or undermine his auteur-voice? Is this an experiment in which Bergman set himself up to be critically deconstructed by Ullmann, dissected in the same way he psychologically dissects his characters on screen? Was this his way of discovering whether Ullmann had internalized his cinematic style to such a degree that she was able to visually and sonically (re)-create a Bergman film? In this way, Ullmann *is* the ultimate transgressor of boundaries, metaleptically seizing control of a screenplay to implement Bergman's own directorial voice through indirect means as she projects an image of Bergman back onto a constructed vision of the great auteur. In the end, the muse eats the artist and assumes his identity. It is a cannibalistic theme that Bergman returned to many times over his career.[85]

As I have shown, Bergman's script and Ullman's direction play with different kinds of metareference and metalepsis to create wonderfully multilayered cinematic magic. One of the most powerful devices they use in this shared creative endeavor is music. Music can break the rules, transgress the walls of different realities, and thus become an active force in the film, almost like a character or an object passed around between different temporalities and ontological spaces.[86]

In *Faithless*, the auteur's voice appears to be silent while director Liv Ullmann speaks. But these identities and the identities in the various plots of the film inevitably meld. This forces viewers to question whose film they are watching, whose presence they feel, and whose voice they heard.

Upon its release, reviewers of *Faithless* were divided over whether to praise Ullmann for internalizing Bergman's cinematic language, to applaud her for being true to her own directorial voice, or to chastise her for copying Bergman's style.[87] Ultimately, *Faithless* is Bergman *and* Ullmann's film. It appears to assume the guise of a love story—but it might more accurately be understood as a modernized *Persona* for the millennium. Undeniably though, it is a brilliant demonstration of Ullmann's ability to play on narrative and sonic planes, with concepts of meta-cinema.

Notes

1   Heartfelt thanks to Maaret Koskinen and Louise Wallenberg and to Bergman workshop members, friends, and ghosts at Fårö: Paisley Livingston, Linus Tunström, Katinka Faragó, Måns Reutersward, and John Skoog.
2   Ingmar Bergman, *Trolösa*, Filmberättelser 33 (Stockholm: Norstedts, 2018).
3   Thomas Hanzon had previously acted in another Ullmann/Bergman film of infidelity, *Enskilda samtal/Private Confessions* (1996), where he played Ingmar Bergman's father. Irving Singer interprets the love triangle in *Faithless* as a version of the Tristan myth. See *Ingmar Bergman, Cinematic Philosopher: Reflections on His Creativity* (Cambridge, MA and London: MIT Press, 2007), 91–6. Screen couple Hanzon and Endre were an actual married couple (1986–99) and divorced shortly before *Faithless* premiered.
4   Stan Schwartz, "New York Film Festival 2000 Interviews: Liv Ullmann on Faithless," *IndieWIRE* (September 16–21, 2000) in Long, *Liv Ullmann Interviews*, 170.

5   Josephson, a lifelong friend and longtime actor in Bergman films was an obvious choice while Endre had performed for Bergman at Stockholm's Royal Dramatic Theater in *Romeo and Juliet*, *The Misanthrope* and *Peer Gynt*. Bergman claims he saw Lena Endre's face before him when he wrote the screenplay for *Trolösa*. Bergman dedicates the screenplay to *Lena and Liv*, referring to Liv Ullmann and actress Lena Endre.
6   Richard Porton, "Actress Behind the Camera: An Interview with Liv," *Cineaste* (Spring 2001): 32; in Robert Long, *Liv Ullmann Interviews*, 211.
7   Manuscript is dated Fårö, September 10, 1997. Bergman Archives, b197Arbetsmanus, Långfilm. Thank you to Jan Holmberg and Hélène Dahl for permission to view this manuscript. For a modern edition of this first version of the screenplay see Swedish publishing house Norstedts's 2000 and 2018 publications.
8   Performed by Sveriges Radios Symfoniorkester; conducted by Joakim Unander.
9   Performed by Stefan Bojsten (piano), Ulf Forsberg (violin), Pascal Siffert (viola), Ola Karlsson (cello).
10 Performed by Kungliga Teaterns kör; conducted by Kjell Ingebretsen (Caprice Records).
11 Performed by Dragspelsimprovisation: Love Malmsten. Although Bergman had drawn from the repertory of these composers (with the exception of Börtz) for other films, the precise musical excerpts chosen by Ullmann are unique only to *Faithless*. Note that in Bergman's original screenplay, only *Backanterna* and the Brahms quartet are referenced.
12 Alexis Luko, *Sonatas, Screams, and Silence: Music and Sound in the Films of Ingmar Bergman* (New York and London: Routledge, 2016).
13 We learn later that Marianne has drowned and that old Bergman is plagued with guilt because he did not support her after leaving the relationship.
14 Bergman staged Luigi Pirandello's *Six Characters in Search of an Author* in 1967. Like the play's characters in search of an author, Marianne searches for a screenplay writer and Bergman seeks out a director/voice for his work. Thanks to Maaret Koskinen for bringing this to my attention. According to Ullmann: "To me, the most fascinating of the two stories is between the writer and the woman. . . . you really see this back and forth [tension] between the writer/director and the woman/actress, the play of power, and all of that. So that is what attracted me." See Schwartz, "New York Film Festival 2000 Interviews," 169.
15 Besides Strindberg's *Dreamplay*, one might also think of Isaak Borg of Bergman's *Smultronstället/Wild Strawberries* (1957), who looks back at pivotal life episodes of love and regret. In the interview, Ullmann claims that she conceived of the David-character as the writer in his younger years: "The writer in the story must be you because he's called Bergman." Quoted in Stephen Pizzello, "Through a Glass Darkly:

Ullmann Analyzes Bergman," *American Cinematographer* 82 #1 (January 2001): 24–8, in Robert Long, *Liv Ullmann Interviews*, 173.
16 Ibid., 175.
17 Porton, "Actress Behind the Camera"; in Robert Long, *Liv Ullmann Interviews*, 209.
18 TIFF Talk: *Faithless* with Liv Ullmann (October 23, 2018), youtube.com/watch?v=zzdk9yPi1z8. Accessed June 2, 2020.
19 In *Unquiet*, the autobiographical novel by Linn Ullmann (daughter to Liv Ullmann and Ingmar Bergman), she complains "but the truth is you can never know much about other people's lives, least of all your parents', and certainly not if your parents have made a point of turning their lives into stories that they then go on to tell with a God-given ability for not caring the least about what's true and what's not" (p. 4).
20 An artist, ghosts, an island, music from *The Magic Flute*, and a story told from a woman's perspective (by Alama played by Liv Ullmann) are also narrative elements found in *Hour of the Wolf*.
21 Roger Long, "Interview with Liv Ullmann: Ullmann as a Director," in *Liv Ullmann Interviews*, 222.
22 Gerald Peary, "Interview with Liv Ullmann," *Boston Phoenix* (March 2–8, 2001), in Robert Long, *Liv Ullmann Interviews*, 200.
23 Ingmar Bergman, *The Magic Lantern: An Autobiography*, trans. Joan Tate (New York: Viking, 1988), 158–71.
24 Maaret Koskinen, "Out of the Past: Saraband and the Ingmar Bergman Archive," in *Ingmar Bergman Revisited: Peformance, Cinema and the Arts*, ed. Maaret Koskinen (London and New York: Wallflower Press, 2008). Koskinnen's chapter is republished at ingmarbergman.se/en/universe/bergman-revisited, accessed June 2, 2020.
25 Jan Holmberg, *Författaren Ingmar Bergman* (Stockholm: Norstedts, 2018), 162.
26 Ingmar Bergman Archives, F:093.
27 Bergman, *The Magic Lantern*, 161.
28 Björn Larsson and Karin Thunberg, "På Fårö avslöjades sanningen om papa," *Svenska Dagbladet* (November 13, 2004). svd.se/pa-faro-avslojades-sanningen-om-pappa. Accessed June 2, 2020.
    Ingmar Bergman and Maria von Rosen, *Tre dagböcker* (Stockholm: Norstedts, 2004).
29 Jan Holmberg, "Afterword," in *Trolösa*, ed. Ingmar Bergman (Stockholm: Norstedts, 2018), 117. Holmberg describes the "enmeshed layers" of *Faithless* (the screenplay) "in an intricate embroidery where the threads can hardly be followed even if you turn the fabric over and look to the back for clues." Jan Holmberg, *Författaren Ingmar Bergman* (Stockholm: Norstedts, 2018), 162.

30 Linda Rugg, *Self-Projection: The Director's Image in Art Cinema* (Minneapolis and London: University of Minnesota Press, 2014), 10.

31 For a similar discussion of metalepsis, music, and film, see Alexis Luko, "Dream weaving and sonic metalepsis in Jan Troell's Land of Dreams," *Journal of Scandinavian Cinema* 11(3): 243–265.

32 See Werner Wolf, "Metalepsis as a Transgeneric and Transmedial Phenomenon: A Case Study of the Possibilities of *Exporting* Narratological Concepts," in *Narratology Beyond Literary Criticism: Mediality, Disciplinarity*, ed. Jan Christoph Meister (Berlin and New York: Walter de Gruyter, 2003), 83–108 (quoted here at 91). Also see Gérard Genette, *Narrative Discourse: An Essay in Method* (Ithaca: Cornell University Press, 1972) and Gérard Genette, *Métalepse: De la figure à la fiction, Collection Poétique* (Paris: Seuil, 2004).

33 Werner Wolf, ed., *Metareference Across Media: Theory and Case Studies*, Studies in Intermediality 4 (Amsterdam: Rodopi, 2009).

34 Wolf, "Metalepsis as a Transgeneric and Transmedial Phenomenon," 91. Sonja Klimek provides an easy-to-grasp example of how, at the level of character, transgressions can occur in two different directions: "when things or characters from the level of representation introduce themselves on the level of what is represented (ascending metalepsis); and descending metalepsis when fictitious things or characters come to life on the level that includes the representation of their own fictitious world." Sonja Klimek, "Metalepsis and Its (Anti-)Illusionist Effects in the Arts, Media and Role-Playing Games," in *Metareference across Media*, 170.

35 Janet H. Murray, *Hamlet on the Holodeck* (New York: Free Press, 1997); Alison McMahan, "The Effect of Multiform Narrative on Subjectivity," *Screen* 40, no. 2 (1999): 146–57; Matthew Campora, "Art Cinema and New Hollywood: Multiform Narrative and Sonic Metalepsis in Eternal Sunshine of the Spotless Mind," *New Review of Film and Television Studies* 7, no. 2 (2009): 119–31; Matthew Campora, *Subjective Realist Cinema: From Expressionism to Inception* (Oxford and New York: Berghahn Books, 2014). Stavros Halvatzis, "Multiform and Multistrand Narrative Structures in Hollywood Cinema," PhD dissertation (University of Southern Queensland, 2011).

36 It was Gérard Genette who first established a vocabulary to describe narrative structure: "diegetic" (for a narrative event that is part of the diegesis) and "extra-diegetic" or "non-diegetic" (for a narrative event external to the diegesis).

37 On limitations of diegetic/non-diegetic definitions, see Robynn Stilwell, "The Fantastical Gap Between Diegetic and Nondiegetic," in *Beyond the Soundtrack: Representing Music and Cinema* (Berkeley and Los Angeles: University of California Press, 2007), 184–202; Jeff Smith, "Bridging the Gap: Reconsidering the

Border between Diegetic and Nondiegetic Music," *Music and the Moving Image* 2, no. 1 (Spring 2009): 1–25; Alexander Binns, "Desiring the Diegesis: Music and Self-Seduction in the Films of Wong Kar-Wai," in *Cinemusic? Constructing the Film Score*, ed. David Cooper, Christopher Fox, and Ian Sapiro (Newcastle: Cambridge Scholars Publishing, 2008), 127–40. Ben Winters, "The Non-Diegetic Fallacy: Film, Music, and Narrative Space," *Music & Letters* 91, no. 2 (2010): 224–44.

38 Claudia Gorbman, *Unheard Melodies: Narrative Film Music* (Bloomington: Indiana University Press, 1987). Gorbman, "Narrative Film Music," *Yale French Studies* 60 (1980): 183–203. Edward Branigan, *Narrative Comprehension and Film* (London and New York: Routledge, 1992), 87.

39 Guido Heldt, *Music and Levels of Narration in Film: Steps across the Border* (Bristol and Chicago: Intellect Books, 2013), 80–4.

40 Campora, "Art Cinema and New Hollywood."

41 In Bergman's original screenplay, Isabelle is mentioned in four scenes: (1) Isabelle tells a story about an ugly troll-boy under her bed with a blue shawl and a ghost with a yellow face who steals the shawl and consequently turns blue; (2) Isabelle tells a story about a dream of an angel in red with red wings and red hair, with yellow broken teeth. She jumps out the window to try to fly; (3) Isabelle's dream of a woman eating a child; and (4) a final scene in which Marcus attempts to hurt her and turn her against her mother by telling her about an aborted half-sibling (a product of her mother's adulterous affair) and testimonial of her mother's lack of love for her daughter. Bergman's odd parenthetical denouement to Isabelle's story reads like a clinical assessment:

"Isabelle got married when she was just 23 years old. The relationship was happy and she became pregnant. A few months after her descent, she suffered a severe depressions which in turn resulted in hospital stays and extensive analytical treatment. Eventually she was haunted by conversations with her father. . . . She instinctively knew that her father . . . wanted to hurt her even though he continually assured her that he loved her."

42 Schwartz, "New York Film Festival," in *Ullmann Interviews*, 170.

43 Porton, "Actress Behind the Camera"; in Robert Long, *Liv Ullmann Interviews*, 210.

44 On cinematic auteurship, Linda Rugg has written how, "One sign of the auteurist film's construction of a palpable subjectivity . . . is the frequent employment of autobiographical gestures." Rugg, *Self-Projection*, 9.

45 Birgitta Steene reports on a press conference held on May 9, 1998, in *Ingmar Bergman: A Reference Guide* (Amsterdam: Amsterdam University Press, 2005), 350.

46 Rugg, *Self-Projection*, 11.

47 Ibid., 10.

48 Roger Ebert, "Liv Ullmann and Memories of Bergman," *Interviews* (February 16, 2001), rogerebert.com/interviews/liv-ullmann-and-memories-of-bergman. Accessed June 2, 2020.
49 August Strindberg, "A Dream Play," in *Five Plays* (Berkeley and Los Angeles: University of California Press, 1983), 205.
50 *The Bacchae*, arguably one of Euripides's greatest tragedies, is known as idiosyncratic for having a chorus that is integrated into the plot and a god that is an actual character in the play. This in itself is a type of narrative transgression, where Dionysius and the chorus leap from their own worlds to populate scenes within the main diegesis. The Bacchanalia myths involved cultic rites with loud music and ecstatic dancing that would purportedly become so frenzied that the souls of the bacchae would attain release from their bodies. In these rituals, music played a dual role, simultaneously liberating the bacchae and violently tearing them apart.
51 How *faithful* Ullmann remains to the script is up for debate. She explains that she "didn't change a word or comma . . . because I knew he's very protective of his lines." But, in the same breath she also admits, "since it was a 5 hour script, I had to do a lot of cutting" (206–7). Porton, "Actress Behind the Camera"; in Robert Long, *Liv Ullmann Interviews*, 206–7.
52 From the end of Act I of the Bachae by Bergman and Börtz.
53 Robert Emmet Long, "Interview with Liv Ullmann," in *Liv Ullmann Interviews*, ed. Robert Emmet Long (Mississippi: University of Mississippi Press, 2006), 223.
54 Bergman, *Trolösa*, 11.
55 Here, embedded within the title itself, where the words of a script are referred to as a soundtrack to be paired with images, Bergman plays with the notion of "transmedial transposition." This keeps with Bergman's lifelong preoccupation with playing with the individual elements that make up the medium of film (e.g., still photographs, single frame sounds of off-screen film crews, single pitches, reading letters/scripts). By shattering cinema into pieces and revealing the seams, he reduces film to its elemental properties (visual, narrative, and aural), thereby exposing medial "in-betweenness." To this end, while the Wagnerian Gesamtkunstwerk seeks to bring things together, the Bergmanian aesthetic often delights in fragmentation of the whole into its constituent parts. Paraphrased from Luko, *Sonatas, Screams and Silence*, 228.
56 As described by Ullmann—the first take was as Marianne the "actress," and the second was as Marianne "the character." Emmet Long, "Interview with Liv Ullmann."
57 Ullmann's shooting script has the instructions: "Alla scener med Mariannes voice over i manus ska spelas in i arbetsrummet/närbild/ Detta gäller även alla andra voice over" ("All scenes with Marianne's voice over in script should be recorded in the study/close-up/ This also applies to all other voice overs.") The shooting

script can be viewed at the Bergman Archives in Stockholm: b218, Version: Fårö 5, dialogmanus. May 26, 1999, 2. Thanks to Jan Holmberg and Hélène Dahl at the Bergman Archives for permission to view this document.
58 Michel Chion, *The Voice in Cinema* (New York: Columbia University Press, 1999), 49.
59 Ibid., 51.
60 Chion points out that the i-voice must be dry for it to be intimate enough to resonate "in us as if it were our own voice." Reverb situates the voice in a space, distancing the voice, making it less of a "subject with which the spectator identifies." 51.
61 A beautiful *Magic Flute* tapestry, made by Anita Grede, hangs in his private cinema on the island of Fårö (the movie theater also served as the humble site of the premiere of his opera). "The tapestry Trollflöjten på Fårö," by Anita Grede, 1975. See Bukowskis Catalogue, *The Ingmar Bergman Auction: 28 September 2009*, 97.
62 See liner notes by Ingmar Bergman for: *Trollflöjten/The Magic Flute/Die Zauberflöte*. LP-box, SR Records RXLP 1226/28 (1974/1975). The original sound recording for Ingmar Bergman's television film "The Magic Flute" Radiokören and Sveriges Radios Symfoniorkester, conducted by Eric Ericson. Also see *Trollflöjten*, Directed by Ingmar Bergman and Conducted by Eric Ericson (Sweden: Svensk Filmindustri, Svenska Filminstitutet, 1975). And *Tystnad! Tagning! Trollflöjten!* Directed by Måns Reuterwärd and Katinka Faragó (Sveriges Television, 1975).
63 Are the miniature puppets an ode to the miniature people of James Whale's 1935 *The Bride of Frankenstein*? Tamino cries out, "O dark night, when will you disappear? When will I find light in darkness?" The chorus answers ambivalently, "Soon, soon or never more." Bergman describes how this passage has "the most agitating music . . . twelve measures [that] involve two questions at the outermost limit of life."
64 For example, in *Smiles of a Summer Night*, an astronomical clock plays the religious hymn tune "I Himmelen I himmelen," self-consciously punctuating the three metaphorical "smiles" of the film, while a mechanized bed, which plays a delightful tune on the celesta, brings two unsuspecting lovers together through a secret panel in a wall. In the case of the clock and the mechanical bed, these are machines that operate automatically, or "possessed," without human control.
65 The odd makeup of the music box is remarked on by Bergman in his liner notes to *The Magic Flute* LP: "Papageno's bells have always surprised me. . . . some sort of lyre with bells hung up on traverse sticks . . . probably set in motion by keys which cause little hammers to strike bells tuned to different notes—at least that's what the music sounds like."

66 Continuation of *Ein Mädchen oder Weibchen* . . .

Dann schmeckte mir Trinken und Essen;	Then drink and food would taste good to me;
Dann könnte' ich mit Fuersten mich messen,	Then I could Measure myself with princes,
Des Lebens als Weiser mich freun,	Enjoy life as a wiseman,
und wie im Elysium sein.	And feel like I'm in Elysium.
Ach, kann ich denn keiner von allen den reizenden Mädchen gefallen?	Ah, can I not please any of all Those charming girls?
Helf' eine mir nur aus der Not,	If only someone would help me out in this need,
Sonst gräm¹ ich mich wahrlich zu Tod.	Otherwise I will worry myself to death.
Wird keiner mir Liebe gewähren,	If no one will grant me love,
So muss mich die Flamme verzehren;	Then the flame must consume me;
Doch küsst mich ein weiblicher Mund,	Still, if a womanly mouth kisses me,
so bin ich schon wieder gesund.	Then I will be immediately healthy again.

67 A shot of a rowboat on the water serves as a not-so-subtle homage to Bergman's *Smiles of a Summer Night*.

68 In Bergman's screenplay the setting is supposed to be Bois de Vincennes. Bergman, *Trolösa*, 46.

69 A comparable music box is found in *Shame*, where Jan and Eva temporarily escape the horrors of war by listening to a Meissen music box.

70 Movement III of the Brahms quartet introduces a pathos-laden sequence of descending thirds in the upper-register of the cello. The cello was a favorite Bergman instrument, with the slow thoughtful *Saraband* movements of Bach's unaccompanied cello suites figuring prominently in many of his films (e.g., *Saraband, Through a Glass Darkly*, and *Cries and Whispers*). See Luko, *Sonatas, Screams, and Silence*, Chapter 5.

71 I located a score of the quartet in Bergman's private home library and curiously, the second movement is lightly marked with annotations.

72 Luko, *Sonatas, Screams, and Silence*, Chapter 5. Adding a level of meta-perplexity, musical repetition also happens to be a central aspect of Liv Ullmann's sonic style, particularly obvious in her films *Miss Julie*, and *Private Confessions*.

73 Other examples of Bergman's camera studying the faces of musical listeners can be found in *Höstsonaten/Autumn Sonata* (1978), *Ansikte mot ansikte/Face to Face* (1976), *The Silence, Persona, Hour of the Wolf, Saraband*, Bergman's 1975 television production of Mozart's *The Magic Flute* (and many other films).

74 Porton, "Actress Behind the Camera"; in Robert Long, *Liv Ullmann Interviews*, 210.

75 Pizzello, "Through a Glass Darkly," 24–8; Robert Long, *Liv Ullmann Interviews*, 177. The ignored/silent child theme surfaces in *The Silence, Fanny and Alexander, Autumn Sonata* and *Persona* (among other films).
76 On mutes and acoustical beings, see Luko, *Sonatas, Screams, and Silence*, Chapter 6.
77 Schwartz, "New York Film Festival 2000 Interviews," in Robert Long, *Liv Ullmann Interviews*, 169.
78 Pizzello, "Through a Glass Darkly," 24–8; Robert Long, *Liv Ullmann Interviews*, 174.
79 Quoted in Wolf, "Metalepsis as a Transgeneric and Transmedial Phenomenon," 109.
80 Schwartz, "New York Film Festival 2000 Interviews," 170–1.
81 Shane Danielsen, "Liv Ullmann Part II," *The Guardian* (January 23, 2001), in Long, *Liv Ullmann Interviews*, 198.
82 Gerald Peary, "Interview with Liv Ullmann," *Boston Phoenix*, March 2–8, 2001; in Long, *Liv Ullmann Interviews*, 201.
83 TIFF Talk: *Faithless* with Liv Ullmann (October 23, 2018), youtube.com/watch?v=zzdk9yPi1z8. Accessed June 2, 2020.
84 Rugg, *Self-Projection*.
85 *Persona* and *Hour of the Wolf* serve as the best examples of this cannibalistic theme.
86 On music's negative powers over musicians and listeners, see Luko, *Sonatas, Screams, and Silence*.
87 See a summary of reviews in Birgitta Steene, *Ingmar Bergman: A Reference Guide* (Amsterdam: Amsterdam University Press, 2005), 351.

10

Bergman's *The Magician*

The Art of Creating Illusions

Allan Havis

To discuss Ingmar Bergman's philosophical propensities on screen thirteen years after his death is an invitation to examine his recurring lifelong fascination with a secret self and—more to the point—a self that is not readily discernible to oneself. This leads to the problems of divine faith and a world that is suffering a sacred negligence. It is a question that circumvents the fabric of entertainment and cultural comforts. Subsuming the question is the tracing of threads linking the artist to a deity and the same threads linking the artist to the combative commoner scorning the artist. This inquiry should also have a double needle: for the film director's sense of self and for the imagined characters' sense of self on screen.

The phenomenology on human personality and on critical self-narrative might share the rubric that the concept of "self" in the modern world most likely has a true core and not a particle or matter subject to the mercurial uncertainties of Quantum Mechanics. On this principle, perhaps a genuine, unique, and constant face can be found in the privacy of a bedroom mirror or in an actor's dressing room. Humanity has evolved to rely on masks and the sophisticated fluency of camouflage. The nineteenth-century Danish philosophy Søren Kierkegaard, known for melancholic existential and complex ontological polemics, wrote using many pseudonyms and disguises until he unveiled himself to Scandinavia as the Christian theologian who employed countless *nom de plumes*. He suffered painfully for this reveal more than he anticipated he would. Kierkegaard surpassed his initial doctoral work, *On the Concept of Irony with Continual References to Socrates*, with numerous publications and treatises on the concept of dread in an age of high individuality over society.

Kierkegaard in his publications passed himself off first as a cerebral narcissistic aesthete, then a respectable, civic ethicist, and eventually as an intense person of faith. Despite being a devout denizen of Copenhagen, he was hazed relentlessly like a wandering parasitic gadfly (not unlike Socrates in Athens) or a nomadic philosopher/artist of anarchy. He was so ridiculed in a satirical journal *The Corsair* for these excessive masquerades and his didactic pronouncements, that Danish families avoided naming their sons Søren for years to come. The very name Søren was fraught with shame but he pioneered intellectual culture which hungered for a commanding authenticity of thought tied to personal experience.

Italian playwright and novelist Luigi Pirandello, born a dozen years after Kierkegaard died, was equally engrossed by theatrical ironies and paradoxes of a single core identity and tandem to personal experience. These concerns were literary and sometimes ponderous, but not jargon for Freud and Jung per se. Undoubtedly, the challenge of a character in fiction without fixed mooring offered both tragic and comic possibilities, and Pirandello pursued in theater writings the dynamic, non-comedic contest between mask and face, posture and soul. With respect to the latter, Kierkegaard also was profoundly fixated on the dance for dominance between posture and soul. All of which helps give a vital framework in understanding Kierkegaardian chords of irony and dread along with Pirandello's morbid masking obsessions in Ingmar Bergman's oft-underappreciated, transitional film on the artist's ipseity of the late 1950s *Ansiktet* or *The Magician/The Face*.

While *The Magician/The Face* may not make the top tier of praised Bergman film works, there is something strangely brilliant, sardonic, and neurotically precise about this 1958 black-and-white tale starring Max von Sydow as the gaunt, title character. *The Magician* is artfully agile, concise, philosophical, and mysterious about the issue of identity within the realm of the exotic traveling thespian purporting to be a supernatural medium, mixing the masks of charlatan and mystic effortlessly, deliberately, playfully, and deceptively. Bergman's roving actors and grifters set in Sweden's 1840s (concurrent coincidently with Kierkegaard's life in Denmark) are charming cinematic creatures seen as an extended family of survivors or misfits, leaning heavily on two supporting female players that nearly match the mystique of the central character: a rascal grandmother and the illusionist's spouse as both powerbroker and cross-dresser (Figure 10.1).

Frank Gado, author of *The Passion of Ingmar Bergman*, presses the case about the dissonant blend of terror and humor that was justified by Bergman's

Figure 10.1 Perpetual performance by the charming cinematic creatures in *The Magician* (1958).

obligation to expand his screenplay for the contracted players of his company.[1] Material featuring the very glib Tubal (Åke Fridell), Vogler's impresario, spins like boulevard comedy or a spry divertissement. Fridell reprises the frothy, non-threatening role he created in Bergman's *Sommarnattens leende/Smiles of a Summernight* (1955). Seen in this construct, the comic relief scenes are deftly executed but can seem like accessories to a garment that was succinct. Gado went on to write that similar to many Bergman movies, *The Magician/The Face*:

> vibrates with echoes of earlier works. The filmmaker himself has repeatedly stated that *The Face* "corrects" *Evening of the Jesters*, although he has left unsaid what he corrected and how. Obviously, Albert Emanuel Volger resembles Albert Johansson in his humiliation, but the deeper connection—reflected by another Albert, Joakim's "important" alter ego in "The Fish"—seems embedded in the circus film's previously described psychological underlayers.[2]

Film scholars, critics, and cinephiles embraced *The Magician* for a variety of intriguing motifs on performance versus substance (art versus science), in contradiction to the discernible diorama of two clashing societies—church-going conventional homesteaders and shifty vagabonds without the umbrella of Christianity. Therefore, the movie as parable or period drama lent open analysis and interpretation about three discernible themes within: (1) the existential freedoms and vices of rootless artists and charlatans; (2) the powers of suggestion on stage and off (performance, hypnosis, and love potions); and (3) pagan folk legends with death's shadow over hypocritical villagers and all individuals of false piety and mendacity. Bergman's film casts judgment harshest on those having the most surface respectability. The moral pronouncement has a light, elliptical touch. The director adjusted his aesthetics and canvas for *The Magician* by degree, wit, and mood from his two previous richly heralded classics *Smultronstället/Wild Strawberries* (1957) and *Det sjunde inseglet/The Seventh Seal* (1957), for he had concocted a clever, personal, horror story that teases both the artist's tenuous self-respect and the problematic respect of a materialistic society. Unmistakably, the fixation on death is found in all three films. Still, as *The Magician* comes to what might be called a tragicomic finale, Bergman has argued for a happy, comedic ending—specifically for the acting troupe—while upending conventional bourgeois power structures and the police superintendent, along with tarnishing the dignity of the hosting villagers.

The Magician impressed critics as a scurrilous depiction of Malmö City Theatre during Ingmar Bergman's residency. Others critics and scholars found that the screen story was quite close to Gilbert Keith Chesterton's less-known one-act play *Magic* which Bergman had staged at the Gothenburg City Theatre between the staging of two of his own plays—*The Day Ends Early* and *Unto My Fear* in 1947. Most remarkable, Chesterton's play had as its primary idea the clash between a cold, skeptical scientist and a brash, eponymous conjurer—a platform which Bergman underscored in *The Magician*.[3] The dramatic performance in *Magic* was seen as a broadside against prominent entrepreneurs and scientists without ethics and social principle. The playwright sided with absolute faith, against a facile pragmatism fueled by money and material lust.

Underscoring the forensic thematic evidence from Pirandello's stage literature and Bergman's investigations on the artist battling autonomous invented identities, during his six-year term at Malmö City Theatre, his production of Pirandello's most celebrated drama, *Six Characters in Search of an Author*, was Bergman's major stage success to date. There were a few visual components (e.g., kerosene stage lamps, the old-fashion backdrop) of the Malmö City Theatre production of Pirandello that prefigured the sensibility of the climatic stage show in the parlor room of hosting gentleman Egerman.

> In Pirandello's intricate play marrying illusion with reality, Bergman allowed scenographer Per Falk to frame the stage as in a Baroque theatre peepshow, with a stucco-deck of gold and white and a kerosene lamp ramp. A sort of show of Russian dolls on stage. The old-fashioned backdrop enabled the audience to adjust to the suspense between the stage's illusion and the theatre's sparse reality, as there was no curtain in place beforehand. Within the frame of the mirror, one's gaze once again encountered the bare stage: an empty floor and naked walls without coulisse.[4]

In Bergman's production, he makes it known firsthand how the theater artists sense the double standard of being within the community of non-artists. "The public believes that it loves us when it sees us in light of our work and our public persona. But if we are seen without masks, we are instantly transformed into less than nothing."[5]

Bergman's *The Magician* aptly guides his audience to sense the myriad conceits of role, status, and even totem. The movie deftly frames the practical and ephemeral notions of identity many times throughout the narrative, in the linear scripted action and notably lighting Max von Sydow's character Albert Vogler with harsh-edged lines. The painterly illumination of Vogler manages to project a poseur's grandeur in tension with a penetrating inner misery of religious penitents. In addition, arch expressionistic cosmetics highlights the critical significance of the magician's blatant unambiguous naked continence that constitutes the face as *The Face*. As described in Bosley Crowther's *New York Times* 1959 film review:

> Max von Sydow as the magician is a haunting figure who floats between the realms of an agonized mystic and a vulgar charlatan. And he recalls the late Lon Cháney in his sad unmasking scene and in the one he plays with the surgeon, brilliantly performed by Gunnar Bjornstrand.[6]

There is something capricious in Vogler's mien and disposition. His service to others tips to the conjurer's role over the role of thespian. When a film clip of *The Magician* is shown in universities, it often is of Albert Vogler removing his performance disguise in the presence of his wife or Vogler without moustache and beard terrorizing Dr. Vergérus during the film's climactic autopsy scene. It is this dual persona and dichotomy of identity that is sometimes alluded to in some thread of Bergman cinematic theory regarding a "double self" divided into two characters (intuitive vs. analytic; feminine vs. masculine) as well as a Dr. Jekyll and Mr. Hyde compact inside one individual.[7] Perhaps the striking Pirandellian concern herein regarding fictional characters and their artifice in dispute with the creator of the illusion, the unveiling of the rootless actor/magician and the interface between actor/magician and spectator. In Pirandello's *Six Characters in Search of an Author*, the existential malcontent of fictitious creations challenge the thin conceits of the so-called playwright; the playwright as an inferior god if you will.

While Bergman's film script avoids polemics and overt philosophical speculation on human truth, the unfolding tale presents an arresting example of the acute frisson between illusion and reality of his lead figures, between the realms of existence and imagination, between the empirical world and the unseen supernatural world, between sanity and madness, and finally between the fleeting notion of temporal life versus the eternal arc demarcated by death. Pirandello's stage characters like Bergman's travelers in *The Magician* are assigned to a perpetual performance and, on occasion, are allowed to drop the masks of deceit and subterfuge. Doing so frees them momentarily and transcends the stigma of being typed into one person, and frozen as it were between narrative and dramatic form. In their life on stage or on screen, characters enact a routine that passes as identifiable truth but is only a fraction of the truth. These heightened, self-posturing characters attempt to possess themselves forcefully as they work to sustain a cast of their own whether or not incongruent to the current circumstances, attempt to tell their life-stories, and attempt to press themselves before their most prominent antagonist, which is either the requisite threatening skeptic on stage/screen or perhaps the reigning film director/storyteller. According to Olivier Assayas in his short essay. "A Portrait of the Artist: on Bergman's 'The Magician'": "For in the center of his moving universe, this baroque forest of signs and symbols, we find a figure, the mesmerist Vogler, Bergman's first major self-portrait."[8]

Wonderfully amoral, roguish, and spirited, Granny played by Naima Wifstrand has fewer restraints and inhibitions than her troupe colleagues. Claiming to be 200 years old, she is a portrait of a geriatric Rabelaisian bathed in stark, chilling light. "And who is that weird old woman who tags along with the troupe?"[9] Tagged bawdily by this bald question in Crowther's *New York Times* review, Granny could be the less charming precursor to Ruth Gordon's iconographic anarchist approaching her eightieth birthday nearly a dozen years later in Hal Ashby's black comedy on the fetishes of suicide and ceremonial death, *Harold and Maude*. Bergman's aberrant Granny has discernible traces to Georg Büchner's Grandmother figure in his 1833 early modernist, sardonic theater work

Woyzeck. In it, Grandmother recounts in spare prose a dreary fairytale about a young child to whom everything in life became a disappointment, carrying the darkest philosophical statement in Büchner's view on this lonely planet devoid of any love from supernatural beings. Bergman's Granny is rendered, by contrast to Büchner, more rogue and slightly less ghoulish, holding superstitious practices from the early 1800s.

In Bergman's *The Magician*, we see again the elegiac horse-drawn carriage from the two previous period movies of this decade—*The Seventh Seal* and *Wild Strawberries*; we see innocent maids flirting about, superfluous but necessary love potions, understated demonic apparitions leading to a stunning vengeance, and a surprise happy ending. The entourage is named, "Vogler's Magnetic Health Theater," which entails a contradiction whether villagers will be healed, heralded, or entertained. They are coming from Kierkegaard's stately Copenhagen and will eventually go to Stockholm. Sometimes Vogler is addressed as Doctor Volger, and other times he is not afforded the honor. Nonetheless, in the movie's central locus, the tall, imposing mesmerist Vogler is both faker and fakir. Vogler might also be the understudy for Bergman himself to inhabit the contents of Bergman's story. If you will, Bergman's alter ego—a mute magician bankrupt of belief knows only how to entertain others in a one-night's stand. He must leave by morning lest he be captured—imposter that he is. All that remains for the tall illusionist is his obligations to his select entourage and to the secret love of his wife played sharply by Ingrid Thulin as if she were in a crime thriller. Through the Manda/Mr. Aman gender switching which is revealed later in the film without a direct explanation, Manda pretends to be a man of great discipline. This disguise is pivoted within the intimacy of the bedroom, where she lets herself don sexy negligees with hair luxuriously long and fair. It is in these private scenes between Vogler and Manda where the audience is privileged to hear Volger's voice and glean his inner life as a married man, sensing that he is far from impotent as a husband.

Examining the uncomplicated narrative track, the movie's opens with a quirky mobile troupe responding to a village summons, and in transition to the next town Vogler wandering desolate land stumbles upon an incapacitated stage actor John Spegel who requests alcohol and a quiet rescue. Spegel (the name means mirror in Swedish) unmasks his rescuer instantly telling Vogler he sees the fake beard and moustache which undresses Vogler absolutely. Spegel identifies Vogler's wife despite her male disguise as well which enhances the paranormal capacities of this tertiary character. Symbolically, Vogler is Spegel's next of kin in this deserted landscape, much more than a compatriot of theater. Entering the carriage, Spegel joins them on the voyage ahead which is short lived for this drifter. Looking cursed and abject, the actor dies while locking eye contact with Vogler. This incident hits rather suddenly and portends further death encounters to come. The posthumous Spegel, symbolically, is both the mirage and the supernatural mirror image for Vogler. Vogler happens upon this lost actor as if in a nightmare and Vogler may wonder if his fate is foretold by Spegel's anonymous fatality. Moreover, Bergman makes efficient use of Spegel's corpse for a macabre plot device in the game of Vogel's retribution to a common nemesis. It could be interpreted as well that Spegel's corpse gives Vogel a poetic resurrection, supporting some interpretations that Vogel is a Christlike figure in the tale.

Adding to the troupe's woes upon arrival at the mansion of a condescending politician, played by Erland Josephson, Vogler's band is held overnight on suspicion of chicanery and unlawfulness. Adding insult to injury, Vogler is forced to demonstrate in front of an informal jury his magical powers and the capacities of animal magnetism. Most skeptical of them all stands the unlikeable arrogant scientist Dr. Vergérus, played by Gunnar Björnstrand. Rounding out the biased panel is Starbeck the commissioner, performed by Tovio Pawlo. The quick outline of this impromptu contest turns out to be a dramatic event severely harsh, preordained, presentational. Reason, which assumes the form of Dr. Vergérus's absolute materialism battles the open mechanics of the shamanistic Dr. Vogel. The parlor room performance entails cheaply sensational stunts, including levitation and an invisible chain which overcomes the muscular powers of a healthy man. Coldly rendered, Vergérus signifies an aggressive certainty and supremacy about modern science and elite European empiricism which override centuries of human intuition, the disreputable occult, and—by inference—any and all spiritual faith about invisible life. Vergérus serves as an early malevolent archetype for Bergman's subsequent films, a bully obsessed with the desire to unmask Vogler, to publicly humiliate him, and destroy Vogler's future. As film director, screenwriting and critic Olivier Assayas states in *Cahiers du Cinéma*:

> Beneath this hideous figure, one of the worst incarnations of Bergman's phobia of criticism and exegesis—which he nonetheless frenetically feed in *The Magician*—we find the first sinister incarnation of the kind of evil that moves throughout his cinema, and that we will reencounter bearing the same name, appearing each time more terrifying, as in *The Serpent's Egg*, already growing in *The Magician*, and of course in the very similar *Fanny and Alexander*.[10]

Vergérus is akin to the pernicious theater/gallery critic who unconsciously despises the fecund creativity of the celebrated artist and who tears into the official assessment of the mysterious art proffered. He is that sort of critic who gains indomitable joy delivering pain and failure to the vulnerable talent on stage or displayed on the museum wall. Bergman had confirmed that motivation.

> The health official [. . .] was born out of an irresistible desire to take a small revenge on Harry Schein. Schein was the movie critic at Bonniers litterära magasin, which at the time was a heavyweight cultural organ. Schein is intelligent and arrogant, and what he wrote was echoed in the inner circles. I felt that he treated me in an exceedingly humiliating manner, which he later insisted that he did not do.[11]

Vergérus is the sterile authority personified, an empty suit cloaking a negating agenda atop the contour of enlightened hypothesis and rationalism. This self-confident, reptilian figure holds nothing but contempt for Vogler. His envy is seen in his secondary behavior, in his small movements and gestures as well as his sharp verbal taunts. One might assume that he craves Vogler's charismatic stature, Vogler's access to silence and to the miraculous, which escapes Vergérus, just as he lusts after Manda, Vogler's clandestine wife. Vergérus secretly despises himself. Ironically, this visiting troupe is the agency of Vergérus's unmasking. We learn eventually that Vergérus does not doubt; in his panic attack upstairs in the attic he comes to believe in Vogler's powers, he's convinced. But he also knows Vogler's torments as common to his own, Vergérus's hidden uncertainty and how vulnerable it makes Vergérus, how much dignity and control Vergérus abandons to this philosophical vanity. Much of this disdainful, prejudicial dynamic occurs when Vergérus, with degrading dehumanization, examines Vogel's mouth and throat, proving to Vergérus and the spectators that Vogler has no medical pathology to take away his voice.

Perhaps not serving strictly as a ghostly sensational omen and certainly not the gothic chord of cinematic horror, the inexplicable actor's death early on exposes Bergman's anxiety over fragile human existence; beneath Vogler's phony carnival whiskers and hypnotically fatigued visage there's a self-doubting, aging man caught inside a private unflattering mirror. Quietly the film registers an indescribable dread about the precise moment of dying, of vacating the body, of losing speech forever, of losing all ties to other human beings, of forfeiting forever ownership of one's own existence. This may be a cinematic moment which aptly captures Kierkegaard's *Sickness Unto Death*, which is to say that the

Vogler is in despair when his soul does not align to God or God's plan for Vogler. Finally, there is prominent symmetry on this point with respect to Vergérus.

A shallow mesmerist in dissonance against evolving nineteenth-century reason and technology, Vogler is a little more than a jobless actor who finds himself trapped by his last successful role. The script's inane subplots seem to detract from the elegance of the moral crisis or at best deflect for lesser comic effect the profound ramifications of the climatic performance of the itinerant magician who can mesmerize and achieve near Godlike abilities. Again, without trickery the film's intense focus on Vogler's true self and on Vergérus's synthetic faith carry the contours of Kierkegaard's obsession with essence and façade, with person and persona. In Michael J. Stern's essay on Kierkegaard and Bergman, he writes:

> As a persona masks one appearance with another, a pseudonym masks an author identity, or a proper name. It too acts as a screen, and in Kierkegaard's case the pseudonym functions as an existential possibility that he claims has little or no relation to him.[12]

Stern delineated this theme with specific inquiry regarding Bergman's *Persona* (1966) and the psychiatric interplay between *Persona*'s two central characters Alma and Elizabeth. Further, it is Stern's fascination with the discarded attributes of the false front which illuminates the ineluctable nuances of the true soul. He applies an interesting and functional term—oscillation—about the psychic space between personae and the irony of the construction by the guiding character. With respect to Kierkegaard himself, Stern identifies Kierkegaard's more famous alias Constantin Constantius along with Bergman's twin, feminine avatars in *Persona*:

> The oscillation in the space between personae allows Contantin, Alma, Elizabeth, and us to move into *ek-stasis*, allows us to be both inside and outside of ourselves. The irony of the persona represented in the movement between the opaque border categories of subject and object creates the multiple masks of the decisionist text: persona, personae.[13]

When Tubal tries to seduce Sofia with moronic aphrodisiacs, she doesn't hesitate and returns the overture with unromantic candor like a shark merchant on a swift street sale. Not surprising, Tubal does not flinch or think twice; he accepts the crass bargain for the bargain that it is. Moreover, when Vogler's coachman, Simson, initiates sex with young Sara, Simson drinks the awful elixir, resounding the male impotence and artistic impotence ailments as intertwining. No matter which angle one inspects *The Magician*, how curious it is that Bergman imagined that the select target in his screen fiction was not Vogler, but Vogler's wife:

> But the actual focal point of the story is, of course, the androgynous Aman/ Manda. It is around her and her enigmatic personality that everything rotates. Manda represents the belief in the holiness of human beings. Vogler, on the other hand, has given up. He is involved in the cheapest kind of theater, and she knows it [. . .]. If Vogler is a magician, who, even though he is tired to death, keeps repeating his by now meaningless hocus-pocus, Tubal is the exploiter, the salesman of art.[14]

The slow building revenge scene in the claustrophobic attic with Vogel's corpse pits Vergérus against the illusory tricks of Vogel. Bergman and his masterly cinematographer Gunner Fischer fabricate a daunting, disquieting *mise-en-scène* transforming the commonplace into the sepulchral, the familiar into the extraordinary. First, Vergérus spies an eye in the ink well. Then a disembodied hand reaches out and touches his hand. The viewer realizes that this is a prosthetic but Vergérus does not. He then finds himself locked inside this dimly lit, confined space. Vergérus approaches a tilted full-length mirror and spots Vogel's face looking directly at him. The ashen corpse, it turns out, is of another individual. This is not Albert Vogel. Vergérus, visibly shaken loses his eyeglasses. The importance of his spectacles is dire, since he accidently steps on the glasses, victimizing himself again, and rendering Vergérus even more vulnerable to the punishing illusions of Vogel. Vergérus exclaims aloud that either he is dreaming or going insane. The onslaught continues, like cat and mouse, orchestrated by a fatalistic drumming, with hands from a wall section grabs Vergérus by the throat. This stagecraft and unnerving signature by Bergman in this sequence is one of humiliation by the puppeteer to the lowly godless puppet, with Vergérus forced into the subordinate role. It is a pattern tracked in several Bergman films by Birgitta Steene.[15] Finally, Vogler materializes without the false black beard and dyed eyebrows, showing his trim blonde head of hair. This would be the *coup de grâce*, as the film viewer senses Vergérus's death. Desperately Vergérus steps back and falls down the stairs, but does not die.

There is a second death in this story, coming immediately after Vogler's Magnetic Health Theater presentation. The coachmen, who was mesmerized and humiliated by imaginary chains bonding his hands, ends up killing himself outside the manor. In Bergman's script, Granny is first to find the coachmen hanging dead from the tree but she magically breathes life into him. Apparently, Bergman preferred a crueler and credible reality worked best in the film version.[16]

If we were to imagine *The Magician* to end differently and perhaps following the logic of just desserts with the certain demise of Vergérus, Bergman's film would occupy thoroughly the vehicle known as the modern black-and-white horror movie. For Bergman's purposes, however, Vergérus does not perish and should not perish. The aftermath of the horrific scare to Vergérus and Vergérus's self-consciousness are more important to Bergman's teaching story. Bergman's audience happens upon a glimpse of Dr. Vergérus as though he were the clinical specimen. After the autopsy, Vergérus demands to know whose corpse he examined. Vogel replies curtly and poetically that it was a "poor actor." This only enrages Vergérus more, as he proclaims how much he deplores the troupe's performance. Bergman's dramatic irony follows suit with Vergérus paying the troupe for the entertainment, coins tossed with indignation upon the floor.

Despite the harrowing episode in the attic for Vergérus, the observed human behavior returns to a social comedy built on the clash of two societies that do not coalesce harmonically. We are witnessing serious drama grafting onto a vaudevillian circus. As observed by Paisley Livingston in his study on Ingmar Bergman *Ingmar Bergman and the Rituals of Art*, there is a striking chord of theatrical circus within Bergman's cinema which matches the direct equivalents of the universal artist's risky social conditions and the circus star's plight on the trapeze, the clown's mock battles with powerful enemies. Moreover, Livingston writes:

> Bergman's interest in the denizens of the circus, his methods of illustrating his own role by depicting nomadic performers of every sort, may seem anachronistic, but this does not lessen the validity of his approach. The chronology of art is never simple.[17]

Returning to the more mundane plotting, Bergman has us consider too that Manda instructs Simson to hitch up the horses, but Tubal stuns Manda that he will remain with Sofia who we imagined to be a disposable affair. Just as unexpectedly, Granny informs Manda she will stay in town and live on her meager savings. Wanting to join the troupe, however, is lovestruck Sara who wishes to accompany Simon. Sara asks Manda and Vogler for permission and her wish is granted. The police interrupt and Manda and her husband assume they will be arrested for some damning transgression. The Police Superintendent Starbeck to his chagrin conveys the news that The Royal Palace now requests their presence. The troupe's carriage then leaves for Stockholm and a command performance for the King of Sweden.

Filmmaker Woody Allen, noted lifelong Bergman admirer and apostle, had this to say about the high-minded Kierkegaardian scaffolding co-existing with the tangible greasepaint artifacts inside *The Magician*:

> Shortly after *Wild Strawberries*, I saw *The Magician*, an audacious black-and-white dramatization of certain Kierkegaardian ideas presented as an occult tale and spun out in an original, hypnotic camera style that reached its crescendo years later in the dreamlike *Cries and Whispers*. Lest the Kierkegaardian reference make the movie sound too dry or didactic, please be assured. *The Magician*, like most of Bergman's films, had one foot brilliantly planted in show business.[18]

Kierkegaard's central proposition about mortal existence which fits closely to *The Magician* is that "subjectivity is truth" and that validates the duality of the conjurer facing off in the presence of the modern scientist. It is an ineffable, dark idea about what the soul senses between comprehension and apprehension. Albert Vogel—a creature of show business—is a million miles from clinician Vergérus, and Vogel will never be looking for objective, scientific knowledge. Therefore, he has an advantage over Vergérus about the wounds we deny each day, about the death sentence everyone must face. Vogel, despite his personal dread, starts each day with an individual human soul, his own soul, and that soul's direct experience of life on this silent, eerie planet. Interesting to cite in conclusion that the filmmaker's childhood fixation with cinema initiated by his creative play using a rudimentary opaque projector, a precursor to Vogler's magic lantern.[19] Ingmar Bergman and Albert Vogel are seeing themselves as each other inside an eschatological looking glass caught between the realms of Kierkegaard and Pirandello.

Notes

1 Frank Gado, *The Passion of Ingmar Bergman* (Durham, NC: Duke University Press, 1986), 230.
2 Ibid., 237.
3 Ingmar Bergman Foundation, Holmberg, Jan, curator https://www.ingmarbergman.se/en/production/magic.

4 Henrik Sjögren, *Stage and Society in Sweden: Aspects of Swedish Theatre Since 1945* (Stockholm: The Swedish Institute/Ann Arbor: University of Michigan, 1979). 113.
5 Ingmar Bergman, *Images: My Life in Film*, trans. Marianne Ruuth (New York: Arcade Publishing, 1994), 164.
6 Bosley Crowther, *New York Times* Movie Review (August 1959), 27.
7 Michiko Kakutani, "Ingmar Bergman, Summing Up a Life in Film," in *New York Times Magazine* (June 1983), Section 6, 24.
8 Olivier Assayas, "A Portrait of the Artist: on Bergman's 'The Magician,'" in *Cahiers du Cinéma* (October 1990), 16.
9 Crowther, *New York Times* Movie Review, 27
10 Assayas, "A Portrait of the Artist: on Bergman's 'The Magician,'" 16.
11 Bergman, *Images*, 164.
12 Michael J. Stern, "Persona, Personae! Placing Kierkegaard in Conversation with Bergman," *Scandinavian Studies* 77, no. 1 (University of Illinois Press on behalf of the Society for the Advancement of Scandinavian Study, Spring 2005): 32.
13 Ibid., 50.
14 Bergman, *Images*, 164.
15 Birgitta Steene, *Ingmar Bergman: A Reference Guide* (Amsterdam: Amsterdam University Press, 2005), 31.
16 Stig Björkman, Torsten Manns, and Jonas Sima, *Bergman on Bergman, Interviews with Ingmar Bergman* (New York: Simon & Schuster, 1973), 122.
17 Paisley Livingston, *Ingmar Bergman and the Rituals of Art* (Ithaca: Cornell University Press, 2019), 67–8.
18 Woody Allen, "Through a Life, Darkly," in *The New York Times* (September 18, 1988), Section 7, 1.
19 Philip Mosley, *Ingmar Bergman, The Cinema as Mistress* (London: Marion Boyars Ltd, 1981), 94.

Author, Auteur, Actor

Twenty-one Fragments on Bergman, Ullmann, and *Persona*

James Schamus

Prologue
From a 1978 interview with Ingmar Bergman, Liv Ullmann, and David Carradine:

> **Bergman** (to Carradine and Ullmann): What is important is not the words you exchange, but the atmosphere, the relationship between both of you. Silence will speak on your behalf. (To Liv Ullmann) You're good at silences.
> **Liv Ullmann**: David and I are silent actors.
> **Bergman**: And I'm so talkative!
> **Liv Ullmann**: No, you are a silent director.
> **Bergman** (to J[ames] J[acobs]): Liv is very generous when she calls me a "silent" director. In 1943, when I met my drama teacher, who had been working in the theater for fifty years, he told me that a director should know two things: shut up, and listen to the actors.[1]

1.
Praising the German theater director Peter Palitsch, Liv Ullmann writes in her memoir, *Changing*, that he "never told me what I should think or do every moment of the time."[2] This directorial reticence is a mark, for Ullmann, of directorial talent: "It is only the untalented director who imagines himself in every part, wants his own thoughts and emotions portrayed; it is only the untalented who makes his own limitations those of the actor as well."[3]

Rather than *telling* the actor what to think or do, the talented director, according to Ullmann, "works on the actor's imagination and musicality."[4] That is, in whatever form the director communicates with the actor, "work" must always, in the end, replace words—must, indeed, do the work of words. Tellingly, though, for Ullmann, the actor, for their part, must also oddly refrain from putting their *own* thoughts and emotions legibly on the stage or screen: "I, who for years had kept Stanislavski's book on the art of acting by my bedside table, now began to look for other ways."[5] Turning away from the practice of so-called "Method" acting, in which the actor is called upon to mobilize their own, "real" emotions and memories—a practice Ullmann would throughout her later career loudly decry[6]—Ullmann instead embraces "technique," a focus on "details": "Less feelings, more concentration on giving expression to feelings."[7] And this expression, like the direction that inspires it, is not verbal, but, rather, and rather abstractly, "musical," an embodied if unheard harmony.[8]

Ullman gives as the exemplary instance of such technique—and the direction that spurs it—an anecdote from the set of *Persona* (1966), the first of many collaborations between Ullmann and Ingmar Bergman (and the film during the shooting of which they commenced a years-long romantic partnership).[9] Most of these collaborations figured Bergman as writer and director—as, we might say, author and auteur—and Ullmann as actor: *Skammen/Shame* (1968), *Vargtimmen/Hour of the Wolf* (1968), *En passion/The Passion of Anna* (1969), *Viskningar och rop/Cries and Whispers* (1973), *Scener ur ett äktenskap/Scenes from a marriage* (1973), *Ansikte mot ansikte/Face to face* (1976), *Ormens ägg/ The Serpent's Egg* (1977), *Höstsonaten/Autumn Sonata* (1978), *Saraband* (2003). But in later years, Ullmann became a director in her own right, and Bergman provided the screenplays for two feature films she directed, *Enskilda samtal/ Private Confessions* (1996) and *Trolösa/Faithless* (2000). Over the years, Ullmann and Bergman used the changing dynamics and oscillations they experienced between and through these roles—of author, auteur, and actor—as occasions to theorize their functions (we might call them *actantial* functions)[10] in the process of cinematic art-making.

The scene Bergman was shooting when he gave the direction Ullmann celebrates in *Changing* depicts Liv Ullmann's character, Elisabet Vogler (an actor who has been placed under psychiatric care after going silent while on stage during a performance of *Electra*), listening as the young nurse Sister Alma (Bibi Andersson), tasked with tending her, drunkenly recounts the story of an impromptu infidelity, a beachside orgy.

Here, from Bergman's account, quoted by Ullmann: "When we were going to shoot it, I told Liv that she must gather all her feelings into her lips. She had to concentrate on placing her sensibility there—it's possible, you know, to place your feeling in different parts of your body. . . . And that is what I insisted she did."[11]

The results of this direction were for Bergman readily apparent in Ullman's performance: "If you look at Liv's face, you can see that all the time it's swelling. It's fascinating—her lips get bigger, her eyes darker, the whole girl is transformed into a sort of greed. . . . One can see her face transformed into a sort of cold, voluptuous mask."[12]

Bergman and Ullman returned, over the years, and with some regularity, to this anecdote, one that became famous among critics, fans, and scholars.[13] But as we shall see, the story changed—wildly so—as the anecdote's meaning and its place in Bergman and Ullmann's creative histories were repurposed, revised, and reconsidered. In the notes and fragments that follow, I attempt to figure out why that moment on the set of *Persona* took on the roles it did in their public *personae*. My method is aleatory, fragmented, associative. I'll be connecting a lot of dots, but the resulting image will be, at best, a palimpsest, a kind of worried meditation on the stakes this seemingly trivial anecdote, with its lips, feelings, masks, and orgies, raises.

And if our main focus is on *Persona*, Ullmann's first collaboration with Bergman, and her depiction in that film of the rigorously silent actress Elisabet Vogler, we'll also keep in our sights Ullmann's final collaboration with Bergman, her rather, as we shall see, less-than-faithful directorial adaptation of Bergman's screenplay *Faithless*, a film whose two main characters are an actress named Vogler and a director named Bergman.[14] It is time to listen carefully to Ullmann's voice—or, as in *Persona*, to Ullmann's silence. For that silence—and the lips that embody it—have much to say about our received ideas of cinematic authorship and of auteur cinema, and thus of cinema as art, ideas entangled in contested material practices we call writing, directing, and acting, practices that Ullmann and Bergman relentlessly interrogated.

2.

So Ullmann's face became a "cold, voluptuous mask." Bergman has chosen his words to mark that face as a synecdoche of the film itself: in the ancient theater, for example, the one in which *Electra* would originally have been presented, the actors would have performed behind masks—*personae* in Latin—and Bergman, in preparing the film (and in changing its title, at the request of his producer, from *Kinematograph* to *Persona*), made much of the ambiguous and ambivalent slippage between the Latin meanings of *persona* as both person and mask.[15] We can thus get a sense of just what an accomplishment this directorial transformation of Ullmann's swelling lips might have meant for Bergman.

3.

Kinematograph—"writing in movement"—a perfect title for the kind of "self-reflexive," auterist, modernist film that is *Persona*. For Bergman, a writing incorporated into the lips of a silent/silenced mouth, transforming a face into a . . . *Persona*. And, as with Ullmann, a process in which *techne*, technique, replaces, does the work, of *graphé*, writing, and its directorial analog, telling. But let's not forget: the ancient theatrical mask may well also have been a *megaphone*, designed not simply to emblematize a character or type, but, according to some theater scholars, to modify and amplify the actor's voice and to clarify the text that voice carried.[16] According to Marco Mancini, for example, the tragic masks used by Roman actors "functioned as a sort of full face helmet for the actor and, thus, as proper filters, allowing the reinforcement of some bands of the laryngeal frequency, with an effect similar to that of lip protrusion."[17] Ullman's protruding, "swollen" lips visually mirror the sonic effects of the mask itself.

4.

Ullmann, again, from *Changing*: "We were so much alike. What he had not known about himself he began to see in me—as if in a mirror—despite the fact that I was a woman and much younger and perhaps unlike him in ways he didn't know."[18]

This passage describes the start of Ullmann and Bergman's relationship while they were shooting *Persona* on the island of Fårö. It begins with an acknowledgment of their alikeness—a major theme, of course, of *Persona* itself, and of the soul-sharing and soul-destroying relationship between the silent Mrs. Vogler and the chatty young nurse, Sister Alma, that the film depicts. Indeed, Ullmann here figures Bergman relating to his beloved as if he were seeing himself in a mirror, but what he sees there is something very odd. He sees what he had *not* known about himself. According to Ullmann, the amatory relationship here is founded on Bergman's overweening narcissism, but this is a narcissistic love not of a self for its own known self, but of a self in a state of epistemological lack regarding itself; love discloses the self to itself by placing what it doesn't know about itself in the image of the other.

5.

What, then, was Bergman looking at while seeing what he had not previously known about himself? While on the set of the film, he was looking of course at an *actor*, but an actor playing an actor—and not just any actor, but an actor who refuses, in a sense, to say her lines. If the mirror speaks only what is spoken to it, what is told to it, what is disclosed when the "talented" director in front of the mirror tries to preserve his silence, to refrain from "telling"?

6.
Except Ullmann wasn't portraying an actor: she was *pretending* to portray an actor in order really to portray a *director*. Here is how Ullmann explains it in a radio interview from 1993:

> I was 27, and the one thing I did understand was that I was doing Ingmar Bergman. And that's what I continued to do in a lot of the films, and just because he wanted to work with me, he made the role into a woman's role instead of a man's role. I was too young really to understand what an existential crisis was, and I was kind of a happy person, and it hadn't occurred to me that one had such crises. And today I understand much more. But I think my luck was that I somehow recognized Bergman and saw it's him I'm portraying. So I watched him and I did him on camera.[19]

We are meant thus to understand that the character of Elisabet Vogler is not who Ullmann is portraying; Vogler is herself a figure standing in for the male character of Bergman, the director, himself. Which is to say, for many years before she *became* a director, Ullmann *portrayed* a director, or, rather, represented a director—she "did him on camera." As she put it in another interview, "if at the time of *Persona* (Bergman) hadn't met me, and hadn't sensed that I understood him and the part, I think my role would have been written for Max von Sydow."[20]

7.
A further complication: Who was Bergman seeing when looking into the mirror that was Ullmann? Not, it seems, just himself. As many scholars have noted, the blending in *Persona* of Elisabet and Alma is a kind of remaking or mirroring of Bergman's own relationship to his most important artistic forebear, the nineteenth-century dramatist August Strindberg: "If you live in a Strindberg tradition," according to Bergman, "you are breathing Strindberg air. After all, I have been seeing Strindberg at the theater since I was ten years old, so it is difficult to say what belongs to him and what to me."[21]

Birgitta Steene calls this relationship between Bergman and Strindberg one of "symbiosis." As Bergman situates himself in this relationship, he figures it also as a kind of *loss* of self, a loss that can only be redeemed through control of an

Other. Very much as Ullmann will describe in *Changing* her relationship with Bergman.[22] And how Bergman describes his relationship with Strindberg: "It is difficult to say what belongs to him and what to me," says Bergman.

It is a difficulty actors are familiar with, as they merge with the characters they embody, every working day, and where the "what" that belongs to each is often primarily embedded in the actor's *lines*; they belong to the playwright or screenwriter, but they must also, as they say, be "owned" by the actor. Bergman and Ullmann constantly return to the question of what happens as the title to that language gets transferred from writer, through director, to actor. Here is Bergman: "Words ... are ... always ... difficult. Now we're back to the beginning. The musician writes notes on a score, which are the most perfect signs that exist between creator and performer. But words are a very very bad channel between writer and performer."[23] And, as we saw, Ullmann is very much in agreement with Bergman here—only untalented directors tell their actors what to do and think; the talented ones work on their actors "musically."

Suspiciously, though, Bergman, at least in Ullmann's framing, may be "talented" by working musically, but his aims seem oddly "untalented": "It is only the untalented director who imagines himself in every part, wants his own thoughts and emotions portrayed; it is only the untalented who makes his own limitations those of the actor as well."[24] Ullmann "does" her director on screen, but without being told, and without telling. Except, we might note, in the one moment in the film where she repeats a single word: *ingenting*, nothing. For Ullmann, as we shall see, it is precisely this nothing, as a kind of supplement or remainder to the work, that creates the space for her own authority, not just as an actor, but, perhaps, as an auteur as well.

8.
Words are "very very bad" as conductors of intention from writer to actor. Is that why Bergman describes his screenplay for *Persona* as "more like the melody line of a piece of music ...?"[25] Perhaps, but there's more to it. This conduction of intention is, in the Strindberg tradition, also the threat of a transfer of power, of soul. Strindberg's famous ideas about soul-murder, of the battle between the stronger, who creates ideas and language, and the weaker, who steals the stronger's power by appropriating the stronger's language, are central to the inheritance he gave to Bergman, and have been much (and with great insight) discussed by many Bergman scholars.[26] This battle was often staged in Strindberg's works between powerful male textual authorities and the weaker women, who, in

subjecting themselves to parroting the language of their masters, actually end up winning the "battle of the brains," as Strindberg called it, by transmuting this parroting into a kind of theft, a vampiristic draining of the soul-stuff of the seemingly stronger author.[27]

9.
This puts the authorial soul in a paradoxical position: it must be both an auteur, a creator—but it must also jealously guard its words, keep them to itself, as it were. Strindberg wrote a play, suitably titled *The Stronger*, in which this dynamic is explored, if hardly resolved. It's a two-hander, consisting of a lengthy lunch date played out between two actresses, Mrs. X and Mlle Y, and—here's the *Persona* part—only one of them, Mrs. X, speaks.

Bergman was clearly inspired by Strindbergs play *Den starkare/The Stronger* (1889) when it came time to making *Persona*, as evidenced by this outburst:

> Everything, everything came from you to me, even your passions! Your soul crept into mine like a worm in an apple, ate and ate, dug and dug until only the skin was left with a little black meal! I wanted to flee but I could not; you lay there like a snake with your black eyes and kept me spellbound. . . . I hate you, hate you, hate you! But you, you only sit there silent, calm, indifferent.[28]

Is this Sister Alma speaking in *Persona* or Mrs. X speaking in *The Stronger*? In essence, it's both of them, though the passage I quote is from Strindberg; Bergman uses much of it, though, in *Persona*.

Steene sees *Persona* as a subversion of *The Stronger*, for, interestingly, it appears that the weaker character is the one forced into speech; the silent character at least appears to be stronger. Why is this? It comes back to the paradox I mentioned above—the creator must create and articulate but somehow also *not* communicate. A very odd idea, until you start to think of the last century or so of avant-garde and modern artistic production. How much of it do you understand? How much of it were you meant to understand? You'll see how this relates to Bergman and Ullmann when we look at this problem specifically in the context of so-called auteur cinema.

10.
Why do we use the word "auteur" when speaking of certain kinds of film directors? What makes one director an auteur and another "merely" a director? Perhaps the word is simply a laudatory honorific, like an honorary degree:

auteurs are just really good directors. But clearly that does not explain the word's cultural valence: why is simply being a great director not good enough? Indeed, in the word auteur's common usage, we tend to imagine that it describes a *type* of directing, regardless of achievement: after all, most of us have seen enough art films to encounter the work of more than a few bad auteurs. For while the *politique des auteurs* originally was used to identify directors with distinct personalities working within the Hollywood system, it morphed into a way of identifying auteur cinema as a distinct industrial or artisanal practice, like reality television or Broadway musicals. Christopher Orr summarizes this practice as having "two dominant traits . . . authorial expressivity and ambiguity."[29] Auteur cinema is "authored"—and its authors practice a studied ambiguity.

Note how in this formulation—one I think most of us take at face value, at least I tend to—authorial expressivity is paired not with clarity and communicability, but with ambiguity. The closer we get to cinematic authorship, the more opaque the film text becomes, at least up to a point. If it weren't at least a bit difficult to decipher, it wouldn't be art, and thus it wouldn't be the work of an auteur. But . . . why?

11.
Persona is often pointed to as a perfect exemplar of this kind of cinema.[30] Susan Sontag, in her famous appreciation of the film, shows how "Bergman . . . intends the film to remain partly encoded,"[31] that is, it is intended to be willfully undecipherable in parts. *Persona*, she writes, "is constructed according to a form that resists being reduced to a story,"[32] story here being conflated somewhat with clarity.

In this dominant version of what makes an art film an art film, film auteurs are auteurs to the extent to which they do like Bergman in *Persona*—enticing viewers and critics with enough narrative and coherence to solicit our interpretations, but always being ambiguous enough to ensure that no interpretation is ever going to be definitive. This is a truly strange idea, which doesn't make it a wrong idea, by the way. I just want you to keep its strangeness present as we continue.

12.
Why am I spending so much time parsing this term here? Because doing so leads us to one of the major matrices that informs the Ullmann/Bergman dyad, and that is the obvious, but oft-overlooked, relationship between the idea of auteur and the idea of author.[33] Why is it that art film practice has imported this word-

heavy idea of authorship into its cinematic domain? Is it because we believe that auteurs should not only direct but also write their films? Many of them do, but of course many do not. Somehow, though, writing haunts our idea of art cinema, and it haunts in very specific and different ways the art cinema of Bergman, as so much Bergman scholarship has shown us.

Maaret Koskinen has diligently tended Bergman's manuscripts and notebooks, and has unearthed and articulated Bergman's anxious relationship to authorship as a key aspect of his art; in particular, Bergman's generic struggles with screenwriting as a practice and its relation to his finished films were the site of an enormous creative struggle, and the screenplay of *Persona* is no exception.[34] It is a screenplay Bergman himself proclaims "does not look like a regular scenario."[35] It does not look normal because, like many of Bergman's scripts, it pulls in two very different directions—toward its instrumentality as a guidebook for Bergman and his team of actors and technicians, and toward its self-sufficiency as a work of prose written by the *author* Ingmar Bergman, as evidenced by his predilection for novelistic description in his screenplays. Let me quote Koskinen at length on this subject:

> [W]hat we encounter in [Bergman's] literary descriptions is just as much the creative power of a (frustrated) writer, one who very much kept his literary powers in check but still could not help but indulge in them. It was only later in his career . . . that he let go of those inhibitions related to his literary aspirations. The screenplay for *Fanny and Alexander* is essentially a nineteenth-century novel, full of generously described rounded characters, personifications, and other literary excesses. But again these did not come about until after a number of lamentations, which in Bergman's notebook for this film are of an almost ritualistic nature, as to the "unnecessity" of such descriptions: "Now, don't write things that can't be translated into images," reads one of his many pieces of advice to himself, "really, I'm very tired of it, this kind of half-literary snobbery which doesn't belong anywhere." But for all such admonishments, Bergman persisted in writing in ways that could not always be "translated into images."[36]

To put this another way: for Bergman, the proof that he was an author, as well as an auteur, lay in the fact that his screenplays could not be fully "encoded," to use Susan Sontag's term, into the films he made that were based on them. In order to be an auteur, he needed to be an author; but in both roles, his achievements were based on very specific kinds of failure: failure to write words that could ever translate fully on to the screen (if he succeeded, he would be a bad author, just a merely adequate screenwriter); and, on the other end, failure to reflect faithfully the specificity of the screenplay (if he succeeded, he would not be an auteur, he would just be a director filming an author's work). The "half-literary snobbery which doesn't belong anywhere" is actually a structural requirement for his art—suspended between text and image, clarity and ambiguity, this *failure* was the key to Bergman's art house *success*.[37] Was Ullmann's success as an actor dependent on a similar failure?

13.

So, what do we have so far? Some trouble about authorship and auteurship; some trouble about clarity, translatability, and ambiguity; some symbiosis with Strindberg which also leads to some trouble about gender and power relations, which are themselves caught up in the dynamic between words and images; some thoughts about the paradoxical need for the author to keep his words to himself, to remain silent, and for the director to remain silent too, and for the actor, portraying an actor, but actually "doing" a director, to say, at most, *ingenting*. And yes, soon all this will lead to Ullmann, but before we get back to her decisive intervention in these and other matters, one more detour through *Persona*, and yet another pair of swelling lips.

14.

One of the most disquieting shots in *Persona* comes during the opening credits, the famous sequence that also included another startling shot, a shot of an erect penis—an image which was, for nearly thirty-five years, excised from the American and UK versions of the film.[38] The removal of the penis shot was one of two notable censorings *Persona* suffered, the other being a bit subtler; I remember the first time I saw the film, in the 1970s, when I had just enough of an understanding of spoken Swedish to realize that the subtitles accompanying the famous scene of Sister Alma recounting her orgy to Elisabet Vogler were, well, a bit *selective*, especially when it came to the mention of oral sex. I have a feeling Bergman must have known some such censorings might be inevitable in at least some territories, and I do not recall evidence of him raising much of a protest about them.

But the shot to which I am referring is not the penis shot, but rather one of a pair of lips, photographed (or at least projected, depicted) sideways, that is, on a vertical axis, in a sense, erect.[39] The positioning gives the lips a distinctively labial look; indeed, critic Gwendolyn Audrey Foster calls the shot "one of the first images that performs the lesbian phallus of desire. . . . Set on their side, these

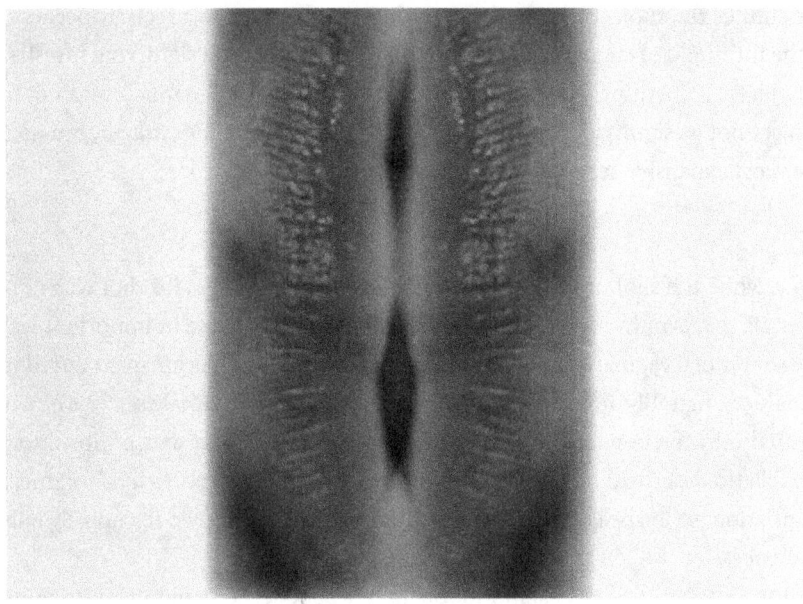

Figure 11.1 Still from the opening credits of *Persona* (1966).

lips immediately connote and perform the image of the vagina as it is viewed by French feminists, as Kristeva's 'chora,' or a space that precedes patriarchal and heterosexist hegemony" (Figure 11.1).[40]

I haven't the space here to unpack fully Foster's claims regarding the "choric" nature of the image here—they are claims I am very sympathetic with—but I will note how the reference to Julia Kristeva aligns with our "swollen lips" anecdote. Kristeva's theories on the relationship between what she calls "the semiotic" and "the symbolic" do seem *a propos*; her account of how humans, as speaking subjects—subjects-in-process—create meaning in a constant oscillation between somatic drives, with their rhythms and sonic ejaculations, and symbolic meanings—linguistically recognizable utterances—can tell us a lot about what might have been going on in, and on, Liv Ullmann's lips as she received Bergman's "technical" direction to place her (and, by extension, his) "feelings" in them.[41] Perhaps more than the "choric," pre-symbolic lips that Foster sees in the credit sequence, they might embody what Kristeva calls the "thetic" in her landmark work *Revolution in Poetic Language*: "[Thetic] signification is a stage attained under certain precise conditions during the signifying process, and . . . it constitutes the subject without being reduced to his process precisely because it is the threshold of language."[42] This notion of the subject as a signifying threshold articulates something very close to what we will see as Ullmann's notion of the subject not as signifying *author*, not as directing and "telling" *auteur*, but as, in the most expansive sense of the term, *actor*.

15.
Now, while the shot of the penis was censored, the sideways lip shot was not—after all, it was only a pair of lips, not a vagina. But of course in important ways the shot *is* of a vagina: it only escaped censorship because Bergman conjured the female sex figurally, not indexically. The censorship of the female sex was *already* figured into the poetic conflation of its representation by a pair of lips, just as the fellatio described by Sister Alma in the presence of Elisabet's lips became, in translation, so to speak, meaningless sounds left untranscribed for non-Swedish audiences.

The sideways lips thus stand in, or up, for *both* sets of genitalia, vagina *and* penis, both being and oscillating between them—a thetic emblem.[43]

16.
Where do we take all these associations, images, ideas, and references in our attempt to reckon with the anecdote of the lips? Let us follow Liv Ullmann's lead and see where her own reflections led her, as she was asked often about it.

Here is one of her responses to a query from 1973: "To my recollection, he didn't even say that . . . If you say to someone, concentrate on your lips, you get too self-conscious."[44]

Wait, *what*?

17.
So what shall we make of Ullmann's later recollection? Or is it a forgetting, a mis-remembering, or, simply, a lie? First, let us note the specter and role of "too much" self-consciousness as an impediment to good directing and acting, to the finding and imaging of the kind of truth in her work Ullmann speaks often of reaching for. As Ullmann continues her answer, she replaces the earlier "technical" story with a new one, one filled, in fact, with words, with talk: "We talk about experiences."[45] And then this talk of talk leads her to mark the discussion in strongly gendered ways. "Men are sometimes better directing

women, because they have a certain openness and can make themselves naked in ways women can't."[46]

The transition, from memories of Bergman as the near-silent master of technique to a more loquacious, emotionally naked interlocutor ("We talk about experiences") is, I think, quite meaningful, a reconfiguring by Ullmann of what is at stake in the process, from text, through direction, to acting, of filmic artmaking. Let's move now to how the actor figures in this equation, and in its evolving, always (though contradictorily) gendered, narrative.

18.

The critic Steve Vineberg writes that *Persona* is "centrally about the seduction and power of acting."[47] But for Vineberg, this seductive power takes too strong a hold of Bergman, much to the detriment of his work—indeed, much to the detriment of Ullmann's work, too:

> In Bergman's 1970s pictures, an unanticipated shift begins to occur in the acting of Liv Ullmann, who has certainly become his muse.... Ullmann pioneers a new phase in realism where her submersion into the characters she plays is so complete that the actress disappears entirely, the way Robert De Niro would a decade later in his collaboration with Martin Scorcese. This description is *not* meant as praise. If acting should incorporate both behavior and interpretation, then the approach Ullmann takes to her roles ... is counterproductive.... It seems noteworthy that Ullmann's career faded out after these mid-1970s Bergman films. She had vanished into the screen; there was no actress left.[48]

Well.

I quote Vineberg at length here because he invokes with perverse clarity many underlying ideas that even Ullmann, in her criticism of American-style Method acting, also appears to embrace, even if those ideas are taken by Vineberg I think to the wrong conclusion. These ideas revolve around binaries—of emotion/technique, of being/representation, of self-possession/disintegration, of realism/symbolism—that are commonplace and commonsensical. The social practice of acting creates for us precisely these kinds of paired sets of anxieties: Can a fellow human being be actually so much in the moment, can she be so purely in a state of emotional presence and experience, can she transform herself so completely through play and imagination, that she shows us simply and scarily how fine a line there really is between what we think of our "presence" and "disappearance"? And, in so doing, can she take from us the easy distinctions between, say, *me* and *you*, *life* and *art*, *real* and *unreal*, that we lean on to make sense of our common human culture? Vineberg's attack on Ullmann resides in the fear that she exceeds and erases these binaries (in Kristevan terms, she goes full "chora," and thus lapses into a chaotic, asymbolic real). What is missing from her performances is, for Vineberg, "interpretation," a category that fulfills an appositional and defining role vis a vis its opposite, what Vineberg calls "behavior." These terms are of course quite loaded—we associate "interpretation" with language, the manipulation of symbols, the reference to regimes of meaning that exist outside or alongside pure phenomena and raw experience, while we tend to associate "behavior" as instinctive, pre-linguistic, uninflected with codes of meaning and significance, immediate. But this opposition (one traditionally heavily gendered: the feminine, material, animal versus the masculine, articulate, thus "human") supposes that "behavior" is itself not already in some deep sense of the word "interpretation," and that interpretation can itself not be reduced to a kind of behavior.

The scandal of Ullmann's achievement for Vineberg is the excess of her performance, its outstripping of its function as symbolic of her role as Bergman's "muse" and into some other territory not contained within or containable by the auteur construct.[49] And it is that territory, now, in our final fragments, into which we shall follow Ullmann, as she crosses the threshold from in front of the camera to a place behind it.

19.

"When I played Elizabeth Vogler, I didn't know very much, but I just knew I was playing Ingmar. That's why I said that Max von Sydow could have played that part. I thought at that time, 'I will just watch Ingmar and I will try to act like him.' In the current film [*Faithless*], the character called Bergman is like the character he made into a woman and I played as Elizabeth Vogler in *Persona*. You can have great fun with this."[50]

Indeed you can.

20.

Ullmann was well aware, when she took on the task of directing Bergman's screenplay for *Faithless*, that "it will always be considered a Bergman film—if it's good it's still a Bergman film. It's a privilege, but it's still a difficulty."[51] That is, the film could never fully be recognized as an "auteur" film, because the auteur who authored the script was not directing it. Or, to put it another way, at this point in their careers, and after the decades of "self-fashioning" that Bergman had crafted around his auteur persona, his role as *author* would now finally fulfill the role of *auteur* too.⁵² Part of that self-fashioning was Bergman's oft-stated insistence that there be little or no improvisation on set, that the dialogues as written in his screenplays were sacrosanct.⁵³ So when it comes time to direct from a Bergman screenplay, the text remains supreme.

21.
Or does it? Here, from an exchange between Ullmann and an American critic:

> *Cineaste*: Although you made many distinctive choices as a director [of *Faithless*], you didn't change any of Bergman's dialog, did you? *Ullmann*: No, I didn't change a word or a comma, because I knew from acting with him that he's very protective of his lines. But, since it was a five-hour script, I had to do a lot of cutting. The film is mainly composed of Lena Endre's monologs, but people don't seem to notice this.⁵⁴

So not a word was changed—except that *hours of script* were removed! And what is primarily left? Lena Endre's monologues, though "people don't seem to notice this." That is, Ullmann, *totally faithful* to Bergman's lines, *cuts out the male bits* and turns the film into a *Persona*-like series of female monologues? And no one seems to notice. How is this possible?

Ullmann gives us a clue:

> The limit is the text, and much more in the theater than in film. Because in film you can always add by a closeup. You may say a stupid line but your face can defy it and make the line inconsequential, for your face is telling what the feeling really is. On the stage you can't do this; you stand there with a line and that's your line.⁵⁵

If I had more space, I would expand on just how important an intervention Ullmann's words are into the long-standing debates within film theory, going all the way back to Hugo Münsterberg in 1916, on the relationship between theater and film, including André Bazin's great essays from the 1950s on the role of language and text in filmed theater.⁵⁶ But for our present purposes there is enough to say, for here Ullmann definitively plays her cards: the text may be the limit, but the moment it is put in her hands as a film director, she fulfills Bergman's worst nightmares about just how bad—how, as he put it, "very very bad"—language works as a conductor of authorial intentions to the work of the actor on the screen. A simple facial expression in a close-up of an actor can overturn authorial intention—embodied in a "stupid line"—inscribed on the page. For it is the face that "tells" the "feeling," that thing Bergman did and did not tell Ullmann to swell her lips with.

And there you have it. For Ullmann and Bergman, an actor, to fulfill the auteur's work of bringing the author's words to the screen, must stupefy, dumbfound, silence the very lines that, with the language of authorial intention, crease, fill, and inscribe her face. And thus the actor's sublime role as the emblem of the structuring failure of communication that defines the very essence of so-called art cinema, the "uncoded" work of the film auteur that Susan Sontag so eloquently celebrated in her essay on *Persona*. And if, as Ullmann claims, with Bergman she was able, in close-up, to "discard the mask and show what is behind it," we should not be disappointed if what is revealed is another mask, its lips distended, as they haltingly form the only word that could possibly signify art cinema's paradoxical success: *ingenting*.[57]

Notes

1 James Jacobs, "Ingmar Bergman at Work," in *Ingmar Bergman: Interviews*, ed. Raphael Shargel (Jackson: University Press of Mississippi, 2007), 144.
2 Liv Ullmann, *Changing* (New York: Bantam, 1978), 120.
3 Ibid.
4 Ibid.
5 Ibid.
6 "Virginia Wright Wexman: What Do You Think of the American Style of Method acting? 'I think it's bullshit. I don't believe in it. I've worked with some method actors, and they're very difficult to work with because you never know who's coming in on the stage,'" in *Liv Ullmann: Interviews*, ed. Robert Emmet Long (Jackson: University Press of Mississippi, 2006), 85.
7 Ibid.
8 For a deep dive into the role of music and the idea of "musicality" in Bergman's work, see Alexis Luko, *Sonatas, Scream, and Silence: Music and Sound in the Films of Ingmar Bergman* (New York: Routledge, 2015). Chapter 7, "Music Lessons with August Strindberg," connects this musical aspect of Bergman's relationship to Strindberg in wonderful detail; we'll be talking about Bergman and Strindberg shortly.
9 Ullmann's *Changing* deftly functions as both artistic manifesto and romantic memoir; its second half, titled "Islanders," gives at once a detailed account of her relationship with Bergman but also manages the neat hat-trick of transmuting that story into one of the ongoing development of craft and "technique" as well; toward

the end of the book, in the form of a production diary from the set of *Face to Face* (1976), a film made years after their break-up, Ullmann will reach a crescendo of praise for Bergman's "genius" in an *excursus* on his use of close-ups. "I love close-ups. To me they are a challenge" (*Changing*, 282). And this challenge is specific to Bergman and Ullmann's joint quest to "discard the mask and show what is behind it," for "to work with Ingmar is to go on a journey of discovery within my own self" (ibid.). We shall see below how this language mirrors almost exactly Ullmann's description of the journey she believes Bergman was on when he cast and directed her in *Persona*.

10 The year of *Persona*'s release, 1966, was also the year of the publication of A.-J. Greimas's *Sémantique structurale*, a towering achievement of structuralist linguistics, which proposed to understand narrative events through the lens, among other things, of what Greimas called "actants," boiled down to six narrative actantial functions: Subject, Object, Sender, Receiver, Helper, and Opponent. One certainly appropriate reading of *Persona* would track how its lead characters embody, test, trade, and empty these functions as human subjects provisionally and differentially coming into being and non-being in the course of the narrative events they figure in. "Actant" would be a reasonable addition to author, auteur, and actor; Bergman and Ullmann certainly tried on each of Greimas's actantial functions vis a vis each other in the course of their careers. See A.-J. Greimas, *Structural Semantics: An Attempt at a Method*, trans. Danielle McDowell, Ronald Schleifer, and Alan Velie (Lincoln and London: University of Nebraska Press, 1983). Recently critics have returned to Greimas to discover that his very structuralist work can be fruitfully read to enable *post*-structuralist understandings of human agency as dispersed and "networked." See Matthew Burroughs Price, "Old Formalisms," *New Literary History* 50, no. 2 (2019): 47.

11 Ingmar Bergman, *Bergman on Bergman*, trans. Paul Britten Austin (New York: Simon and Schuster, 1973), 208. Quoted in Ullmann, *Changing*, 121.

12 Ibid.

13 *Liv Ullmann: Interviews*, 32.

14 The Ingmar Bergman Foundation website has a fun brief essay on Bergman's re-use of character names. See "Egerman, Vogler & Co.," https://www.ingmarbergman.se/en/universe/egerman-vogler-co.

15 Peter Goodrich, in a wonderfully learned and imaginative essay so rich in detail and association I can hardly do justice to its pertinence here, traces just one fascinating strand in the history of *persona*, beginning with the observation of the curious homonymy found in early modern English common and Anglican ecclesiastical law that gives us the word for person as *parson*. Goodrich pulls on this thread to show the essentially theatrical nature of subjective investiture, showing that "the person

is in origin a theological creation. The person is someone nominated by a higher authority, a patron.... The *persona* hides the machinery, the apparatus of staging and so instituting subjects within the spectral spaces of governance.... It is the optical apparatus that makes the person appear, the event of staging and inducing ..." in "The Theatre of Emblems: On the Optical Apparatus and the Investiture of Persons," *Law, Culture and the Humanities* 8, no. 1 (2012): 65–6. The *Kinematograph* is such an "ocular apparatus." And a reminder: Bergman's father was a "parson," a Lutheran minister, and he grew up in what in English we would call a parsonage, one Bergman explicitly associates with the theater in his autobiographical writings: "Our [the family's] drama was acted out before everyone's eyes on the brightly lit stage of the parsonage." Ingmar Bergman, *The Magic Lantern* (New York: Viking, 1988), 139; quoted in Maaret Koskinen, "Ingmar Bergman, the Biographical Legend and the Intermedialities of Memory," *Journal of Aesthetics and Culture* 2, no. 1 (2010). Koskinen's detailed pioneering work on Bergman as "author" informs much of this essay. See Koskinen, *I begynnelsen var ordet:: Ingmar Bergman och hans tidiga författarskap* (Stockholm: W&W, 2002) and *Ingmar Bergman's* The Silence*: Pictures in the Typewriter, Writings on the Screen* (Seattle: University of Washington Press, 2010).

16 Thanos Vovolis, "Acoustical Masks and Sound Aspects of Ancient Greek Theatre," *Clássica* (São Paulo) 25, no. 1–2 (2012); Thanos Vovolis and Giorgos Zamboulakis, "The Acoustical Mask of Greek Tragedy," https://www.didaskalia.net/issues/vol7no1/vovolis_zamboulakis.html; and Christian Zimmer, "*Persona*—Une fugue à deux voix," *Études Cinématographiques* 45 (1999): 53.

17 Marco Mancini, "Terentianus Maurus, *sonus tragicus* and the masks," *Glotta* no. 93 (2017): 79.

18 Ullmann, *Changing*, 137.

19 Interview with Terry Gross, https://freshairarchive.org/segments/actress-liv-ullman-filmmaker-ingmar-bergman.

20 *Liv Ullmann: Interviews*, 32. This gender switching is not limited to *Persona*: "Ester in *The Silence* could just as well have been a man. In fact, in my original draft, she *was* a man." *Bergman on Bergman*, 18. For the parallels between if not identity of Bergman and Vogler in *Persona*, see, among others, Birgitta Steene: "At the end of the film (if it has an end), Elisabet is seen in the same Electra makeup as in the beginning vignette from her stage performance, but now she is filmed in a studio. Her story thus parallels Bergman's own professional and personal experience of resignation from stage work, withdrawal, illness, and eventual recovery before turning again to the film medium." "Bergman's *Persona* through a Native Mindscape," in *Ingmar Bergman's* Persona, ed. Lloyd Michaels (Cambridge: Cambridge University Press, 2000), 25–6.

21 Steene, "Bergman's *Persona* through a Native Mindscape," 25, citing Frederick and Lise-Lone Marker, *Ingmar Bergman: A Life in the Theater* (Cambridge: Cambridge University Press, 1992), 57.
22 Ullmann, *Changing*: "Terrified, I felt I only had him. And when his jealousy placed limits on my freedom, I entered into his territory, in order to create the same limits there for him. Experienced my own security only as far as I could control his life" (136).
23 Quoted in *Ingmar Bergman: Essays in Criticism*, ed. Stuart Kaminsky with Joseph F. Hill (London and New York: Oxford University Press, 1975), 112.
24 *Changing*, 120.
25 Ingmar Bergman, *Persona and Shame*, trans. Keith Bradfield (New York: Grossman, 1972), 21.
26 In addition to the studies by Koskinen, Steene, and Luko referenced here, see Egil Törnqvist, "Bergman's Strindberg," in *The Cambridge Companion to August Strindberg*, ed. Michael Robinson (Cambridge: Cambridge University Press, 2009) and John Fletcher, "Bergman and Strindberg," *Journal of Modern Literature* 3, no. 2 (1973). Törnqvist makes the strong case for the influence of Strindberg on Bergman's relationship to language: "The most common way of establishing contact with others is through language. Yet, as a stage and screen director, Bergman distrusts language as a means of communication in any deeper sense. In accord with Hummel's remark in *The Ghost Sonata* that languages are 'codes' invented 'to conceal the secrets of one tribe from the others', he often demonstrates how language masks reality" (153).
27 I discuss this Strinbergian inheritance at length in James Schamus, *Carl Theodor Dreyer's Gertrud: The Moving Word* (Seattle: University of Washington Press, 2008), 22.
28 Steene, "Bergman's *Persona* through a Native Mindscape," 32.
29 John Orr, *The Demons of Modernity: Ingmar Bergman and the European Cinema* (New York: Berghahn Books, 2014), 86.
30 Though Hamish Ford perceptively and provocatively turns this exemplary auterishness on its head: "The excessively foregrounded appearance, or 'function', of Bergman's authorial signature—in late modernist tradition, to the point of extreme auto-critique and crisis—that Matthews highlights, is precisely what makes an attempt to try judge the films in auteurist terms unconvincing." "Great Directors: Bergman, Ingmar," http://www.sensesofcinema.com/2002/great-directors/bergman/.
31 Susan Sontag, "Bergman's *Persona*," in Michaels, *Ingmar Bergman's* Persona, 67.
32 Ibid.
33 Though not overlooked in Bergman scholarship. See Linda Haverty Rugg, *Self-Projection: The Director's Image in Art Cinema* (Minneapolis: University of Minnesota Press, 2014), and Koskinen, *I begynnelsen*.

34 See also the detailed scholarship of Anna Sofia Rossholm, in particular her essay "Tracing the Voice of the Auteur: *Persona* and the Bergman Archive," *Journal of Screenwriting* 4, no. 2 (2013). Rossholm illuminates how Bergman's process reflects on "the transitory nature of the text," 135.
35 Ingmar Bergman, *Images: My Life in Film* (New York: Arcade, 1994), 61.
36 Koskinen, *Silence*, 102–3.
37 Peter Ohlin gives a tremendously nuanced account of what's at stake in Bergman's embrace of the "instability of interpretation" in "The Holocaust in Ingmar Bergman's *Persona*: The Instability of Imagery," *Scandinavian Studies* 77, no. 2 (2005): 242. See also Peter Ohlin, *Wordless Secrets: Ingmar Bergman's* Persona: *Modernist Crisis and Canonical Status* (Welsh Academic Press, 2011).
38 Robert Koehler, "A New 'Persona' Stirs Old Passions," *Variety*, April 16, 2001. Accessed online at http://bi.gale.com/essentials/article/GALE%7CA73828097?u =columbiau.
39 A shot which serves as the pretext for a fascinating essay by Daniel Humphrey aptly titled "Persona's Penis," in *Ingmar Bergman: An Enduring Legacy*, ed. Erik Hedling (Lund: Lund University Press, 2021).
40 Gwendolyn Audrey Foster, "Feminist Theory and the Performance of Lesbian Desire in *Persona*," in Michaels, *Ingmar Bergman's* Persona, 132.
41 Kelly Oliver gives a useful summary of Kristeva's ideas and the feminist debates around them in "Julia Kristeva's Feminist Revolutions," *Hypatia* 8, no. 3 (Summer, 1993): "Kristeva uses 'semiotic' (*le sémiotique*) as a technical term that she distinguishes from 'semiotics' (*la sémiotique*). The semiotic element within the signifying process is the drives as they discharge within language. This drive discharge is associated with rhythm and tone. And because these sounds and rhythms are primarily associated with the sounds and rhythms of the maternal body, the semiotic element of language is also associated with the maternal. The semiotic is the subterranean element of meaning within signification that does not signify. The symbolic, on the other hand, is the element of meaning within signification that does signify. The threshold of the symbolic is what Kristeva calls the 'thetic phase,' which emerges out of the mirror stage. The symbolic is associated with syntax or grammar and the ability to take a position or make a judgment that syntax engenders. The semiotic gives rise to, and challenges, the symbolic. Kristeva describes the relation between the semiotic and the symbolic as a dialectic oscillation. Without the symbolic we have only delirium or nature; without the semiotic, language would be completely empty, if not impossible" (96).
42 Kristeva, *Revolution in Poetic Language* (New York: Columbia University Press, 1984), 100.
43 Koskinen, in her brilliant study of *The Silence*, discusses how Bergman's notion of the human subject is constantly "oscillating between the poles of masculinity and

femininity." *The Silence*, 56. Quoted in Daniel Humphrey, *Queer Bergman: Sexuality, Gender, and the European Art Cinema* (Austin: University of Texas Press, 2013), 4. Humphrey's book builds masterfully on earlier, particularly feminist, scholarship to paint a detailed and convincingly queer portrait of Bergman's work.
44 *Liv Ullman: Interviews*, 32.
45 Ibid.
46 Ibid.
47 Steve Vineberg, "Persona *and the Seduction of Performance*," in Michaels, *Ingmar Bergman's* Persona, 111.
48 Ibid., 114.
49 Indeed, as Maaret Koskinen convincingly argues in her overview of Ullmann's acting career in its transnational context, Ullman can productively be regarded as "a kind of auteur star," a productive nodal point for understanding the history of Western art house film culture. See Koskinen, "Reception, Circulation, Desire: Liv Ullmann and the Transnational Journeys of a Scandinavian Actress," *Journal of Transnational American Studies* 7, no. 1 (2016): 12.
50 *Liv Ullman: Interviews*, 211.
51 Ibid., 32.
52 See Janet Staiger, "Analysing Self-Fashioning in Authoring and Reception," in *Ingmar Bergman Revisited: Performance, Cinema, and the Arts*, ed. Maaret Koskinen (London: Wallflower Press, 2008).
53 Though there are of course many notable exceptions to this rule. Indeed, for our purposes, there is one very notable exception; it turns out that Bergman almost didn't shoot our anecdote scene, Sister Alma's account of her orgy. Bibi Andersson recounts that it was she who convinced Bergman to shoot the scene, though on the condition that she revise the script: "On one occasion Bergman said of Andersson that she needed to believe in something before she could act it." This might sound like a limitation, yet in Bergman's eyes it was a sign of integrity. One example of this in *Persona* is Alma's famous monologue about a sexual adventure she once had on a beach with another woman and two young boys. During the shooting Bergman wanted to scrap the scene, perhaps because he thought it was too explicit. But Andersson insisted that they keep it in. Reminiscing in an interview in *American Film*: "I said, 'Let me shoot it, but let me just alter certain words no woman would say. It's written by a man, and I can feel it's a man. Let me change certain things.' He said, 'You do what you want with it. We'll shoot it, and then we'll go and see it together.'" See "Persona," https://www.ingmarbergman.se/en/production/persona.
54 *Liv Ullmann: Interviews*, 120.
55 Ibid.

56 See in particular André Bazin, "Theater and Cinema," in *What is Cinema? Vol. 1*, ed. André Bazin, trans. Hugh Gray (Berkeley: University of California Press, 1967).

57 The seed for this essay was planted in the form of an informal talk given at the Norwegian Film Institute in 2010, at a symposium in honor of Liv Ullmann. Many thanks to Jan Erik Holst and the team at the Institute for their gracious hospitality that summer. I have retained some of the informal tone and much of the substance of that presentation here, while also benefiting from the following decade's worth of tremendous scholarship that has continued to deepen many of the topics I touch on. Indeed, the above is much more an invitation to the reader to explore the riches of Bergman scholarship I reference than it is an addition to it.

12

Dear Director

Adapting Bergman's Failures and Leftovers into a Play, and a Fan-letter into a Film

Marcus Lindeen

When I was about to do my fourth play, I decided to work with fiction for the first time. I had earlier written and directed documentary projects and used methods from my journalist background to stage stories. I thought fiction was presumptuous and reality held enough fantastic material to create interesting theater. But I had begun to have doubts. Perhaps fiction could offer possibilities I did not recognize earlier. I started reading plays and watching films to see if I could find a reasonable way in.

Bergman's films had been produced on stage for many years, but as a young Swedish director I found Bergman hard to approach. His legacy was hefty and his presence could still be felt in the Swedish cultural sphere through the constant anecdotes of older actors and film and theater staff about how it was to work with the great master. I had just seen *Ur marionetternas liv/From the Life of the Marionettes* (1980), one of Bergman's two German films, and was fascinated by its strange, experimental form and I was particularly captivated by the complex gay character Tim, in whom I recognized myself and by whom I was also deeply provoked. The film had earlier been produced as a play in Germany and I thought that it could be good material for me to stage for the first time in Sweden. I bought the script as a book and read Bergman's own introduction where he wrote that *Ur marionetternas liv* was the waste product from a script he had finished but never managed to film. The failed film would have been titled "Kärlek utan älskare" ("Love Without Lovers").

My curiosity was immediately piqued. What a fantastic title—"Love Without Lovers." Could it really be true that the master director Bergman, at the pinnacle of his career, wrote a script that was rejected? He would probably have been able to film whatever he liked. I called the Ingmar Bergman Foundation and asked whether the unfilmed script had been preserved. It had, and I was welcome to come the following day and read it.

Ingmar Bergman always denied saving any old working material. He said all the old, unfinished scripts and sketches had been burned and were gone for good. As it turned out, he had saved most things and today his archive is one of the world's most comprehensive personal archives of an individual filmmaker, and it was added to the UNESCO World Heritage List in 2007. When I arrived at the archive in the fall of 2011, all material had not yet been worked through or digitalized. I sat with the original documents in a basement storage area and carefully paged through them wearing cotton gloves. "Kärlek utan älskare" had been saved in a yellow plastic file and the sprawling script was finalized in Munich in 1978. Ironically, the plot is about a director who fails to complete a film. His name is Marco Hoffman, and he disappears without a trace during the editing phase and leaves Anna, the editor, with hours of recorded material without a script. Finally, she finds Marco out cold and blind drunk at the home of his lover Tim. Marco promises Anna that he will return to the cutting room and complete the film but instead he takes a gas can and sets fire to the whole film studio so that all the material is consumed in flames.

So tremendously symbolic, a failed script on a director who fails to complete a film. The first page of the original script includes a handwritten note in ink, where Bergman writes: "This script was rejected by three impeccably conscientious producers. Their reasons varied but the basic message was the same: it's impossible to make a film from this material. Expensive. Would end in catastrophe. Suicide. Eventually, I came to share their sorrowful opinions and consigned my script to the archives, filed away under unrealizable dreams and visions."

I'm still skeptical about whether the script actually had been read by any "conscientious producers" or whether this was some kind of affectation for posterity. Presumably the script was rejected by Bergman himself in pure self-censure. But *Arkivet för orealiserbara drömmar och visioner* (*The Archive for Unrealizable Dreams and Visions*) set my imagination going and this also became the title of the play that I directed for the Stockholm City Theater in the spring of 2012. The text was based on fragments from "Kärlek utan älskare" and other unfilmed Bergman scripts preserved in the archive. Six actors from the theater ensemble staged characters and scenes from the failed film projects, interspersed with excerpts from his workbooks. At first, I thought that this would be the perfect way for me as a young director to take on Bergman. Instead of staging yet another theater production of one of his classic films, I would showcase the failed waste products and attempts at fiction the master never managed to realize.

During my own writing process I quickly had to let go of this cocky attitude. I spent several months in Bergman's archive reading his handwritten diaries and gradually became deeply fascinated by his dedicated, arduous efforts to create fiction. It was both impressive and inspirational to follow the development of ideas over several years, successful as well as unsuccessful ones. More than fifty notebooks are preserved in the archives, creating a kind of log that he kept parallel to his scriptwriting and in which he reasons with himself on the fiction he tries to create. Perhaps I could learn something about how fiction is created by turning over Bergman's trash can.

One of the most interesting methods I found was that he sketched out his characters in a kind of interview format, where he let them put questions to him about who they were or were busy becoming: "How do I look?"; "Do I have any lovers"; "What do I want from my life?" In the workbooks, Bergman answered in page after page of long dialogue. This was actually not a completely different approach to research than what I was used to as a journalist. However, instead of interviewing real people about their lives, he conducted conversations with his imagined figures and did the research inside himself. Perhaps the step from telling stories based on reality to imaginary construction was not as great as I had previously wanted to believe?

When Bergman did not know what to write, he just wrote, "the pen goes and goes and oh, how good this pen smells . . ." until something suddenly came. It may seem banal, but is still evident of enormous discipline: he actually sat there writing although he did not know what to write. He did not rely on romantic ideas about waiting for artistic inspiration. He knew that a proper, dedicated work effort was required to actually achieve a result. (Not completely unlike the writing method I saw Oprah Winfrey recommending on her talk show, when she addressed audience members who wanted to write books but did not know where to start. Her trick was to set an egg timer next to her computer and set the timer on three minutes and then force her fingers to dart across the keyboard, even if the resulting text was about nothing at all. Eventually, after a few minutes' writing, one's imagination takes control and starts creating.)

In addition to the fascinating workbooks with Bergman's inner research, I was reading loads of more polished script materials that did not result in anything. Both well-advanced feature film projects and other more sketch-like scenes and fragments. It was liberating to see that even a master like Bergman had an archive full of failed attempts at fiction that never made it. To realize that all creation demands its sacrifices.

The residues for example included a collaborative film with Fellini and a finished Italian TV film script based on the last forty-eight hours in the life of Jesus. I also found an erotic feature-length comedy on a sexually inhibited prince on the cover of which Bergman himself wrote with a black marker: "Buried 1977. Never lived!" From his earliest writing years, I discovered a play on a cannibal who has eaten thirty people and when he cuts up his own stomach finds his soul, in the shape of stinking smoke.

I found the amount of queer material hidden in Bergman's failures both surprising and interesting. When he at the start of the 1960s wrote *Tystnaden/ The Silence* (1963), he for instance first had the idea that the film should be about a relationship between two men. In the workbooks from this period I also found a fantasy about two men who meet at a porn cinema and go home together. And in the film that would have been a collaboration with Fellini, several of the storylines are set in a lesbian club. I decided to pull some of the queer characters out from archival oblivion and into what would become my play.

Another recurring theme in the rejected or incomplete material was several scenes set in the womb; Freudian fantasies about wanting to again become a little fetus and longing to be allowed to crawl into and lay down inside "a nice and warm hen." The most advanced project in this genre is a puppet show in ten acts, written by Bergman as late as the 1990s, with the title "Från sperm till spöke" ("From Sperm to Spook"), and which I at first found ridiculous in its silliness. But later I recognized its greatness. Talk about existential storytelling ambitions. Not only portraying a life from "cradle to grave," but starting already *before* birth and continuing *after* death.

Arkivet för orealiserbara drömmar och visioner became a kind of playful portrait of a writer who struggles with his creation and who, just like the rest of us, is forced to give up on many of his ideas and projects. Yet it proved difficult to put together a collage of the material from a film director's failed attempts at fiction and create a new associative play that would hopefully present new meaning to the audience. I exchanged scenes and rewrote parts late into the rehearsal process. We tested loads of material and had to abandon much before the performance found its final shape.

I decided that the play may only include quotations from unfilmed scripts, the workbooks or different fiction sketches such as torn-out sheets with lists of possible film titles or character names that never came to anything. One type of material from the Bergman archive never made it into my play—the letters. In addition to Bergman's own scripts and workbooks, the archive preserves thousands of letters he had received from people who had seen his films and wanted to praise him or ask questions or just tell him about their lives. These made for fascinating reading and I realized that you so rarely get to see the audience's reactions. When film is discussed, the critics, film scholars, or directors themselves always make pronouncements, but hardly ever those who actually watch and experience the films. I decided to present this perspective and make a short film titled *Dear Director*.

A few years after my play opened, I was again in the Bergman archive together with an assistant. We went through the thousands of letters, hunting for one that could form the basis of a new short film. My hope was to track down the letter writer to see whether there's a character with a story worth telling. Most of the letters included the expected tributes from fans who wanted to congratulate him, or autograph hunters who just wanted a signature from their idol. But then we found two letters that stood out.

The first was from the Serbian psychologist Snežana Milenković. In the fall of 1991, she was on a trip to Oslo and decided to ask her great idol Bergman if she could come to visit him in Sweden because she thought that they would have much to exchange. She described herself as "alone in the wilderness, lost in the jungle, searching" and concludes the letter with a poem she had written about her dreams and a quotation from *Hamlet* in a postscript: "The rest is silence."

I found her easily online and made contact. She remembered the letter and wrote that she was obsessed with Bergman and had seen all his films. Snežana admired him because he was a director who used art as a type of psychotherapy and had described himself as having a double nature in a newspaper interview, something she could identify with:

> I feel very familiar with what he said about himself. All my life I have struggled to connect both sides of me: the rational and the emotional. The philosophical, psychological, scientific, objective, verbal part of myself with the artistic, spiritual, intuitive, symbolic, nonverbal part. I have chosen as my metaphoric theme "How can I know the dancer from the dance?" to reflect all the creative challenges I am faced with in this phase of my life. And my answer is: there is no dancer, only dance.

I was intrigued and curious. What did she mean by that? Maybe this woman had something valuable to teach me about the meaning of artistic creation. Bergman had never answered her letter. Then, many years later, she was working in Belgrade as a psychotherapist and used art therapy and psychodrama exercises to help groups to process their traumatic experiences from the Yugoslav Wars. She sent me some photos from one of the exercises: several participants standing in a circle with brown-colored water up to their waists in something appearing to be a tiny lake with a huge sewage pipe in the background. I thought it could be perfect. A psychologist who processed war trauma through group therapy in Belgrade's sewage system and possibly possessed truths about art.

Then the other letter surfaced.

A fall evening in 1980, the jazz pianist Liz Gorill emerged from a cinema in New York after seeing Bergman's *Ur marionetternas liv*. Over a period of five months, she wrote a sixteen-page letter to Bergman, in which she in a kind of diary format told him about her life and why she had been so deeply moved by his film. She described scenes that had brought back memories and reactions and revealed everything from her recent suicide attempt and the abuse she had been subjected to in her youth to her art and music quests. The letter is gripping and portrays a woman suffering a complete breakdown who, thanks to Bergman's film, discovers hidden aspects of herself. I decided to find her.

But when I googled the name Liz Gorill I could not find much, only a few old albums from the 1970s, and after 1980 there was nothing. I turned to the United States' Internal Revenue Service to find out if there was a person named Liz Gorill, but they couldn't find anything registered under that name. Perhaps she was no longer alive. What if her letter to Bergman was a farewell? But then I came in contact with a man who worked at the record label that had sold her first jazz album and he told me that she had later changed her name to Kazzrie Jaxen. He gave me a phone number and within a few hours I was speaking to her.

At first she was almost shocked when she heard that the private letter she had written over forty-five years ago was still preserved in an archive in Stockholm, and that a director had read it and wanted to make a film based on the letter. But she was curious and willing to talk. During our two-hour-long conversation she told me about her life both before and after the letter. A few years after the life crisis triggered by Bergman's film, she had left the metropolitan stress of New York and moved to a small town on the banks of the Delaware in upstate New York. Aided by Taoism, qigong, and the suggestive natural environment of the river she had reinvented herself as Kazzrie Jaxen, a type of artistic shaman who today not only makes experimental jazz albums but also offers people healing therapy sessions. She invites them to her house where they lie down on a mattress under her grand piano and meditate while she senses their energy and improvises jazz piano. Fascinating, I thought, that also the second letter writer who interested me in Bergman's archive should be someone using art as a form of therapy.

Then she told me about a strange discovery she had made later in life. After a doctor's appointment, she realized that she is a so-called vanishing twin survivor, someone who should have had a twin but whose twin died in the womb. The remains of the undeveloped twin fetus were absorbed into her own body and had stayed there in the form of a small fatty lump on her back. She had quite simply discovered a type of tumor called a teratoma, the medical term for when unborn twin fetuses are transformed into tumors in the surviving twins' bodies, which sometimes even includes still-growing hair or nail tissues. Some regard this as an entirely physical or medical defect, while others think that teratomata are souled and can affect people mentally. The syndrome has given rise to an entire movement in which teratoma patients regard it as an explanation for the psychological problems they have experienced throughout their lives. To Kazzrie, it meant that her feelings of absence and emptiness could finally be explained. The absence she had felt was simply grief for the twin she never had but who was still there in the form of a small fatty lump on her back. I immediately realized that the film had to be about Kazzrie and her unborn twin. But the letter she had written to Bergman was not about the twin at all, because she only came to this realization later. However, Kazzrie said that the letter may have been about her twin, because she experienced the film as full of obvious twin and womb associations. I asked her whether she would consider participating in a film in which the letter she wrote to Bergman is partially rewritten so that the story of her unborn twin could be included. She agreed and within a few weeks I was on a plane to New York with a small three-person film crew.

Together we were going to spend ten days in Callicoon, two hours north of New York City, and film the short about Kazzrie as a kind of improvisational game. The only thing I knew in advance was that Kazzrie would play herself before the camera without us interviewing her and later we would rewrite and let her read her own letter as narrator. Callicoon is a sleepy little town of 3,000 inhabitants in Sullivan County. We rented a house not far from Kazzrie's and made ourself at home. The first day we drove around to find locations: a swimming pool, a clearing in the woods with an abandoned piano, a concert venue at a hotel, a music studio, and a classic old cinema.

At Kazzrie's house we rearranged the living room into a suggestive massage parlor drenched in red light. There she would improvise a dialogue with Thomas, one of her closest friends and an art school teacher, who had agreed to participate in the film. Kazzrie says that sometimes when she goes to the cinema she afterward has the feeling that she is wearing the film characters outside on the street as kind of masks, behind which she no longer sees through her own eyes but through someone else's. Thomas answers by telling a story about his fragmented childhood and how he, through his homosexuality, experienced his body as containing multiple bodies simultaneously. He massages her and they try to contact the contents of the small lump on her back. They talk about the remains of the dead twin that may be inside and how it affects her. Perhaps her experience of doubleness is a premonition of a future attitude to our identities? That we will gradually realize that identity is never unique or stable, but that we bear multiple egos in constant flux. A thought that would upset the whole idea of self-realization as a life project. It is simply futile to try to understand "who you really are, deep inside," because we are never just one; we are always many.

The most central scene in *Dear Director* was filmed at the local cinema, which has not been revamped since it was built at the end of the 1940s. It is a fantastic cinema with beautiful red velvet armchairs and a classic domed ceiling. We filmed Kazzrie while she sat alone in the theater watching scenes from *Ur marionetternas liv* as well as sequences from Lennart Nilsson's celebrated 1970s macro photographic shots taken of a fetus inside the womb.

Kazzrie tells me how she sees the cinema as an artificial womb for adults, which through its enveloping darkness with images and sounds from the outside world allows us to reach our ultimate origin. In the rewritten letter to Bergman that she reads as a voice-over during the cinema scene she describes her experiences from that earth-shattering night in 1980, when she saw *Ur marionetternas liv* and felt the film changing her life:

> It was as if your film catapulted me out of the theater and deep into myself. I was transported back through all the memories of my life to the very beginning, before I was even born. I felt like the movie screen collapsed and the images came pouring out of the screen like a flood of water, filling the theater and slowly transforming it into a gigantic womb. And there I was, captured inside of it, like a fetus.

In the letter, Kazzrie continues to describe how she inside the amniotic fluid of memory feels the presence of someone else, a twin who had been beside her

Figure 12.1 Marcus Lindeen and Kazzrie Jaxen.

but who was never born and whose absence has left her with an inexplicable longing. After shooting Kazzrie sitting in the cinema we together climbed on stage and went in behind the screen. There we filmed her while she, exactly like the little boy in the opening of Bergman's *Persona* (1966), caressed the images projected on the screen with her hands. But from the back, as if hidden inside the film itself. The light from the black-and-white images of *Ur marionetternas liv* penetrates the screen and plays on her face.

As we stand there, on the other side of the screen, I feel that we all three meet—Kazzrie, Bergman, and me—in a fantasy of unborn twins, failed script ideas, and everything that might have been but never was (Figure 12.1).

13

Making (the) Silence Speak

Remake, Retake, Rectify

Louise Wallenberg

Introduction

For the 2018 centennial anniversary of Ingmar Bergman, in Sweden known as *Bergmanåret* ("the Year of Bergman"), six filmmakers were invited by Public Swedish Television and the Swedish Film Institute to create one short film each that was to investigate the legacy of Bergman's cinematic oeuvre in contemporary Swedish film. This compilation—spanning from typically Bergmanesque dramas (as in Pernilla August's *Scener ur natten/Scenes from the Night*), via dreamy reveries showing well-known yet slightly changed Bergmanesque characters (as in by Tomas Alfredson and Jesper Waldersten's *Bergmans Reliquarium*) to animated satire and critique (as in Jane Magnusson's *Fettknölen/Vox Lipoma*)— was titled *Bergman Revisited*.[1]

The series of films were screened on Swedish television in the summer of 2018, marking the height of the many Bergman festivities and celebrations that occurred in Sweden (and abroad). While all six of these films constitute interesting examples of advancing and interrogating Bergman's film work, and surely deserve a critical and insightful reading, for this chapter I will focus on Lisa Aschan's *Guds tystnad/God's Silence*, based on a script by Isabel Cruz Liljegren. Perhaps the most obvious example of remaking out of the six, this film refers back to and aligns itself with *Tystnaden/The Silence*, one of the three Bergman films that is often said to deal with God's absence. Yet, as we will see, *God's Silence* offers an indeed unbashful remake—what I would deem a rectification—of the original oeuvre.[2]

Hence, in what is to follow, questions regarding cinematic revisiting—as in remaking, retaking, and rectifying—in relation to *The Silence* as original and *God's Silence* as remake will drive the analysis. And while Bergman will be present, it is actor and film and stage director Gunnel Lindblom who will occupy center stage. Lindblom's importance for this chapter is directly connected to an interview that I, together with a colleague, conducted with her back in 2018. In this interview, held at *Dramaten* (the Royal Dramatic Theatre) in Stockholm, we asked about her life and work, about her experiences of working in the Swedish film industry, and naturally, about her longtime work with Bergman.[3] Enthused by the generous and candid outcome of that interview (but also, by the pre-pandemic, i.e., physical, meeting with her), I find Lindblom, and, as we will see, her first feature film, *Paradistorg/Summer Paradise* (1977), to be a most interesting link between *The Silence* and *God's Silence*. Another central link is the character Anna (who in *The Silence* is played by Lindblom, and in *God's Silence*' is played by Nina Gunke). In the hands of Aschan and Cruz Liljegren, Anna evolves into a more embracing and loving character, hence clearly breaking with the younger Anna. Some fifty-five years separate the two films, and the suffocating and painful lesbianism that is only allowed to surface in Bergman's *The Silence*, is turned into an affirmative desire that is fully—and joyfully—expressed in Aschan and Cruz Liljegren's rectifying remake.

Gunnel Lindblom, Actor Turning Director

Before discussing the two films, let me start off with a short presentation of Lindblom—and a discussion of the first film that she directed, *Summer Paradise* (1977), a film that Bergman initially was supposed to direct, but who, due to "troubles" with the tax authorities, decided to hand it over to Lindblom.

To the international audience, Lindblom is most probably known as one of "Bergman's actors" (or rather, as one of his actresses). They collaborated for approximately four decades, and their professional relationship would change over time, and it would span over theater, film, and television. Lindblom started out as a stage and film actor in the early 1950s, and would turn director in the 1970s, and she remained active as both theater and film director—and as actor—up until 2020. One of her very last performances for the screen—and one that again connects her with Bergman—was in the role as the mean bishop in Alfredson and Walderstens's *Bergman's Reliquarium*.[4] In late January 2021, she passed away, at the age of eighty-nine.

Bergman had first hired Lindblom in 1954, when theater director at Malmö City Theater. There she appeared in the leading female roles in his productions of Henrik Ibsen's *Peer Gynt* (1957) and Johann Wolfgang von Göthe's *Faust* (1958). By then, she was already quite experienced as a screen actor, having starred in Gustaf Molander's *Kärlek/Love* (1952) and *Sången om den eldröda blomman/ Song about the Scarlet Flower* (1956), and in Alf Kjellin's *Flickan i regnet/The Girl in the Rain* (1955). And while appearing in Bergman's *Peer Gynt*, she worked with him on two of his most iconic 1950s films: *Smultronstället/Wild Strawberries* and *Det sjunde inseglet/ The Seventh Seal*, both which premiered in 1957.

After that, Lindblom came to play both major and minor parts in his film and television productions: she starred in his early TV productions *Venetianskan* (1958) and *Rabies* (also 1958). In 1960, she appeared in *Jungfrukällan/The Virgin Spring* and in 1963, she starred with Ingrid Thulin in *The Silence*, while also playing a minor role in *Nattvardsgästerna/Winter Light* (1963). A decade later, in 1973, she appeared in the televised series *Scener ur ett äktenskap/Scenes from A Marriage* (1973). While filming with Bergman, she continued working with him on stage, as actor, but also, from the early 1970s, as his directing assistant (at the Dramatic Royal Theatre). In 1973, she directed her first theatrical play, and in 1976, she was approached by Bergman to direct her first feature film, *Summer Paradise*.[5] The film was based on a novel by Swedish author Ulla Isaksson, and together with Isaksson, Lindblom would co-write the film script.[6] Bergman had worked with Isaksson on two of his previous films, *Nära livet/Brink of Life* (1958) *The Virgin Spring*, and for *Summer Paradise* he would stand as producer, and Lindblom as director. However, as stated above, due to tax problems, Bergman decided to escape the country, and the film was filmed without Bergman's presence—much to Lindblom's initial despair. But as they started filming, "it all went very well." Production leader was Katinka Faragó, and it would not be farfetched to assume that Faragó (with Bergman out of the picture) was in charge on the production side, taking up the position both as producer and as production leader.

Summer Paradise in fact makes an interesting "feminist," and for its time—the mid-1970s—"timely" example: apart from a male photographer and four smaller male characters, this was an all-women film: From the editor, the set designer, the production leader, the costume designer, to the director and the two main protagonists. It is also worth pointing out that the two main protagonists differ from most films with women in the lead: in *Summer Paradise*, the story revolves around two women best friends, Katha (a medical doctor) and Emma (a social worker), who both are in their mid- to late sixties, and who both happen to be single. While Katha's two daughters seem to be both free and comfortable in their sexual relations with men, Katha and Emma are presented if not as asexual, then as "post-sexual."

In the interview conducted with Lindblom, she told us that the next to all-women crew was indeed a conscious choice on her part. And when interviewing Faragó in 2018, she explained to us that the filming of *Summer Paradise* was one of the happiest work experiences that she ever had ever had, emphasizing that the women-dominated crew was a strong contributing factor.

And while the film did well in the cinemas—and was met with critical acclaim—it also managed to incite a vivid debate on parenting, and especially, on motherhood.[7] Further, the film was initially met with some resistance for being a "women's pic." As Lindblom tried to get the film screened at the Cannes Film Festival, Harry Schein, CEO of the Swedish Film Institute, was indeed unenthusiastic. His reluctance had to do with the film's focus on elderly women. In our interview with Lindblom she recalled how he has asked her: "Who wants to see a film about two old women [*kärringar*]?." Despite Schein's dislike, the film was chosen to be screened at Cannes' *Les yeux fertiles*, and it was met with standing ovations and went on, overnight, to be sold to fourteen countries. Lindblom recalled how Schein had gone to an extreme, trying to

> persuade "the French" not to pick my film and to take another one instead—but I got in. And I knew he didn't like it and I knew he would be in Cannes so I tried to hide because I did not want to bump into him at some a café or at a street corner. And yes, I was absolutely alone. . . . But it was wonderful, I participated in a symposium, and I met with Rossellini, and . . .

Schein, of course, had to swallow his pride and participate in the press conference and the festive reception that followed. And together with some of Bergman's films, including *Viskningar och rop/Cries and Whispers* (1973) and *Scenes from a Marriage, Summer Paradise* became one of Sweden's largest film exports in the 1970s. This anecdote puts light on the double bind that women filmmakers find themselves in: whereas (director) Bergman—who could count Harry Schein as his friend and his most fervent supporter—could make uncountable films about women, young and old, and have his "women's pics" screened at international film festivals with support from the SFI, (actress) Lindblom was indirectly questioned as a director, and her film was considered uninteresting due to its focus on (middle-aged) women. It would have been interesting to know who

Bergman would have casted had he gotten to make the film: Women in their mid-sixties, or women much younger?

The questioning of *Summer Paradise*, however, did not stop with Schein's apparent dislike: When screening her film to twelve men at the Swedish Film Institute ("all dressed in dark suits"), she got one positive comment from producer Bengt Forslund ("Gunnel, you have made a really good film"), whereas all the other questioned her work. She recalled how Jörn Donner (who in 1978 took over as CEO of SFI after Schein) had asked her why she had decided not to make it "a costume film," as if the problems investigated in the film were not topical any more. This is indeed interesting taken that the film critically discusses the societal weight put on women as sole caretakers (even with a partner/father present), and how patriarchal structures hinder women from having both a professional career and a family.[8]

For the screen, Lindblom came to make four feature films, all of which focus on women's stories and experiences. After *Summer Paradise*, she directed *Sally och friheten/Sally and Freedom* (1981), a drama focusing on a young woman's dilemma in regard to abortion, freedom, and choice; hence, a film that indeed, like *Paradistorg*, was engaged with some of the more pertinent questions (for women, at least) of that era. The two other films were *Sommarkvällar på jorden/ Summer Nights on Earth* (1986) and *Sanna kvinnor/True Women* (made for Swedish television in 1991), both of which also tell about women's lives and experiences.

Telling Women's Stories, Refusing Nudity—and Being Excluded

Lindblom was adamant about the importance of telling women's stories, and while this was emphasized in the interview that we conducted with her at *Dramaten*, it was also brought up when she was interviewed by Swedish television in 2018, when asked about her subject matters in retrospect: "stories about women were missing and I felt a need to tell them." And further, she pointed out that it was not Bergman who was her inspirer when it came to filmmaking—it was Mai Zetterling, who in the 1960s made no less than four feature films dealing with women's stories and feminist issues, with Lindblom appearing in two of them: *Älskande par/Loving Couples* (1964) and *Flickorna/The Girls* (1968). In our interview, she pointed out that while Bergman indeed helped her when she first moved into directing film, he did not play an important role after *Paradistorg* was made: "When returning from München he had closed down his production company and then he was not so interested anymore . . . from then on, it was mostly theater and his own films that mattered to him."

During the Bergman Centennial, in the close aftermath of the MeToo-movement, questions regarding Bergman's possible misconduct in relation to his many women actors and co-workers came to the fore, as mentioned by Maaret Koskinen in her contribution to this collection. In an interview with Swedish tabloid paper *Expressen*, in conjunction with Lindblom receiving the Achievement award at the Stockholm Film Festival in 2018, she was asked how (and if) Bergman would have survived the MeToo-debate:

> O dear, he probably would have been punched. He was so macho. Very bossy, and he did not want to discuss things. But he did care for his actors in a genuine way like no other director I have ever met. And he wasn't physical. He would never have been accused for groping.[9]

Still, as the MeToo-debate blazed up just a couple of months before the inauguration of the Centennial in January 2018, everyone who had been working on and curated film screening series, talks and exhibitions, myself included, held their breath and waited for a bomb to explode. Known for notoriously bedding his actors, and going from one woman to the next, leaving a string of children behind him, there was of course cause for anxiety. Yet, there was little, if any, complaints about his misconduct.

But how come Lindblom did not appear in any of his films made between 1963 and 1973? While supportive of her directing *Summer Paradise*, he had not engaged her for his films in the ten years that followed *The Silence*. When she was offered a minor role in *Scenes from a Marriage* in 1972, Bergman had just warmed up to her again after a decade of keeping her in the cold.[10] She had assisted him when directing theater plays at *Dramaten*, but he had not employed her for his films. According to Lindblom, this had to do with her refusal to appear naked and demanding a body double in *Tystnaden*.

In an article written for the Swedish film magazine *Chaplin* in 1988, she recalled Bergman being infuriated when she had turned up for the sex scene (in the hotel) in a negligé, and that cinematographer Sven Nykvist and costume designer Marik Vos, who were present on the set, quickly had both hid behind a cabinet—Bergman's outbursts were infamous—yet she would not give in.[11] At one point he uttered (for everyone to hear): "What is so fucking important about those hellish goddamned cursed globs of fat!?!" Lindblom had just given birth, and probably felt that her "globs of fat," more than ever, were her business. While she admitted to feeling a bit foolish, and that she later felt "unforgivably stupid and prudish," at the time this occurred she "had only one thought in my head: 'It's OK to turn my soul inside out, but I want to keep my clothes on.'"[12] As mentioned by Koskinen, Bergman excluded her when making *Persona* (1966), *Vargtimmen/Hour of the Wolf* (1968), *En passion/The Passion of Anna* (1968), and *Skammen/Shame* (1968). And he did not include her in *För att inte tala om tala dessa kvinnor/All These Women* in 1964—a film depicting an almost all-female scenario and engaging most of his favorite actors. Lindblom's experiences of filming *The Silence*, followed by the silent retribution she would experience after having finished filming, together with her dual professional position as both actor and as director, are indeed remarkable, and say a lot about women's cinematic representation as well as of their working conditions (Figure 13.1).

The Silence is probably Bergman's most sexually provocative film, together with *Ur marionetternas liv/From the Life of the Marionettes* from 1980 in which Bergman dealt with nudity, prostitution, and overt homosexuality. In 1963, *The Silence* was met with both harsh and favorable critique—as director and filmmaker he had definitely crossed the line for what was considered morally

Figure 13.1 Lindblom refusing nudity in the bathroom scene in *The Silence* to Bergman's dismay (1963).

acceptable. While the film puts emphasis on *female sexuality*, it would, however, be a mistake to say that this is a film about female sexuality. This is Bergman's vision of what that may encompass—and this vision is carried out and constructed under his instruction and supervision.[13] Lindblom knew that her character Anna—the younger sister who engages in casual sex with strangers—is far from amicable, to say the least. Yet, she trusted Bergman, and she willingly took the risk. How bad was it? Well, pretty bad: Bergman has her character leave her young son and her dying sister in a hotel room in a foreign city to look for casual sex. And finding it, Bergman chooses to depict her sexual encounter as overly masochistic and degrading—with Bergman positioning her at the center of the frame, making her the sexual object to whom sexual acts are carried out. Hence, there is sadism in the way she is treated on the set (as she refuses to be naked), and there is sadism in how her character is being represented on screen. Lindblom is blamed for being prude, and her character is blamed for asking for it—hence she is doubly punished. And in both scenarios, Bergman gets away with it.

Yet, there is another act of sadism that sneaks into the setting, one that is directed toward the other woman on the set, Anna's sister Ester, who is played by Ingrid Thulin. As has been pointed out by Maaret Koskinen, "the strangely sadistic uglification of this then-still extremely beautiful actress" is striking.[14] There are rumors that Bergman had tried to court her in the early 1950s, but she had turned him down—only to marry Harry Schein. Surely, Ester indeed needed to be uglified—she is, after all, terminally ill and dying—but this is taken to an extreme. Every pore, every irregularity in her face, is emphasized by the unforgiving harsh light and the intrusive camera. Further, Bergman has her drink and smoke like a sailor, twisting in cramps, in sweat, and in pain.

This kind of sadistic treatment of women actors on the film set and on screen is not unique for Bergman.[15] The MeToo-movement has taught us that the film business is no walk in the park for women who want to break into—and stay in—film. In 1963, the same year as *The Silence* premiered, Alfred Hitchcock made *The Birds*, and the year before that Henry Hathaway made *How the West was won*. In 1971, Sam Peckinpah's *Straw Dogs* premiered, containing one of film history's most controversial and sadistic rape scenes, and the following year, Bernardo Bertolucci's *Last Tango in Paris*, crossed yet another boundary in terms of sadistic treatment of a leading lady, on film and on set. In all of these films, the female leads were pushed to their physical and mental limit, degraded and harassed—all while being filmed.[16] These films not only represent sexual violence and other forms of violence; their film sets *do* violence. Hence, representations are not just representations—they come from somewhere and refer to and visualize real acts. Acts that are carried out on the screen, then, are not just fantasies: in order for them to be represented, they have to be carried out, and hence, violence—sexual or other—toward women characters *on* film is also carried out toward women *in* film.

When Lindblom makes *Summer Paradise* in 1976, she sets out to counter and decenter the male gaze as well as the objectification of the female naked body. Further, she refuses to portray female sexuality and desire as one shaped by masochism (and sadism). Lindblom includes a couple of explicit sex scenes, yet these are characterized by equality between the sexes and bodies. This entails the male body being portrayed in its full naked state, which is still very uncommon in film, and it is shown as sensitive and as receptive as the female body. Further, in Lindblom's framing of the shots, both bodies are positioned as central: she does not objectify the female body in favor of a male gaze, instead, both bodies—and their joyful encounters—are there to be enjoyed by us, hence surpassing the old cinematic trap of women being left excluded from desiring, "all they can desire is to desire," to speak with Mary Ann Doane.[17]

Guds tystnad/God's Silence: *Remaking and Breaking the Silence*

Let me now move on to the 2018 remake of *The Silence*. Fifty-five years later, *God's Silence* again portrays Ester and Anna, yet this time they are not sisters, but longtime friends. And while Bergman's sisters were in their thirties, here the two women friends are well into their sixties and seventies. Shot in black and white, using the train (in transition) and the hotel room (a static space) as settings, and applying a mid- to late twentieth-century aesthetics, the film clearly plays tribute to *The Silence*—while also stressing lesbian desire, a desire that was only implicit and depicted as destructive in Bergman's film.

Lisa Aschan had—by the making of *God's Silence*—only two feature-length films behind her: in 2011 she had made the critically acclaimed *Apflickorna/She Monkeys*, focusing on the complicated relation between two teenage girls, and in 2015, she made *Det vita folket/White People*, a drama about a society dominated by surveillance. For the *Bergman Revisited* series, Aschan teamed up with screenwriter and playwright and stage director Isabel Cruz Liljegren, and together they decided to do a remake of *The Silence* and their chosen title is in fact the same that Bergman initially had intended for *The Silence*.[18] And silence was indeed a recurrent motif in Bergman's early career, and most fully explored in *Såsom i en spegel/Through a Glass Darkly* (1961) and *Winter Light* (1963), next to *The Silence*.

For the *Bergman Revisited* series Aschan and Cruz Liljegren wanted to explore the female and lesbian gaze in relation to Bergman's female universe, and *The Silence* proved for both to be the most interesting and fruitful "entrance" for their endeavor.[19] The film is 13.43 minutes long and as for the remaking—and retaking—of the story, Cruz Liljegren says that they wanted

> to take Bergman further through the two of us, to look at his work through and with our eyes, to be inspired by him but also to do something different from him, perhaps at odds with what he had wanted. There is a queer potential in his film, and there is room for a variety of interpretations. [When making the film] we wanted to explore how the lesbian gaze differentiates itself from the male gaze. I have no answers. Yet, there must be a reason to why so many queers find a queer leakage in Bergman's art. And that is of interest since he has also been accused for advocating a male gaze . . . and so, what happens when you put these gazes in relation to one another? *God's Silence* and *The Silence* should therefore be read as two different gazes on Ester and Anna during two different periods in their life.[20]

And while Aschan and Cruz Liljegren stay close to Bergman's story, aesthetics and cinematic style, some elements are omitted such as Anna's young son, the hotel butler, and the group of traveling artists. And while Ester is ill, she is not dying. Further, Aschan and Cruz Liljegren tweak the story so as to bring out the lesbian desire as *mutual* between the two protagonists: hence saving Ester from repression, and from her—with Daniel Humphrey's words—"desire to destroy her gender and her sexuality by destroying herself."[21]

Like Bergman, Aschan portrays the two women via close-ups, again paying tribute to Bergman's work, and she lets the camera observe every wrinkle, every pore, in their still beautiful faces. Yet there is no sadism here, no uglification: the women are shown as they are, with the life experiences and the years that they carry visibly in and on their faces (Nina Gunke, who plays Anna, was sixty-three, and Anki Lidén, playing Ester, was seventy-one at the time of filming). The two women friends' stories are also similar to those in *The Silence*: Anna has been married, whereas Ester has always been single, and while Anna engages in casual sex with a silent and much younger stranger, it is apparent that she does so to provoke Ester. Her provocation is indeed performative in the way that it

Making (the) Silence Speak 225

Figure 13.2 Anna (Nina Gunke) and Ester (Anki Lidén) about to kiss in a take evoking the iconic shot in *Persona*.

is used to create a reaction in Ester, but she also performs in terms of speech to try and create change: asking Ester if and why she is jealous, and finally, pushing Ester to ask her if she (Anna) *wants* her to be jealous—until she gets an affirming "yes." "To *say* something," even if it is said as a question, "is to *do* something."[22] In this way, it is in fact Anna who pushes forward, and who initiates the lesbian quantum leap—a leap that includes a joint confession of love followed by a long and passionate kiss (Figure 13.2).

In 1963, the sexual and problematic pseudo-lesbian representation in *The Silence* was difficult to handle for some spectators and critics alike, and in Sweden it soon became known as a film causing "moral shock."[23] In 1976, Lindblom's film *Summer Paradise* about two single middle-aged women was first seen as not worthy of (international) interest and there were efforts made to try and keep it out of the limelight. In this way, *God's Silence* can be said to constitute a two-folded remake—engaging with, and answering back not only to Bergman's film but also, to Lindblom's, placing lesbian and older women at the center. Hence, Aschan and Cruz Liljegren's remaking is nothing but a proud rectifying in which lesbian desire is (finally) allowed to speak loudly.

Acknowledgments

The writing of the chapter was supported by Riksbankens Jubileumsfond and is partly connected to the research project "Representing Women," which they financed between 2018 and 2022 (project number P17-0079:1).

Notes

1 The six short films were Pernilla August and Cilla Naumann, *Scenes From the Night*; Linus Turnström, *Ariel*; Jane Magnusson and Liv Strömquist, *Vox Lipoma*; Lisa Aschan and Isabel Cruz Liljegren, *God's Silence*; Patrik Eklund, *The Infection*; and Tomas Alfredson and Jesper Waldersten, *Bergman's Reliquarium*.
2 The other two are *Såsom i en spegel/Through a Glass Darkly* (1961) and *Nattvardsgästerna/Winter Light* (1963), the latter discussed in depth by Paisley Livingston in Chapter 3.
3 The interview was conducted together with political scientist Maria Jansson at the Royal Dramatic Theatre in Stockholm on April 27, 2018, and was part of a longer research project on women's experiences of working in the Swedish film industry that was financed by *Riksbankens Jubileumsfond*.
4 Hence, besides being connected to the *Bergman Revisited* series through the remake of *Tystnaden*, Lindblom was preeminently also *part* of it: in Alfredson and Waldesten's *Bergman's Reliquarium* she played the part of the evil protestant bishop, echoing the role of Jan Malmsjö in Bergman's last film for the screen, *Fanny och Alexander/Fanny and Alexander* (1982–3).
5 Her debut as stage director was with Gottfried Grafström's play about Swedish poet Gustaf Fröding, *Sjung vackert om kärleken* ("Sing beautifully about love"). The play was successful with both critics and the audience, and was filmed for Swedish television in 1976.
6 In our interview, Lindblom told us that prior to *Summer Paradise*, in 1974, she and Isaksson had worked together on a film script about Viktoria Benediktsson and her feud with Edward Brandes, and that Erland Josephson, Solveig Ternström and Sven Nykvist were to collaborate with her on this production. The film was never made, according to Lindblom because a "film strike brook loose."
7 About the issues of motherhood and childcare discussed in Lindblom's film, see Maria Jansson and Louise Wallenberg, "Negotiating Motherhood in Sweden: On and Off Screen," in *Mothers and Motherhood: Negotiating the International Audio-Visual Industry*, ed. Susan Liddy and Anne O'Brien (London: Routledge, 2021).

8 The (constant) male questioning of women's films (their stories, their characters, their representation, etc.) is something that also came up in the many interviews that I, together with my colleague political scientist Maria Jansson, conducted with women film workers in 2018 and 2019. See Jansson and Wallenberg, "Experiencing Male Dominance in Swedish Film Production," in *Women in the International Film Industry*, ed. Susan Liddy (London: Palgrave, 2020) and Jansson et al., "The Final Cut," in special issue on gender and the screening industries, ed. Louise Wallenberg and Maria Jansson, *Gender, Work and Organization* 28, no. 6 (2021), https://doi.org/10.1111/gwao.12621. See also Wallenberg, "Women in Screen: 1970s-2010s," in *Now about all these women in the Swedish Film Industry*, ed. Wallenberg et al. (London and New York: Bloomsbury, 2022).
9 This view or standpoint has also been supported by Faragó in our interviews with her.
10 She does appear in *Reservatet/The Lie* (1970), directed by Jan Molander, with a script written by Bergman.
11 Gunnel Lindblom, "I skuggan av en vulkan," *Chaplin* 30, no. 2–3 (1988): 100–3. Also discussed and referred to by Maaret Koskinen in her book *Ingmar Bergman's The Silence* (Seattle: University of Washington Press, 2010), 61–4.
12 Ibid. Quoted in Koskinen, *Ingmar Bergman's The Silence*, 63.
13 While Lindblom seems not to have had any problems with the sex scenes—although they are degrading—she made it clear that she did not want to be naked, and Bergman was forced to let her wear a slip in the sex scene and to use a body double in the bathroom scene. See Lindblom, "I skuggan av en vulkan," quoted at length in Koskinen's chapter in this book on pages 61–4. In the documentary *Gunnel Lindblom—ut ur tystnaden* ("out of the silence") (Henrik von Sydow, 2018), she says: "but . . . Ingmar became really angry at me, *really angry* at me, and then he was angry at me for days."
14 Koskinen, *Ingmar Bergman's The Silence*, 60. This uglification, Koskinen writes, had already started in *Nattvardsgästerna* (1961).
15 See for example Laura Mulvey, "Visual Pleasure and Narrative Cinema," *Screen* 16, no. 3 (1975): 6–18; Louise Wallenberg, "Fashion Photography, Phallocentrism, and Feminist Critique," in *Fashion in Popular Culture: Literature, Media and Contemporary Studies*, ed. Joe Hancock, Vicki Karaminas and Toni Johnson-Woods (Bristol and Oxford: The University of Press and Intellect Publishers, 2013), 136–53; Donald Spoto, *The Dark Side of Genius: The Life of Alfred Hitchcock* (New York: Ballentine Books 1983); Spoto, *Spellbound by Beauty: Alfred Hitchcock and his Leading Ladies* (London: Arrow Books, 2009); Tippi Hedren, *Tippi: A Memoir* (New York: William Morrow, 2016); and Edward White, *The Twelve Lives of Alfred Hitchcock: An Anatomy of the Master of Suspense* (New York: W.W. Norton & Company, 2021).

16 On sadism toward women on the set, see for example Spoto, *The Dark Side of Genius*; Kyle Counts, "The Making of the Birds," *Cinemafantastique* 10, no. 2 Fall (1980): n.pag.; Linda Williams, "Women Can Only Misbehave," *Sight & Sound* 5, no. 2 (February 1995): 26–7; Mark Kermode, "A wild bunch in Cornwall," *The Observer*, Sunday August 3, 2003, 9; Martin Barker, "Loving and hating Straw Dogs: The Meaning of Audience Responses to a Controversial Film—Part 2: Rethinking Straw Dogs as a Film," *Particip@tions* 3, no. 1 (May 2006), https://www.participations.org/volume%203/issue%201/3_01_barker.htm. Accessed on July 6, 2022.
17 Mary Ann Doane, *The Desire to Desire: The Women's Film och the 1940s* (Bloomington: Indiana University Press, 1987).
18 While SVT helped produce the film, so did Garagefilm—a film production company led by women. Cruz, a scriptwriter and stage director, had previously only worked in theater, and Aschan had at this point only made two feature-length films.
19 *Persona* (1966), too, would have made a possible entrance in terms of lesbian desire, as has been pointed out by Gwendolyn Audrey Foster, "Feminist Theory and the Performance of Lesbian Desire in Persona," in *Ingmar Bergman's Persona*, ed. Lloyd Michaels (Cambridge: Cambridge University Press, 2000). See also Daniel Humphrey, *Queer Bergman: Sexuality, Gender, and the European Art Cinema* (Austin: University of Texas Press, 2013), and Louise Wallenberg, "Mago's Magic," in *Fashion, Film and the 1960s*, ed. Eugenia Paulicelli, Drake Stutesman and Louise Wallenberg (Bloomington: Indiana University Press, 2016).
20 Interview with Cruz Liljegren with Svenska Yle. https://svenska.yle.fi/artikel/2018/09/25/det-finns-en-queer-potential-i-bergmans-filmer-dramatikern-isabel-cruz-liljegren.
21 Humphrey, *Queer Bergman*, 125.
22 John L. Austin, *How to Do Things with Words* (Oxford: Oxford University Press, 1962), 12.
23 Still, it was picked as the Swedish nomination to the Oscars in 1964, and it won three *Guldbaggar* for best picture, best director, and best actress (Ingrid Thulin).

Conclusion

Maaret Koskinen and Louise Wallenberg

As pointed out in the "Introduction," studying production as a culture often involves gathering empirical data about the lived realities of people in film and media production, and their experiences concerning collaborations, practices, casting, contracts, conflicts, and much more.

The pillars of this book in this regard are no doubt the twin interviews with Katinka Faragó and Måns Reuterswärd. The crystal clear memories of these two octogenarians offer a virtual treasure trove of detailed information about behind-the-scene events, not only from film production but also television and opera sets. In addition this information goes well beyond so-called Bergman studies. For through their detailed reminiscences, covering half a century, it is possible to catch sight also of questions involved in the specifically Swedish national production system and its various studio histories, routines, work organization, and so on.

In addition, what stands forth in the interviews with Faragó and Reuterswärd are the problematic aspects of the degree of power, which undeniably was held by (and given to) Bergman. Their lived experiences and observations of the repercussions of this power are mirrored in Maaret Koskinen's overview of a number of sources, most of them published in Swedish only, which in turn are corroborated by theater and film director Linus Tunström's personal and sometimes shockingly detailed experiences of working with Bergman in the theater toward the latter part of his career.

The fact that Bergman's work, on and behind the scenes, lends itself to a production studies approach is abundantly clear as well from the other contributions in this book. This is the case with Paisley Livingston's contribution regarding the considerations and choices at the director's disposal, gleaned from various sources on the shoot of one single film. This is true also of Atom Egoyan's understanding of similar issues with regard specifically to the contribution of actors, which he considers through the lens of a collegial insider perspective. The importance of the contribution of the actor is taken even further by both

Alexis Luko and James Schamus, specifically in regard to Liv Ullmann's authorial persona—that her creative contribution to Bergman's work must be sought outside of a strict definition of film authorship and the auteur.

But, as mentioned, Bergman's work also lends itself to intermedial perspectives, which in his particular case is closely intertwined with a production studies approach. This is amply illustrated by both Alexis Luko's study mentioned above, regarding the role of music, and Allan Havis's contribution on the intricate relations between film and theater. These relations are illustrated in a fascinating way as well from the viewpoint of filmmaker and playwright Marcus Lindeen, who not only has made a film on Bergman fandom, but has even written an entire play based on Bergman's discarded, unfinished, and unpublished scripts.

The fact that Bergman since long has been a director's director is corroborated in, not least, the "Preface" by Ang Lee, attesting to the power of commonly shared cultural references across borders. This is certainly the case also of Margarethe von Trotta's contribution, written from the insider perspective of a director, and resonating with a joint understanding of literary sources, as well of Jonathan Rozenkrantz's study on "Jewish" elements within a complex national, cultural, and historical context of a postwar Sweden.

Bergman's position as a director's director is even, somewhat unlikely, confirmed by feminist retakes on his deploying female actors in ways that were considered unusual in the day. For, as Louise Wallenberg shows in her study on Bergman through the dual lens of actress Gunnel Lindblom turned director, and the younger Swedish director Lisa Aschan, it is not enough to speak of general "influences" or theoretical "intertextualities," but rather of certain individual works that have made such an impact as to serve as hands-on inspiration for revisiting Bergman, in order to "remake, retake, and rectify."

* * *

What then, finally, can theory and practice "do" for each other? Our hope is that in this book, the possibilities are discernible through example and in the multitude of details offered by the contributors, in their consideration of Bergman's work. For while the various, idiosyncratic approaches taken by each individual writers are illuminating in and for themselves, they could also serve as material for further studies in the context of production studies. Certainly making theory and practice meet and talk does not come without obstacles. But while the individual participants, who did manage to meet in person at our writing retreat, initially spoke wildly different lingos ("what on earth *is* he talking about!?," Katinka Faragó hissed in pure exasperation at some point, listening to one academic's rather lengthy explication), still the participators gradually started conquering common ground. Faragó and Reuterswärd, to their mild amazement, started seeing of how systematic theorization mirrored, albeit sometimes obliquely, their own lived experiences, while, in turn, their anecdotes and crystal clear reminiscences of faces, places, and facts, not only confirmed but threw new light on what scholars had picked up only at a distance—if at all.

While such moments, where the experience of the artistic practitioner collided with the theorization of the academic, may have been illuminating for the individuals involved, they only served to confirm the necessity for further discourse across such boundaries.

Bibliography

Adams, Robert H. "How Warm is the Cold, How Light the Darkness?." *The Christian Century* 81 (1975), 38, reprinted in *Ingmar Bergman: Essays in Criticism*. Edited by Stuart M. Kaminsky, 226–30. New York: Oxford University Press, 1964.

Åhlund, Jannike. "Var Bergman en våldtäktsman?" *Svenska Dagbladet*, April 17, 2019.

Allen, Woody. "Through a Life, Darkly." *The New York Times*, September 18, 1988.

Andersson, Harriet. *Harriet Andersson. Samtal med Jan Lumholdt*. Stockholm: Alfabeta, 2005.

Andersson, Lars M. *En jude är en jude är en jude . . .: representationer av "juden" i svensk skämtpress omkring 1900–1930*. Lund: Nordic Academic Press, 2000.

Assayas, Olivier. "A Portrait of the Artist: On Bergman's 'The Magician.'" *Cahiers du Cinéma*, October, 1990.

Austin, John L. *How to Do Things with Words*. Oxford: Oxford University Press, 1962.

Bachner, Henrik. "Political Cultures of Denial? Antisemitism in Sweden and Scandinavia." In *Politics of Resentment: Antisemitism and Counter-Cosmopolitanism in the European Union*, ed. Lars Rensmann and Julius H. Schoeps, 329–62. Leiden: Brill, 2011.

Baldwin, James. "The Northern Protestant." In *Ingmar Bergman Interviews*, ed. Raphael Shargel, 10–20. Jackson: University Press of Mississippi, 2007. Originally published in James Baldwin, "The Precarious Vogue of Ingmar Bergman." *Esquire* 53, no. 4 (1960): 128–32.

Barker, Martin. "Loving and Hating Straw Dogs: The Meaning of Audience Responses to a Controversial Film – Part 2: Rethinking Straw Dogs as a Film." *Particip@tions* 3, no. 1 (2006). https://www.participations.org/volume%203/issue%201/3_01_barker.htm. Accessed July 6, 2022.

Bazin, André. "Theater and Cinema." In *What is Cinema?* Vol. 1, ed. André Bazin, translated by Hugh Gray, 75–124. Berkeley: University of California Press, 1967.

Béranger, Jean. *Ingmar Bergman et ses Films*. Paris: Le terrain vague, 1959.

Bergman, Ingmar. *Arbetsboken: 1975–2001*. Stockholm: Norstedts, 2018.

Bergman, Ingmar. *Bergman on Bergman*. Translated by Paul Britten Austin. New York: Simon and Schuster, 1973.

Bergman, Ingmar. *Bilder*. Stockholm: Norstedt, 1990.

Bergman, Ingmar. *Fanny and Alexander*. Translated by Alan Blair. New York: Pantheon, 1983.

Bergman, Ingmar. *Fanny and Alexander*. Translated by Alain Blair. London: Penguin Books, 1989 [1982].

Bergman, Ingmar. *Föreställningar: Trolösa, En själslig angelägenhet, Kärlek utan älskare*. Stockholm: Norstedts, 2000.

Bergman, Ingmar. *Il Vangelo secondo Bergman: storia di un capolavoro mancato*. Edited by Pia Campeggiani and Andrea Panzavolta. Genoa: il melangolo, 2018.

Bergman, Ingmar. *Images: My Life in Film*. Translated by Marianne Ruuth. Arcade Publishing, 1994.

Bergman, Ingmar. *Images: My Life in Film*. Translated by Marianne Ruuth. London: Faber & Faber, 1995.

Bergman, Ingmar. *The Magic Lantern: An Autobiography*. Translated from Swedish by Joan Tate. New York: Viking, 1988.

Bergman, Ingmar. *The Magic Lantern: An Autobiography*. Translated by Joan Tate. New York: Penguin Books, 1989.

Bergman, Ingmar. *Moraliteter: tre pjäser*. Stockholm: Albert Bonniers Förlag, 1948.

Bergman, Ingmar. *Persona and Shame*. Translated by Keith Bradfield. New York: Grossman, 1972.

Bergman, Ingmar. *Three Films by Ingmar Bergman*. Translated by Paul Britten Austin. New York: Grove Press, 1970.

Bergman, Ingmar. *Trolösa*. Filmberättelser 33. Stockholm: Norstedts, 2018.

Bergman, Ingmar and Maria von Rosen. *Tre dagböcker*. Stockholm: Norstedts, 2004.

Binns, Alexander. "Desiring the Diegesis: Music and Self-Seduction in the Films of Wong Kar-Wai." In *Cinemusic? Constructing the Film Score*, ed. David Cooper, Christopher Fox, and Ian Sapiro, 127–40. Newcastle: Cambridge Scholars Publishing, 2008.

Björkman, Stig, Torsten Manns and Jonas Sima. *Bergman on Bergman: Interviews with Ingmar Bergman*. New York: Simon & Schuster, 1973.

Björnstrand, Lillie. *Inte bara applåder*. Stockholm: Tiden, 1975.

Blackwell, Marilyn Johns. *Gender and Representation in the Films of Ingmar Bergman*. Columbia, SC: Camden House, 1997.

Blackwell, Marilyn Johns. *Persona: The Transcendent Image*. Chicago: University of Illinois Press, 1984.

Bobrow, Andrew C. "Dialogue on Film: Sven Nykvist." *American Film* 9, no. 5 (1984): 18.

Bobrow, Andrew C. "Sven Nykvist Discusses Ingmar Bergman's 'Face to Face.'" *Filmmakers Monthly Newsletter* 9, no. 7 (1976): 28–34.

Bordwell, David. *Narration in the Fiction Film*. Madison: The University of Wisconsin Press, 1985.

Bourdieu, Pierre. *The Field of Cultural Production*. Cambridge: Polity Press, 1993 [1972].

Brundin, Olof. "Vi levde med en mur omkring oss." *Aftonbladet* (Sunday section), June 14, 1998.

Burroughs Price, Matthew. "Old Formalisms." *New Literary History* 50, no. 2 (2019): 245–69.

Carlsson, Carl Henrik. *Judarnas historia i Sverige*. Stockholm: Natur & Kultur, 2021.

Chion, Michel. *The Voice in Cinema*. Translated by Claudia Gorbman. New York: Columbia University Press, 1999.

Cohen, Hubert I. *Ingmar Bergman: The Art of Confession*. New York: Twayne, 1993.

Counts, Kyle. "The Making of the Birds." *Cinemafantastique* 10, no. 2 (1980): n.pag.

Cowie, Peter. *Ingmar Bergman*. Loughton, Essex: Motion, 1962.

Cowie, Peter. *Ingmar Bergman. A Critical Biography*. New York: Charles Scribner's Sons, 1982.

Cowie, Peter. *Ingmar Bergman. A Critical Biography*, updated edition. London: Andre Deutsch, 1992.

Cowie, Peter. *Swedish Cinema*. London: Barnes, 1966.

Crowther, Bosley. *New York Times* Movie Review, August, 1959.

Diamond, Diana. "In Front of the Camera, Behind the Camera: Ullmann Directs Bergman." *Projections* 5, no. 2 (2011): 51–74.

Doane, Mary Ann. *The Desire to Desire: The Women's Film och the 1940s*. Bloomington: Indiana University Press, 1987.

Donner, Jörn. *Djävulens ansikte*. Lund: Aldus/Bonniers, 1962.

Eco, Umberto. *The Open Work*. Translated by Anna Cancogni. Cambridge, MA: Harvard University Press, 1989.

Ekman, Gösta. *Farbrorn som inte vill va' stor*. Stockholm: Leopard förlag, 2010.

Ekman, Malin. "Överdrev sin kärlek till Hitler för konstens skull." *Svenska Dagbladet*, July 13, 2018.

Elleström, Lars. *Media Borders, Multimodality and Intermediality*. Houndmills: Palgrave Macmillan, 2010.

Elleström, Lars. *Transmedial Narration: Narratives and Stories in Different Media*. Cham: Palgrave Macmillan, 2019.

Elsaesser, Thomas. "Ingmar Bergman in the Museum? Thresholds, Limits, Conditions of Possibility." *Journal of Aesthetics & Culture* 1, no. 1 (2009), doi:10.3402/jac.v1i0.2123.

Emmet Long, Robert, ed. *Liv Ullmann: Interviews*. Jackson: University Press of Mississippi, 2006.

Fletcher, John. "Bergman and Strindberg." *Journal of Modern Literature* 3, no. 2 (1973): 173–90.

Foster, Gwendolyn Audrey. "Feminist Theory and the Performance of Lesbian Desire in Persona." In *Ingmar Bergman's Persona*, ed. Lloyd Michaels, 130–46. Cambridge: Cambridge University Press, 2000.

Gado, Frank. *The Passion of Ingmar Bergman*. Durham: Duke University Press, 1986.

Genette, Gérard. *Métalepse: De la figure à la fiction, Collection Poétique*. Paris: Seuil, 2004.

Genette, Gérard. *Narrative Discourse: An Essay in Method*. Ithaca: Cornell University Press, 1972.

Gervais, Marc. *Ingmar Bergman: Magician and Prophet*. Montreal and Kingston: McGill-Queen's University Press, 1999.

Gill, Jerry H. *Ingmar Bergman and the Search for Meaning*. Grand Rapids, MI: Eerdmans, 1969.

Goodrich, Peter. "The Theatre of Emblems: On the Optical Apparatus and the Investiture of Persons." *Law, Culture and the Humanities* 8, no. 1 (2012): 47–67.

Göranzon, Marie. *Vrålstark & skiträdd*. Stockholm: Norstedts, 2017.

Gorbman, Claudia. "Narrative Film Music." *Yale French Studies* 60 (1980): 183–203.

Gorbman, Claudia. *Unheard Melodies: Narrative Film Music*. Bloomington: Indiana University Press, 1987.

Greimas, A.-J. *Structural Semantics: An Attempt at a Method*. Translated by Danielle McDowell, Ronald Schleifer, and Alan Velie. Lincoln and London: University of Nebraska Press, 1983.

Hedling, Erik. "Book Review." *Scandinavian Studies* 87, no. 2 (2015): 299–303. https://doi.org/10.5406/scanstud.87.2.0299.

Hedling, Erik. "Ingmar Bergman." In *Oxford Bibliographies*, ed. Krin Gabbard. Oxford: Oxford University Press, 2017. https://doi.org/10.1093/OBO/9780199791286-0222.

Hedling, Erik, ed. *Ingmar Bergman: An Enduring Legacy*. Lund: Manchester University Press, 2021.

Hedren, Tippi. *Tippi: A memoir*. New York: William Morrow, 2016.

Holmberg, Jan. *Författaren Ingmar Bergman*. Stockholm: Norstedts, 2018.

Humphrey, Daniel. "Persona's Penis." In *Ingmar Bergman: An Enduring Legacy*, ed. Erik Hedling, 197–210. Lund: Lund University Press, 2021.

Humphrey, Daniel. *Queer Bergman: Sexuality, Gender and the European Art Cinema*. Austin: University of Texas Press, 2013.

Humphrey, Daniel and Hamish Ford. "Situating Ingmar Bergman and World Cinema." Special issue entitled Bergman World in *Popular Communication* 19, no. 2 (2021): 66–79.

Jacobs, James. "Ingmar Bergman at Work." In *Ingmar Bergman: Interviews*, ed. Raphael Shargel, 144. Jackson: University Press of Mississippi, 2007.

Jansson, Maria and Louise Wallenberg. "Experiencing Male Dominance in Swedish Film Production." In *Women in the International Film Industry*, ed. Susan Liddy, 163–78. London: Palgrave, 2020.

Jansson, Maria and Louise Wallenberg. "Negotiating Motherhood in Sweden: On and Off Screen." In *Mothers and Motherhood: Negotiating the International Audio-Visual Industry*, ed. Susan Liddy and Anne O'Brien, 45–62. London: Routledge, 2021.

Jansson, Maria et al. "The Final Cut." In Louise Wallenberg and Maria Jansson, eds., special issue on gender and the screening industries in *Gender, Work and Organization* 28, no. 6 (2021), https://doi.org/10.1111/gwao.12621.

Josephson, Erland. *Doktor Meyers sista dagar och Kandidat Nilssons första natt: två stycken*. Stockholm: Bonnier, 1964.
Josephson, Erland. *Sanningslekar*. Stockholm: Bromberg, 1990.
Josephson, Erland. *Vita sanningar*. Stockholm: Bromberg, 1995.
Kääpä, Pietari and Mette Hjort. "Editorial." *Journal of Scandinavian Cinema* 10, no. 2 (2020): 89, https://doi.org/10.1386/jsca_00015_2.
Kakutani, Michiko. "Ingmar Bergman, Summing Up a Life in Film." *New York Times Magazine*, June, 1983.
Kaminsky, Stuart and Joseph F. Hill, eds. *Ingmar Bergman: Essays in Criticism*. London and New York: Oxford University Press, 1975.
Kawin, Bruce. *Mindscreen: Bergman, Godard and First-Person Film*. Princeton, NJ: Princeton University Press, 1981.
Kermode, Mark. "A Wild Bunch in Cornwall." *The Observer*, August 3, 2003.
Ketcham, Charles B. *The Influence of Existentialism on Ingmar Bergman: An Analysis of the Theological Ideas Shaping a Filmmaker's Art*. Lewiston, Queenston and New York: Edwin Mellen Press, 1986.
Klimek, Sonja. "Metalepsis and Its (Anti-)Illusionist Effects in the Arts, Media and Role-Playing Games." In *Metareference Across Media: Theory and Case Studies*. Studies in Intermediality 4, 169–90. Amsterdam and New York: Rodopi, 2009.
Koehler, Robert. "A new 'Persona' Stirs Old Passions." *Variety*, April 16, 2001.
Koskinen, Maaret. "Au Commencement était le Verbe. Les écrits de jeunesse d'Ingmar Bergman." *Positif* 497/498 (July-August, 2002): 17–22.
Koskinen, Maaret. "From Erotic Icon to Clan Chief: The Auteur as Star." In *Stellar Encounters: Stardom in Popular European Cinema*, ed. Tytti Soila, 81–9. New Barnet: John Libbey Publishing Ltd, 2009.
Koskinen, Maaret. "From Short Story to Film to Autobiography. Intermedial Variations in Ingmar Bergman's Writings and Films." *Film International* 1, no. 1 (2003): 5–11.
Koskinen, Maaret. *I begynnelsen var ordet. Ingmar Bergman och hans tidiga författarskap*. Stockholm: Wahlström & Widstrand, 2002.
Koskinen, Maaret, ed. *Ingmar Bergman Revisited. Performance, Cinema and the Arts*. London and New York: Wallflower Press, 2008.
Koskinen, Maaret. "Ingmar Bergman, the Biographical Legend and the Intermedialities of Memory." *Journal of Aesthetics and Culture* 2, no. 1 (2010): 1–11.
Koskinen, Maaret. *Ingmar Bergman's The Silence. Pictures in the Typewriter, Writings on the Screen*. Seattle: University of Washington Press and Copenhagen: Museum Tusculanum Press, 2010.
Koskinen, Maaret. "Multiple Adaptation Processes: The Case of Alexander Ahndoril's *The Director* and its Predecessors in Feature Film, Television Documentary and Popular Print Media." *Journal of Scandinavian Cinema* 5, no. 1 (2015): 35–47.

Koskinen, Maaret. "Out of the Past: Saraband and the Ingmar Bergman Archive." In *Ingmar Bergman Revisited: Performance, Cinema and the Arts*, ed. Maaret Koskinen, 19–34. London and New York: Wallflower Press, 2008.

Koskinen, Maaret. "P(owe)R, Sex, and Mad Men Swedish Style." In *Swedish Cinema and the Sexual Revolution: Critical Essays*, ed. Mariah Larsson and Elisabet Björklund, 153–67. Jefferson, NC: McFarland & Co, 2016.

Koskinen, Maaret. "Reception, Circulation, Desire: Liv Ullmann and the transnational Journeys of a Scandinavian Actress." *The Journal of Transnational American Studies* 7, no. 1 (2016), https://escholarship.org/uc/item/09h5b6m1.

Koskinen, Maaret and Mats Rohdin. *Fanny and Alexander. Ur Ingmar Bergmans arkiv och hemliga gömmor*. Stockholm: Wahlström & Widstrand, 2005.

Kristeva, Julia. *Revolution in Poetic Language*. New York: Columbia University Press, 1984.

Larsson, Björn and Karin Thunberg. "På Fårö avslöjades sanningen om pappa." *Svenska Dagbladet*, November, 2004. svd.se/pa-faro-avslojades-sanningen-om-pappa.

Larsson, Camillia, ed. "Anteckningar från Bergmanveckan." Special issue of *Filmkonst* 105 (2006).

Lindblom, Gunnel. "Confessions of a Bergman Co-worker." In *Ingmar Bergman. An Artist's Journey. In Stage, On Screen, In Print*, ed. Roger Oliver, 59–63. New York: Arcade Publishing, 1995 [1988].

Lindblom, Gunnel. "I skuggan av en vulkan." *Chaplin* 30, no. 2–3 (1988): 100–3.

Linton-Malmfors, Birgit. *Den dubbla verkligheten: Karin och Erik Bergman i dagböcker och brev 1907–1936*. Stockholm: Carlssons, 1992.

Livingston, Paisley. *Cinema, Philosophy, Bergman: On Film as Philosophy*. Oxford: Oxford University Press, 2009.

Livingston, Paisley. *Ingmar Bergman and the Rituals of Art*. Ithaca and London: Cornell University Press, 1982.

Luko, Alexis. *Sonatas, Screams, and Silence: Music and Sound in the Films of Ingmar Bergman*. New York and London: Routledge, 2015.

Lumholdt, Jan. "Filmskolan special no. 9: Max von Sydow." *Ingmar* 4 (2006): 66–71.

Lunde, Arne. "Ingmar's Hitchcockian Cameos: Early Bergman as auteur inside the Swedish studio system." *Journal of Scandinavian Cinema* 8, no. 1 (2018): 19–33.

Lundegård, Mats. "Svenska judar söker sina rötter." *Dagens Nyheter*, December 31, 1991.

Lundell, Michaela. "Jag vill veta vem jag är." *Judisk Krönika* 77, no. 2 (2009): 6–12.

Luther, Martin. "Eyn sermon von der Betrachtung des heyligen Leydens Christi" (1519). Trans. "A Meditation on Christ's Passion." In *Martin Luther's Basic Theological Writings*, ed. Timothy F. Lull and William R. Russell. Minneapolis: Ausburg Fortress, 2012.

Mancini, Marco. "Terentianus Maurus, *sonus tragicus* and the Masks." *Glotta* 93 (2017): 79–94.

Marker, Frederick and Lise Marker. *Ingmar Bergman: A Life in the Theater*. Cambridge: Cambridge University Press, 1992.
Matteson, Alf. "Ingmar Bergman summerar sitt liv i en generöst myllrande gobeläng." *Nordvästra Skånes Tidningar*, December 19, 1982.
Mosley, Philip. *Ingmar Bergman, The Cinema as Mistress*. London: Marion Boyars Ltd, 2018.
Mulvey, Laura. "Visual Pleasure and Narrative Cinema." *Screen* 16, no. 3 (1975): 6–18.
Mulvey-Roberts, Marie. *Dangerous Bodies: Historicising the Gothic Corporeal*. Manchester: Manchester University Press, 2016.
Nykvist, Sven. "A Passion for Light." *American Cinematographer* 53, no. 4 (1972): 380–81, 456.
Nykvist, Sven and Bengt Forslund. *Vördnad för ljuset. Om film och människor*. Stockholm: Albert Bonniers Förlag, 1997.
Ohlin, Peter. "Bergman's Nazi Past." *Scandinavian Studies* 81, no. 4 (2009): 437–74.
Ohlin, Peter. "The Holocaust in Ingmar Bergman's *Persona*: The Instability of Imagery." *Scandinavian Studies* 77, no. 2 (2005): 241–74.
Ohlin, Peter. *Wordless Secrets: Ingmar Bergman's* Persona. *Modernist Crisis & Canonical Status*. Cardiff: Wales Academic Press, 2011.
Öhrner, Lena. "Replik på [flash symbol] om Fanny och Alexander." *Södermanlands Nyheter*, April 14, 1983.
Oliver, Kelly. "Julia Kristeva's Feminist Revolutions." *Hypatia* 8, no. 3 (1993): 94–114.
Orange, Richard. "Hard-hitting Film Takes Aim at Ingmar Bergman's Flawed Way with Women." *The Observer*, January 6, 2018, https://www.theguardian.com/film/2018/jan/06/ingmar-bergman-beauty-beast-flawed-way-with-women-great-art.
Orr, John. *The Demons of Modernity: Ingmar Bergman and European Art Cinema*. New York and Oxford: Berghahn Books, 2014.
Penley, Constance. "Cries and Whispers." In *Movies and Methods*, ed. Bill Nichols, 204–8. Berkley, University of California Press, 1976. Originally published in *Women and Film* 1, no. 3–4 (1973): 55–6.
Rokem, Freddie. "Bergmans Dibbuk." *Judisk Krönika* 57, no. 1 (1989): 16–17.
Rossholm, Anna Sofia. "Tracing the Voice of the Auteur: *Persona* and the Bergman Archive." *Journal of Screenwriting* 4, no. 2 (2013): 135–48.
Rugg, Linda Haverty. *Self-Projection: The Director's Image in Art Cinema*. Minneapolis and London: University of Minnesota Press, 2014.
Sadoul, Georges. "Ingmar Bergman et le cinéma suédois." *Les lettres francaises*, 626, June 28, 1956, 6.
Sarris, Andrew. "Notes on the Auteur Theory in 1962." In *Film Theory and Criticism: Introductory Readings*, ed. Leo Braudy and Marshall Cohen, 515–18. New York and London: Oxford University Press, 1999. Original edition, 1962.
Schamus, James. *Carl Theodor Dreyer's* Gertrud: *The Moving Word*. Seattle: University of Washington Press, 2008.

Schmidt-Hirschfelder, Katharina. "Odödlig hedersjude?" *Judisk Krönika* 77, no. 2 (2009): 12–13.
Siclier, Jacques. *Ingmar Bergman*. Brussels: Club du livre de cinema, 1958.
Singer, Irving. *Ingmar Bergman, Cinematic Philosopher: Reflections on His Creativity*. Cambridge, MA and London: MIT Press, 2007.
Sjöberg, Thomas. *Ingmar Bergman – en berättelse om kärlek, sex och svek*. Stockholm: Lind & Co, 2013.
Sjögren, Henrik. *Stage and Society in Sweden: Aspects of Swedish Theatre Since 1945*. Stockholm and Ann Aarbor: The Swedish Institute and University of Michigan, 1979.
Sjöman, Vilgot. *L 136 diary with ingmar bergman*. Translated by Alan Blair. Ann Arbor: Karoma, 1978.
Smith, Jeff. "Bridging the Gap: Reconsidering the Border between Diegetic and Nondiegetic Music." *Music and the Moving Image*, 2, no. 1 (Spring) (2009): 1–25.
Söderbergh Widding, Astrid. "What Should we Believe?: Religious Motifs in Ingmar Bergman's Films." In *Ingmar Bergman Revisited: Performance, Cinema and the Arts*, ed. Maaret Koskinen, 194–209. London and New York: Wallflower, 2008.
Sontag, Susan. "Bergman's *Persona*." In *Ingmar Bergman's* Persona, ed. Lloyd Michaels, 62–85. Cambridge: Cambridge University Press, 2000.
Sontag, Susan. "Bergman's *Persona*." In *Styles of Radical Will*, ed. Susan Sontag, 123–45. New York: Farrar, Straus & Giroux, 1969.
Sörenson, Elisabeth. "Bergman vid Fyrisån – nästan på mormors gata." *Svenska Dagbladet*, September 18, 1981.
Spoto, Douglas. *The Dark Side of Genius: The Life of Alfred Hitchcock*. New York: Ballentine Books, 1983.
Spoto, Douglas. *Spellbound by Beauty: Alfred Hitchcock and his Leading Ladies*. New York: Arrow Books, 2009.
Staiger, Janet. "Analysing Self-Fashioning in Authoring and Reception." In *Ingmar Bergman Revisited*, ed. Maaret Koskinen, 89–106. London: Wallflower Press, 2008.
Steene, Birgitta. "Bergman's *Persona* through a Native Mindscape." In *Ingmar Bergman's* Persona, ed. Lloyd Michaels, 24–43. Cambridge: Cambridge University Press, 2000.
Steene, Birgitta. *Ingmar Bergman: A Reference Guide*. Amsterdam: Amsterdam University Press, 2005.
Stern, Michael J. "Persona, Personae! Placing Kierkegaard in Conversation with Bergman." *Scandinavian Studies* 77, no. 1 (2005), University of Illinois Press on behalf of the Society for the Advancement of Scandinavian Study (Spring).
Stilwell, Robynn. "The Fantastical Gap Between Diegetic and Nondiegetic." In *Beyond the Soundtrack: Representing Music and Cinema*, ed. Daniel Goldmark, Lawrence Kramer, and Richard Leppert, 184–202. Berkeley and Los Angeles: University of California Press, 2007.

Strindberg, August. "A Dream Play." In *Five Plays*, ed. August Strindberg. Berkeley and Los Angeles: University of California Press, 1983.

Strindberg, August. *Den starkare*. 1880.

Törnqvist, Egil. *Bergman's Muses: Aesthetic Versatility in Film, Theatre, Television and Radio*. Jefferson, North Carolina and London: McFarland & Company, 2003.

Törnqvist, Egil. "Bergman's Strindberg." In *The Cambridge Companion to August Strindberg*, ed. Michael Robinson, 149–63. Cambridge: Cambridge University Press, 2009.

Törnqvist, Egil. *Between Stage and Screen: Ingmar Bergman Directs*. Amsterdam: Amsterdam University Press, 1995.

Ullmann, Linn. *Unquiet: A Novel*. New York and London: Norton, 2019.

Ullmann, Liv. *Changing*. New York: Bantam, 1978.

Van Belle, Jono. *Scenes From an Audience. The Auteur and the Film Text in Audience Experiences: Ingmar Bergman – A Case Study*, doctoral dissertation. Stockholm University/University of Ghent, 2019.

Vineberg, Steve. "*Persona* and the Seduction of Performance." In *Ingmar Bergman's Persona*, ed. Lloyd Michaels, 110–29. Cambridge: Cambridge University Press, 2000.

Vonderau, Patrick, et al. https://productionstudies.net. Accessed September 7, 2021.

Vos, Marik. *Dräkterna i dramat: mitt år med Fanny och Alexander*. Stockholm: Norstedt, 1984.

Vovolis, Thanos. "Acoustical Masks and Sound Aspects of Ancient Greek Theatre." *Clássica (São Paulo)* 25, no. 1–2 (2012): 149–73.

Wallenberg, Louise. "Fashion Photography, Phallocentrism, and Feminist Critique." In *Fashion in Popular Culture: Literature, Media and Contemporary Studies*, ed. Joe Hancock, Vicki Karaminas and Toni Johnson-Woods, 136–53. Bristol and Oxford: The University of Press and Intellect Publishers, 2013.

Wallenberg, Louise. "Magos's Magic." In *Fashion, Film, and the 1960s*, ed. Eugenia Paulicelli, Drake Stutesman and Louise Wallenberg, 169–89. Bloomington: Indiana University Press, 2017.

Wallenberg, Louise. "Women on Screen: 1970s-2010s." In *Now about all these Women in the Swedish Film Industry*, ed. Wallenberg et al. London and New York: Bloomsbury, 2022.

Wennberg, Anders. "Förmår inte garvade recensenter ifrågasätta Bergmans storhet?" *Gefle Dagblad*, February 2, 1983.

White, Edward. *The Twelve Lives of Alfred Hitchcock: An Anatomy of the Master of Suspense*. New York: W.W. Norton & Company, 2021.

Widerberg, Bo. *Visionen i svensk Film*. Stockholm: Bonniers, 1962.

Williams, Linda. "Women can only Misbehave." *Sight & Sound* 5, no. 2 (1995): 26–7.

Winters, Ben. "The Non-Diegetic Fallacy: Film, Music, and Narrative Space." *Music & Letters* 91, no. 2 (2010): 224–44.

Wirmark, Margareta. *Film och teater i växelverkan*. Edited by Ingmar Bergman. Stockholm: Carlssons förlag, 1996.
Wolf, Werner. "Metalepsis as a Transgeneric and Transmedial Phenomenon: A Case Study of the Possibilities of 'Exporting' Narratological Concepts." In: *Narratology Beyond Literary Criticism: Mediality, Disciplinarity*, ed. Jan Christoph Meister, 83–108. Berlin and New York: Walter de Gruyter, 2003.
Wolf, Werner. *Metareference Across Media: Theory and Case Studies*. Studies in Intermediality 4. Amsterdam and New York: Rodopi, 2009.
Wood, Robin. *Ingmar Bergman*. London: Studio Vista, 1969.
Wood, Robin. *Ingmar Bergman*, 2nd edn. rev. Detroit: Wayne State University Press, 2013.
Wright, Rochelle. "The Imagined Past in Ingmar Bergman's *The Best Intentions*." In *Ingmar Bergman: An Artist's Journey: On Stage, On Screen, In print*, ed. Roger W. Oliver, 116–25. New York: Arcade Publishing, 1995.
Wright, Rochelle. *The Visible Wall: Jews and Other Ethnic Outsiders in Swedish Film*. Uppsala: Uppsala University, 1998.
Zimmer, Christian. "*Persona*—Une fugue à deux voix." *Études Cinématographiques* 45 (1999): 53–68.

Filmography

A Short film about Killing (Krysztof Kieslowski, Poland, 1988)
Apflickorna/She Monkeys (Lisa Aschan, Sweden, 2011)
Anderssonskans Kalle/Mrs. Andersson's Charlie (Rolf Husberg, Sweden, 1950)
Ansiktet/The Face (Ingmar Bergman, Sweden, 1958)
Ansikte mot ansikte/Face to Face (Ingmar Bergman, Sweden, 1976)
Backanterna/The Bacchae (Ingmar Bergman, Sweden, 1993)
Benjamin (Hans Abramson, Sweden, 1960)
Bergman's Reliquarium (Tomas Alfredson and Jesper Waldersten, Sweden, 2018)
Beröringen/The Touch (Ingmar Bergman, Sweden/USA, 1971)
Bröderna Mozart/The Mozart Brothers (Suzanne Osten, Sweden, 1986).
Dear Director (Marcus Lindeen, Sweden, 2015)
Det regnar på vår kärlek/It Rains on Our Love (Ingmar Bergman, Sweden, 1946)
Det sjunde inseglet/The Seventh Seal (Ingmar Bergman, Sweden, 1957)
Det vita folket/White People (Lisa Aschan, Sweden, 2015)
Dokument Fanny och Alexander/Document Fanny and Alexander (Ingmar Bergman, Sweden, 1984)
Double Life of Véronique, The (Krysztof Kieslowski, Franc/Poland/Norway, 1991)
Elvira Madigan (Bo Widerberg, Sweden, 1967)
En lektion i kärlek/A Lesson in Love (Ingmar Bergman, Sweden, 1954)
En passion/The Passion of Anna (Ingmar Bergman, Sweden, 1968)
Enskilda samtal/Private Confessions (Ingmar Bergman, Sweden, 1996)
Fanny och Alexander/Fanny and Alexander (Ingmar Bergman, Sweden, 1982/3)
Flickan i regnet/The Girl in the Rain (Alf Kjellin, Sweden, 1955).
Flickorna/The Girls (Mai Zetterling, Sweden, 1968)
400 Blows, The (Francois Truffaut, France, 1959)
För att inte tala om alla dessa kvinnor/All these Women (Ingmar Bergman, Sweden, 1964)
Greatest Story Ever Told, The (George Stevens, USA, 1965)
Gud tystnad/God's Silence (Lisa Aschan, Sweden, 2018)
Gunnel Lindblom – ut ur tystnaden (Henrik von Sydow, Sweden, 2018)
Harold and Maude (Hal Ashby, USA, 1971)
How the West Was Won (John Ford et al., USA, 1962)
Höstsonaten/Autumn Sonata (Ingmar Bergman, Sweden, 1978)
Jungfrukällan/Virgin Spring (Ingmar Bergman, Sweden, 1960)
Kvarteret korpen/Raven's End (Bo Widerberg, Sweden, 1963)
Kvinna utan ansikte/Woman Without a Face (Olof Molander, Sweden, 1947)

Kvinnodröm/Dreams (Ingmar Bergman, Sweden, 1955)
Kvinnors väntan/Waiting Women (Ingmar Bergman, Sweden, 1952)
Kärlek/Love (Gustaf Molander, Sweden, 1952)
Paradistorg/Summer Paradise (Gunnel Lindblom, Sweden, 1977)
Persona (Ingmar Bergman, Sweden, 1966)
Larmar och gör sig till/In the Presence of a Clown (Ingmar Bergman, Sweden, 1997)
Last Tango in Paris (Bernardo Bertolucci, France/Italy, 1973)
Loffe blir polis/Loffe becomes a cop (Elof Ahrle, Sweden, 1950)
Mamma/Mother (Suzanne Osten, Sweden, 1982)
Marriage Story (Noah Baumbach, USA, 2019)
Min älskade/My beloved (Kjell Grede, Sweden, 1979)
Nattvardsgästerna/Winter Light (Ingmar Bergman, Sweden, 1963)
Nära livet/Brink of Life (Ingmar Bergman, Sweden, 1958)
Rabies (Ingmar Bergman, TV, Sweden, 1958)
Reservatet/The Lie (Jan Molander, 1970)
Riten/The Rite (Ingmar Bergman, Sweden, 1969)
Rosemary's Baby (Roman Polanski, USA, 1968)
Sally och friheten/Sally and Freedom (Gunnel Lindblom, Sweden, 1981)
Sanna kvinnor/True Women (Gunnel Lindblom, Sweden, 1991)
Scener ur ett äktenskap/Scenes from a Marraige (Ingmar Bergman, Sweden, 1973)
Sista skriket/The last Gasp (Ingmar Bergman, Sweden, 1995)
Skammen/Shame (Ingmar Bergman, Sweden, 1968)
Skyddsängeln/The Guardian Angel (Suzanne Osten, Sweden, 1986)
Smultronstället/Wild Strawberries (Ingmar Bergman, Sweden, 1957)
Sommarkvällar på jorden/Summer Nights (Gunnel Lindblom, Sweden, 1986)
Sommarnatttens leende/Smiles of a Summer Night (Ingmar Bergman, Sweden, 1955)
Straw Dogs (Sam Peckinpah, USA, 1971)
Sången om den eldröda blomman/Song about the Scarlet Flower (Gustaf Molander, Sweden, 1956)
Såsom i en spegel/Through a Glass Darkly (Ingmar Bergman, Sweden, 1961)
The Birds (Alfred Hitchcock, USA, 1963)
Trollflöjten/The Magic Flute (Ingmar Bergman, Sweden, 1975)
Trolösa/Faithless(Liv Ullmann, Sweden, 2000)
Tystnaden/The Silence (Ingmar Bergman, Sweden, 1963)
Tystand! Tagning! Trollflöjten! (Ingmar Bergman, Sweden, 1975)
Ur marionetternas liv/From the Lives of the Marionettes (Ingmar Bergman, Germany/Sweden, 1980)
Vargtimmen/Hour of the Wolf (Ingmar Bergman, Sweden, 1968)
Venetianskan (Ingmar Bergman, TV, Sweden, 1958)
Viskningar och rop/Cries and Whispers (Ingmar Bergman, Sweden, 1973)
För att inte tala omt ala desas kvinnor/All these women (Ingmar Bergman, Sweden, 1964)
Älskande par/Loving Couples (Mai Zetterling, Sweden, 1964)

Editors and Contributors

Maaret Koskinen, editor and contributor

Maaret Koskinen is Professor Emeritus at the Department of Media Studies/Film of Stockholm University. She was the first scholar given access to Ingmar Bergman's private papers, which led to the formation of the Bergman Foundation. Books in English include *Ingmar Bergman Revisited. Cinema, Performance and the Arts*, and Ingmar Bergman's *The Silence. Pictures in the Typewriter, Writings on the Screen*. Her Swedish August Prize-nominated book *I begynnelsen var ordet* on Bergman as writer was translated into Spanish as *Ingmar Bergman y sus primeros escritos. En el principio era la palabra* in 2018. Forthcoming books include *Now about All these Women in the Swedish Film Industry* (2022).

Louise Wallenberg, editor and contributor

Louise Wallenberg is Professor of Fashion Studies at the Centre for Fashion Studies at Stockholm University, Sweden. She holds a PhD in Cinema Studies from the same university (2002) and she was the establishing director of the Centre for Fashion Studies between 2007 and 2013. She is the co-editor of *Fashion, Film, and the 1960s* (2017), *Fashion and Modernism* (2018), *Fashion Aesthetics and Ethics* (2022), and the co-author of *Now about All these Women in the Swedish Film Industry* (2022).

Contributors

Paisley Livingston, contributor

Paisley Livingston is Professor Emeritus of Philosophy at Lingnan University in Hong Kong and Visiting Professor of Philosophy at Uppsala University.

He taught previously at the University of Copenhagen (Denmark), Aarhus University (Denmark), and McGill University (Montreal, Canada). He has published various papers and books on aesthetics, including *Art and Intention* (2005), "History of the Ontology of Art" (*Stanford Encyclopedia of Philosophy*), and *Cinema, Philosophy, Bergman* (2009).

Margarethe von Trotta, contributor

German film director Margarethe von Trotta has an extensive body of work in cinema (starting her career in the 1970s). Her most recent films include *Hannah Arendt* (2012), a bio-pic of the German-Jewish philosopher, and the documentary *Searching for Ingmar Bergman* (1918), commemorating Bergman's centennial birthday.

Katinka Faragó, contributor

At the age of seventeen, Faragó started as a script coordinator and in 1955 she was introduced to Ingmar Bergman and soon after started to work with him. They worked together for thirty years as Faragó advanced from script coordinator to production leader to producer. In toto, they made nineteen films together, including *Smultronstället/Wild Strawberries* (1957), *Nattvardsgästerna/Winter Light* (1961), *Tystnaden/The Silence* (1963), and *Fanny and Alexander* (1983).

James Schamus, contributor

James Schamus is a screenwriter (*The Ice Storm*), director (*Indignation*), producer (*Brokeback Mountain, The Assistant*), television show runner (*Somos.*), and the co-founder and former CEO of Focus Features (*Eternal Sunshine of the Spotless Mind, Motorcycle Diaries*). He teaches film history and theory at Columbia University, and is the author of *Carl Theodor Dreyer's Gertrud: The Moving Word*.

Marcus Lindeen, contributor

Marcus Lindeen is a Swedish writer and director who works with both theater and film. His latest theater production is a trilogy of French plays that will premiere at Festival d'Automne in Paris in 2022. His latest feature documentary film *The Raft* (2019) was theatrically released in eleven countries, became a *New York Times* Critic's Pick and was broadcasted on BBC. Marcus lives and works in Paris. He is also a PhD candidate at Stockholm University of the Arts, exploring the subject of "The Staged Conversation" through an artistic project consisting of both film and theater works.

Alexis Luko, contributor

Alexis Luko is a Professor of musicology and director of the School of Music at the University of Victoria. She has published widely on film music, music of the Renaissance, and early music analysis. Her publications include *Sonatas, Screams, and Silence: Music and Sound in the Films of Ingmar Bergman* (2016) and *Monstrosity, Identity, and Music: Mediating Uncanny Creatures from Frankenstein to Videogames*, co-edited with James Wright (2022).

Allan Havis, contributor

Allan Havis is Professor of Theater at the University of California, San Diego. His plays have been produced at major theaters nationally and abroad. He is the author of nineteen full-length published plays and has edited three American Political Plays series—the newest *American Political Plays in the Age of Terrorism*. His two YA novels—*Albert the Astronomer* by Harper/Collins and *Albert Down a Wormhole* by Goodreads Press—preceded his new novel *Clear Blue Silence* in 2022.

Linus Tunström, contributor

Linus Tunström is director for film and television as well as scriptwriter and artistic director. He has directed at major theaters in Sweden, Germany,

Denmark, and Switzerland, from Staatsschauspiel Dresden, where he staged Goethe's *Faust*, to the sold-out musical *Evita* at the main stage of the Malmö Opera, and two works for the legendary, Stockholm-based international dance company Cullberg ballet.

Atom Egoyan, contributor

With eighteen feature films, Atom Egoyan has won numerous awards, including five prizes at the Cannes Film Festival and two Academy Award nominations. His body of work—which includes theater, music, and art installations—delves into issues of memory, displacement, and the impact of technology and media on modern life. Egoyan directed a virtual presentation of Bartók's "Bluebeard's Castle" for Canadian Opera Company in March 2022.

Jonathan Rozenkrantz, contributor

Jonathan Rozenkrantz is the author of *Videographic Cinema: An Archaeology of Electronic Images and Imaginaries* (2020). He is head editor of *Filmpedagogiskt paket för undervisning om de nationella minoriteterna* (2020), a teacher's guide for implementing film in school education about national minorities in Sweden. Rozenkrantz is currently a lecturer at the Department of Media Studies, Stockholm University and at the Department of Arts and Cultural Sciences at Lund University.

Måns Reuterswärd, contributor

Måns Reuterswärd is a renowned Swedish film and television producer. He started out as a television technician in the late 1950s and advanced to being a producer soon thereafter. In the 1970s and 1980s, he worked closely with Ingmar Bergman on several of his documentaries. Together with Katinka Faragó he also produced Bergman's *The Magic Flute* (1975).

Index

actors 183-7
  Bergman, Ingmar with 79-84
  Ullmann, Liv as 184-7
af Klercker, Georg 31-2
After the Rehearsal (1984); see *Efter repetitionen/After the Rehearsal*
Åhlund, Jannike 70-2
Ahndoril, Alexander 78-9
Ahrle, Elof 20
Alfredson, Tomas 215, 217
Allen, Woody 181
All these women (1964); see *För att inte tala om alla dessa kvinnor/All these women*
Älskande par/Loving Couples (1964) 219
Alvfén, Inger 28
ambiguities 39-40, 44-6, 50
Andersson, Bibi 2, 63-4, 72, 79
Andersson, Harriet 2, 21-2, 72, 79, 82-4
Ansikte mot ansikte/Face to Face (1976) 184
Ansiktet/The Magician (1958) 5, 8, 81, 169-81
anti-Semitism 8, 106-12, 115-16, 119 n.32
Apflickorna/She Monkeys (2011) 223
Aschan, Lisa 215
Assayas, Olivier 174, 176
Astaire, Fred 20
August, Pernilla 79, 95, 215
auteurship 189-92
authorship 191-2
Autumn Sonata (1978); see *Höstsonaten/Autumn Sonata*

Babel (2006) 144
Bacchae, The (1993) 30-2, 148
Backanterna (1991) 148-51
Baldwin, James 5
Berggren, Thommy 79
Bergman, Daniel 99
Bergman, Ingmar 1-6
  ambivalent influence 91-101

Ansiktet/The Magician (1958) 5, 8, 81, 169-81
  authorship, notions of 9-10
  Bergman on Bergman 2
  Beröringen/The Touch (1971) 71, 81
  Bilder/Images: My Life in Film (1994/5) 106
  biographical legend 73
  on class 8
  colleagues/co-workers 74-9
  contribution 7
  Det sjunde inseglet/The Seventh Seal (1957) 1, 15, 75, 80-1, 151, 175, 217
  En lektion i kärlek/A Lesson in Love (1954) 80, 141
  En passion/The Passion of Anna (1969) 4, 7, 53-67, 81, 184, 221
  on ethnicity 8
  failures/leftovers 205-13
  Faragó, Katinka and 3, 5-6, 19-36, 121-36
  film work 11 n.1, 13 n.9
  För att inte tala om alla dessa kvinnor/ All these women (1964) 221
  fragments on 183-98
  gossip, notion of 72-4
  Hour of the Wolf (1968) 6, 15-17, 72, 81, 93, 152-3, 184
  Ingmar Bergman Makes a Film (1961) 7, 37
  interviews 20-36
  Jewishness for cinema theaters 8
  Jungfrukällan/The Virgin Spring (1960) 74, 81, 217
  Larmar och gör sig till/In the Presence of a Clown (1997) 33-4, 151
  Laterna Magica/The Magic Lantern (1987) 70-1, 88 n.6, 96, 115-16, 142
  late style 84-6
  Mig till skräck (1946) 106

from musicological perspective 9
Nära livet/Brink of Life (1958) 217
Nattvardsgästerna/Winter Light
 (1962) 4, 37–50, 72, 78, 80, 217
Nazi revelation 115–16, 117 n.9
Persona (1966) 9–10, 15, 140, 178,
 183–98, 199 n.10
powers 8, 69–87, 89 n.18
production studies on 3–6
Rabies (1958) 217
relation with actors 79–84
Reuterswärd, Måns with 3, 6–7,
 19–36, 121–36
Saraband (2003) 141, 184
*Såsom i en spegel/Through a Glass
 Darkly* (1961) 74, 80, 87, 93–4,
 98, 155
*Scener ur ett äktenskap/Scenes from a
 Marriage* (1973) 1, 81–2, 141–2,
 184, 217
on shorter catechism in mind 47–8
Sjöman with 37–50
Smultronstället/Wild Strawberries
 (1957) 23–4, 39, 72, 75, 161
 n.14, 175
*Sommarnattens leende/Smiles of a
 Summer Night* (1955) 22, 25
Swedish theater and 8
Trollflöjten/The Magic Flute (1975) 7–
 9, 91, 100, 121–36, 148, 152–5
Trolösa/Faithless (2000) 5, 10,
 137–60, 184
TV production 30–1
Tystnaden/The Silence (1963) 26–7,
 72, 82, 215
with Ullmann, Liv 9–10, 137–60,
 183–98, 198–9nn9, 10
*Ur marionetternas liv/From the Life of
 the Marionettes* (1980) 99, 205
Venetianskan (1958) 217
Viskningar och rop/Cries and Whispers
 (1973) 26, 50, 72, 85, 184, 218
on whiteness 8
work behind scene 2
working environments 8, 91–101
on younger generation of
 directors 10
Bergman: A Year in a Life 69

Bergman Island (2006) 1, 159
Bergman on Bergman (Bergman) 2
Bergman's Reliquarium (2018) 217
Beröringen/The Touch (1971) 71, 81
Bertolucci, Bernardo 222
Bilder/Images: My Life in Film
 (1994/5) 106
Birds, The (1963) 222
Björnstrand, Gunnar 35, 38, 79–81,
 176
Björnstrand, Lillie 81
Blomberg, Erik 21
Blue Fiddler, The (1947) 109
Bordwell, David 44
Börtz, Daniel 31, 140, 148
Bourdieu, Pierre 73
Brahms, Johannes 155–8
Branigan, Edward 145
Bröderna Mozart/The Mozart Brothers
 (1986) 77
Brooke, Peter 129
Büchner, Georg 174–5

Cahiers du Cinéma 176
Caldwell, John T. 3
Callicoon 211
Campora, Matthew 144
Carlsson, Arne 30, 32
Carradine, David 183–98
Chagall, Marc 109
Chastain, Jessica 1
Chesterton, G. K. 9, 172
Chion, Michel 152
Christmas Oratorio, The (Tunström); see
 Juloratoriet/The Christmas Oratorio
 (Tunström)
cinema projector 91
Cinematograph 28
class 8
Cold, Ulrik 124
Communicants, The (1961); see
 *Nattvardsgästerna/The
 Communicants/Winter Light*
conjecture 73
Crash (2004) 144
Cries and Whispers (1973); see *Viskningar
 och rop/Cries and Whispers*
Crisis (1946); see *Kris/Crisis*

Crowther, Bosley   173
crucifixion   47–8

Dahlbäck, Eva   24
Dåså (1987)   142
Day Ends Early, The (1947)   172
Dear Director (2015)   10, 209–13
Den starkare/The Stronger   189
Det sjunde inseglet/The Seventh Seal (1957)   1, 15, 75, 80–1, 151, 175, 217
Det vita folket/White People (2015)   223
Deuze, Mark   3
Director, Ingmar Bergman Imagined-As Son, as Priest, as Visionary Filmmaker, The   78
Document Fanny and Alexander (1986); see *Dokument Fanny och Alexander/Document Fanny and Alexander*
Doktor Meyers sista dagar (1964)   109–10
Dokument Fanny och Alexander/Document Fanny and Alexander (1986)   30, 32, 74, 85, 92, 96–7, 103–17
Donner, Jörn   50, 127, 219
Doppelgänger   6
Double Life of Veronique, The (1991)   77
Dräkterna i dramat: mitt år med Fanny och Alexander (Vos)   104
dream   38–42
Dreamplay, A   148
Dreams (1955); see *Kvinnodröm/Dreams*
DVD player   91
Dymling, Carl Axel   96

Efter repetitionen/After the Rehearsal (1984)   26
Egoyan, Atom   4, 53–67, 229
 Family Viewing (1987)   53
 Guest of Honor (2019)   53
 interview   53–67
Ein Mädchen oder Weibchen   153–4
Ekblad, Stina   113
Ekdahl, Helena   110–11
Ekman, Gösta   75
Elvira Madigan (1967)   73
En berättelse om herr Silberstein   111
Endre, Lena   139

En lektion i kärlek/A Lesson in Love (1954)   80, 141
Enlightenment   126
En passion/The Passion of Anna (1969)   4, 7, 53–67, 81, 184, 221
Enquist, Per Olov   78
Enskilda samtal/Private Confessions (1996)   139, 184
Ericson, Eric   127, 130–1
Ericsson, Tomas   37
Eternal Sunshine of the Spotless Mind (2004)   144

Face to Face (1976); see *Ansikte mot ansikte/Face to Face*
faith   48–50
Faithless (2000); see *Trolösa/Faithless*
Family Viewing (1987)   53
Fanny och Alexander/Fanny and Alexander (1982/3)   1, 4, 6, 8, 24, 26, 74, 85, 92, 94, 96–7, 103–17
Fanny och Alexander: ur Ingmar Bergmans arkiv och hemliga gömmor (Koskinen and Rohdin)   114
Faragó, Alexander   20
Faragó, Katinka   3, 5–8, 19–36, 121–36, 217, 229, 231
Faust (1958)   217
Feuer, Donya   95
Fischer, Gunner   179
Flickan i regnet/The Girl in the Rain (1955)   217
Flickorna/The Girls (1968)   219
För att inte tala om alla dessa kvinnor/All these women (1964)   221
Ford, Hamish   5, 201 n.30
Forslund, Bengt   219
Foster, Gwendolyn Audrey   192–3
freedoms of rootless artists   8
Fröling, Ewa   134
From the Life of the Marionettes (1980); see *Ur marionetternas liv/From the Life of the Marionettes*

Gado, Frank   41, 170–1
Genette, Gérard   144, 145
Gesamtkunstwerk   4
Ghost Sonata, The (1941/1973)   107–8

Girl in the Rain, The (1955); see *Flickan i regnet/The Girl in the Rain*
Girls, The (1968); see *Flickorna/The Girls*
Giulini, Carlo Maria   130
God   47–50
God's Silence (2018); see *Guds tystnad/God's Silence*
Goodrich, Peter   199 n.15
Gorbman, Claudia   145
Gorill, Liz   10, 210
gossip   72–4
Gothenburg City Theater   9
Grede, Kjell   28
Grut, Gun   142, 149
Guardian Angel, The (1990); see *Skyddsängeln/The Guardian Angel*
Guds tystnad/God's Silence (2018)   10, 215–16, 223–5
Guest of Honor (2019)   53
Gunke, Nina   216, 224

Halvatzis, Stavros   144
Hansen-Löve, Mia   1–2
Hansson, Maud   75
Harold and Maude   174
Hathaway, Henry   222
Havis, Allan   5, 8, 232
Hedling, Erik   72–3
Heldt, Guido   145
Hell, Erik   66
Henriksson, Alf   125
Hitchcock, Alfred   222
Hjort, Mette   3
Hoffman, Marco   206
Hoffmann, E. T. A.   6, 15–17, 106
Holmberg, Jan   85, 115, 142
Höök, Marianne   75
Höstsonaten/Autumn Sonata (1978)   28, 184
Hour of the Wolf, The (1968); see *Vargtimmen/Hour of the Wolf, The*
Humphrey, Daniel   5

I begynnelsen var ordet (Koskinen)   71
Ibsen, Henrik   217
illusions   169–81
Images: My Life in Film (1994/5); see *Bilder/Images: My Life in Film*

Inception (2010)   144
Ingmar Bergman and the Rituals of Art   180
Ingmar Bergman Foundation   2, 10
Ingmar Bergman Makes a Film (1961)   7, 37
intercession   49
internal focalization   145
interviews   20–36, 53–67, 183–98
In the Presence of a Clown (1997); see *Larmar och gör sig till/In the Presence of a Clown*
Isaksson, Ulla   217
Isaac, Oscar   1

Jacob's Ladder (1990)   144
Jansson, Maria   36 n.1
Jaxen, Kazzrie   10, 210–13
jealousy   16
Jewishness   8, 103–16, 120 n.48
Jewish war refugees   21
Josephson, Erland   24, 56–7, 61, 104–12, 117 n.9, 118 nn.28, 29, 119 n.39, 120 n.48, 137, 139, 141–3, 150, 159, 161 n.5, 176, 226 n.6
Judaism   113–14
judegubbe   109–12
Judisk Krönika   112–13
Juloratoriet/The Christmas Oratorio (Tunström)   98
Jungfrukällan/The Virgin Spring (1960)   74, 81, 217

Kääpä, Pietari   3
Kael, Pauline   129
Kärlek/Love (1952)   217
Kierkegaard, Søren   169–70, 177–8
Kieslowski, Krzysztof   77
kippah   107
Kjellin, Alf   217
Kluge, Alexander   15
Koskinen, Lennart   40
Koskinen, Maaret   7, 42, 53–67, 114, 142, 229
Krieps, Vicky   2
Kris/Crisis (1946)   96
Kristeva, Julia   193, 196, 202 n.41
Kvarteret korpen/Raven's End (1963)   79

Kvinna utan ansikte/Woman Without a Face (1947) 71
Kvinnodröm/Dreams (1955) 22, 24, 26
Kvinnors väntan/ Waiting Women (1952) 80

L 136 (Sjöman) 2, 7
Laretei, Käbi 78, 142
Larmar och gör sig till/In the Presence of a Clown (1997) 33–4, 151
Last Gasp, The (1995); see *Sista skriket/The Last Gasp*
Last Tango in Paris 222
Laterna Magica/The Magic Lantern (1987) 70–1, 88 n.6, 96, 114, 115–16, 142
Lee, Ang 66
Lesson in Love, A (1954); see *En lektion i kärlek/A Lesson in Love*
Levi, Hagai 1
Lidén, Anki 224
Lidingö 31
Lie, The (1970); see *Reservatet/The Lie*
Liljegren, Aschan 224
Liljegren, Isabel Cruz 215, 223–4
Lindblom, Gunnel 79, 82–4, 216–23
Lindeen, Markus 4, 10
Lindenstrand, Sylvia 30
Livingston, Paisley 4, 7, 121, 125, 180, 229
Loffe blir polis 20–1
Love (1952); see *Kärlek/Love*
Loving Couples (1964); see *Älskande par/Loving Couples*
Luko, Alexis 5, 9, 232

McMahan, Alison 144
Madame de Sade (1992) 29
Magic (Chesterton) 9
Magic Flute, The (1975); see *Trollflöjten/The Magic Flute*
Magician, The (1958); see *Ansiktet/The Magician*
Magic Lantern, The (1987); see *Laterna Magica/The Magic Lantern*
Magnusson, Charles 31–2
Magnusson, Jane 69–70, 215
Malmö City Theatre 9

Malmsjö, Jan 134
Mamma/"Mother" (1982) 77
Mancini, Marco 186
Marriage Story (2019) 13 n.4
Mattei, Peter 30–1
maxim 48
Mayer, Vicki 3
media production 2–4
Mein Kampf (Hitler) 116
metadiegetic 145
metalepsis 144–5, 152–5
metaleptic practice 148
metaleptic transgressions 145, 155–8, 163 n.33
metareference 143–4, 152–5
MeToo movement 7, 83–7, 220, 222
Mig till skräck/Unto My Fear (1946) 106
Milenković, Snežana 209
Miller, Toby 3
Min älskade/My Beloved (1979) 28
Molander, Gustaf 217
"Mother" (1982); see *Mamma/*"Mother"
Mozart Brothers, The (1986); see *Bröderna Mozart/The Mozart Brothers*
multi culture 126
multiform narrative 144–5
Mulvey-Roberts, Marie 107
Murray, Janet 144
musical metareference 148–51
music boxes 152–5
My Beloved (1979); see *Min älskade/My Beloved*
mystification 38, 42

Nära livet/Brink of Life (1958) 217
Nattvardsgästerna/The Communicants/Winter Light (1962) 4, 37–50, 72, 78, 80, 217
Nazism 115
Norman, Jan-Hugo 122–3
Nykvist, Sven 2, 57, 66, 75, 125–6, 219

Olin, Lena 79
Oliver, Kelly 202 n.41
Oliver Twist (1838) 107
On the Concept of Irony with Continual References to Socrates (Kierkegaard) 169

Orr, Christopher 190
Osten, Suzanne 76–8
Otherness 110

Palitsch, Peter 183
Paradistorg/Summer Paradise (1977) 10, 26, 216–19, 223
Passion of Anna, The (1969); see En passion/The Passion of Anna
Passion of Ingmar Bergman, The (Gado) 170–1
pedagogical outbursts 74–5, 134–5
Peer Gynt (1957) 217
Persona (1966) 9–10, 15, 140, 178, 183–98, 199 n.10
Persson, Jonas 37
Pirandello, Luigi 170–3
powers of suggestion 8, 69–87, 89 n.18
Prenger, Mirjan 3
Private Confessions (1996); see Enskilda samtal/Private Confessions
production studies 3–6
Prüzelius, Gösta 95

quartet Op. 60 (Brahms) 155–8

Rabies (1958) 217
race 5
Raven's End (1963); see Kvarteret korpen/Raven's End
Regissören (Ahndoril) 78
Reitz, Edgar 15
Reservatet/The Lie (1970) 227 n.12
Reuterswärd, Måns 3, 6–8, 19–36, 121–36, 229
Reverence for the Light (Nykvist); see Vördnad för ljuset/Reverence for the Light (Nykvist)
Revolution in Poetic Language (Kristeva) 193
Rite, The (1969) 81
Rogers, Ginger 20
Rohdin, Mats 114
Rokem, Freddie 113
Roth, Tim 2
Royal Dramatic Theater 29–31, 94, 97–8, 126, 133, 136

Rozenkrantz, Jonathan 4–5, 8
Rugg, Linda 72, 143, 146, 159

Sally och friheten (1981) 219
Sången om den eldröda blomman/Song about the Scarlet Flower (1956) 217
Sanna kvinnor/True Women (1991) 219
Saraband (2003) 141, 184
Såsom i en spegel/Through a Glass Darkly (1961) 74, 80, 87, 93–4, 98, 155
Scener ur ett äktenskap/Scenes from a Marriage (1973) 1, 81–2, 141–2, 184, 217
Scenes from a Marriage (1973); see Scener ur ett äktenskap/Scenes from a Marriage
Schamus, James 9–10, 66, 232
Schein, Harry 72–3, 218
Schlöndorff, Volker 15
Schumann, Clara 155
Schumann, Robert 155
Self-Projection: The Director's Image in Art Cinema (Rugg) 72, 143, 146, 159
self-projections 72
self-reference 143–4
self-referentiality 54, 58, 143–4
Serpent's Egg, The (1977) 184
Seventh Seal, The (1957); see Det sjunde inseglet/The Seventh Seal
sexual exploitation 69
Shame (1968); see Skammen/Shame
She Monkeys (2011); see Apflickorna/She Monkeys
Short Film About Killing, A (1988) 77
Sickness Unto Death (Kierkegaard) 177–8
Silence, The (1963); see Tystnaden/The Silence
Sista skriket/The Last Gasp (1995) 31
"Situating Ingmar Bergman and World Cinema," (Humphrey and Ford) 5
Six Characters in Search of an Author (1967) 161 n.13, 172, 174
Sjöberg, Thomas 73
Sjöman, Vilgot 2, 7, 37–9, 42, 48, 78
Sjöstrand, Östen 148
Skammen/Shame (1968) 56, 60, 64, 81, 184

Skyddsängeln/The Guardian Angel (1990) 77
Skytte (1990-3) 108-9
Smiles of a Summer Night (1955); see *Sommarnattens leende/Smiles of a Summer Night*
Smultronstället/Wild Strawberries (1957) 23-4, 39, 72, 75, 161 n.14, 175
Sommaren med Monika/Summer with Monika (1953) 1, 82, 142
Sommarkvällar på jorden/Summer Nights (1986) 219
Sommarnattens leende/Smiles of a Summer Night (1955) 22, 25, 166 n.63, 171
"Söndagsbarn"/*Sunday's Children* (1992) 99
Song about the Scarlet Flower (1956); see *Sången om den eldröda blomman/Song about the Scarlet Flower*
speculation 73
Staiger, Janet 5
Steene, Birgitta 179, 187
Stern, Michael J. 178
Stiller, Mauritz 31
Stilwell, Robin 145
Stormare, Peter 79
Strindberg, August 107, 148
Stronger, The; see *Den starkare/The Stronger*
Summer Nights (1986); see *Sommarkvällar på jorden/Summer Nights*
Summer Paradise (1977); see *Paradistorg/Summer Paradise*
Summer with Monika (1953); see *Sommaren med Monika/Summer with Monika*
Svenska Bio 31-2
Swedish Film Industry 31
Swedish theater and 8
S/Y Glädjen/S/Y Joy (1979) 28
S/Y Joy (1979); see *S/Y Glädjen/S/Y Joy*
symbolism 129
Syriana (2005) 144

Through a Glass Darkly (1961); see *Såsom i en spegel/Through a Glass Darkly*
Thulin, Ingrid 41, 72-3, 79
Top Hat (1935) 20
Törnqvist, Egil 41

Touch, The (1971); see *Beröringen/The Touch*
Trollflöjten/The Magic Flute (1975) 7-9, 32, 91, 100, 121-36, 148, 152-5
Trolösa/Faithless (2000) 5, 10, 137-60, 184
  diegesis in 145-8
  diegetic/extradiegetic narrative circles of 145-8
  female protagonist-ghost 141-3
  love pairs in 149
  metalepsis in 144-5, 152-5
  metaleptic transgressions 145, 155-8
  metareference in 143-4, 152-5
  multiform narrative 144-5
  musical metareference in 148-51
  self-reference 143-4
  voice as metaleptic agent 151-2
True Women (1991); see *Sanna kvinnor/True Women*
Truffaut, Francois 82
Tunström, Göran 98
Tunström, Linus 4, 8
Tystnaden/The Silence (1963) 26-7, 72, 82, 215

Ullmann, Liv 2, 5, 8-10, 16, 58-9, 62-3, 72, 81, 85, 137-60
  as actor 184-7
  Bergman with 9-10, 137-60, 183-98, 198-9nn9, 10
  as director 184, 187
  fragments on 183-98
  interview with 183-98
Trolösa/Faithless (2000) 5, 10, 137-60
Unquiet 162 n.18
Unheard Melodies (Gorbman) 145
universal humanity 126
Unquiet (Ullmann) 162 n.18
Unto My Fear (1946); see *Mig till skräck/Unto My Fear*
Uppsala City Theater 94
Ur marionetternas liv/From the Life of the Marionettes (1980) 99, 205

Vargtimmen/Hour of the Wolf, The (1968) 6, 15-17, 72, 81, 93, 152-3, 184
Venetianskan (1958) 217

Vineberg, Steve 195
violence 58–9
Virgin Spring, The (1960); see
   Jungfrukällan/The Virgin Spring
Viskningar och rop/Cries and Whispers
   (1973) 26, 50, 72, 85, 99, 184,
   218
Vita sanningar (Josephson) 111
Vogler, Elizabeth 139
voice 151–2
Vonderau, Patrick 2
von Göthe, Johann Wolfgang 217
von Rosen, Maria 142–3
von Sydow, Max 2, 16, 61, 79, 81–2, 85,
   93, 170
von Trotta, Margarethe 4, 6
Vördnad för ljuset/Reverence for the Light
   (Nykvist) 75
Vos, Marik 104, 219

Waldersten, Jesper 215, 217
Wallenberg, Louise 10, 42, 53–67

Weinstein, Harvey 69
whiteness 5, 8
White People (2015); see *Det vita folket/
   White People*
Widerberg, Bo 73–4, 79
Wifstrand, Naima 174
Wild Strawberries (1957); see
   Smultronstället/Wild Strawberries
Winfrey, Oprah 207
Winter's Tale, A 94, 98, 126, 133
Wolf, Werner 144
Woman Without a Face (1947); see *Kvinna
   utan ansikte/Woman Without
   a Face*
women's stories 219–23
Woyzeck (Buchner) 9
Wright, Rochelle 5
Writing Cottage 93

"Young German Film" 15

Zetterling, Mai 219